PETE DUNNE
on Bird Watching

SECOND EDITION

Also by Pete Dunne

Tales of a Low-Rent Birder

Hawks in Flight

The Feather Quest

More Tales of a Low-Rent Birder

The Wind Masters

Before the Echo

Small-headed Flycatcher

Golden Wings

Pete Dunne's Essential Field Guide Companion

The Art of Pishing

Prairie Spring

Bayshore Summer

Arctic Autumn

The Art of Bird Finding

Hawks in Flight, Second Edition

The Art of Bird Identification

PETE DUNNE
on Bird Watching

SECOND EDITION

Beginner's Guide to Finding, Identifying, and Enjoying Birds

PETE DUNNE
featuring photographs by Scott Whittle

STACKPOLE
BOOKS

Published by
STACKPOLE BOOKS
5067 Ritter Road
Mechanicsburg, PA 17055
www.stackpolebooks.com

Printed in the United States of America

10 9 8 7 6 5 4 3 2 1

First edition

Photographs by Scott Whittle unless otherwise credited

The original edition of this book was published in 2003 by Houghton Mifflin Company

Library of Congress Cataloging-in-Publication Data

Dunne, Pete, 1951–
  Pete Dunne on bird watching : the how-to, where-to, and when-to of birding / Pete Dunne ; featuring photographs by Scott Whittle. — Second edition.
      pages cm
  Includes bibliographical references and index.
  ISBN 978-0-8117-1576-8
  1. Bird attracting. 2. Bird watching. I. Title.
  QL676.2.D85 2015
  598.072'34—dc23
                                        2015022118

Contents

Acknowledgments

Were honesty to be served, the names of those found here would be as deserving as mine to appear on the cover of this book. As in the spirit of birding itself, Pete Dunne on Bird Watching was very much a community effort. Accordingly, and in this spirit, I extend to all who gave generously of their time and expertise my sincere thanks, and I ask, in the name of courtesy, that you offer them yours. "They" being . . .

Janet Crawford, Scott Edwards, Victor Emanuel, Don Freiday, Eldon Greij, Michael Hannisian, Paul Kerlinger, Daniel Klem, Paul Lehman, Judy Toups, Dick Walton, Peggy Wang, Karen Williams, and Sheri Williamson, for penning one (or more) sidebars on subjects that command their expertise;

Tom Barnes, Alicia Craig-Lich, Bucky Dennerlein, Lynn Hassler, Susan Lenard, Greg Oskay, Chuck Otte, Reese Partridge, Wayne Petersen, Carol Pollard, Patty Van Vlack, and Karen Williams, for offering readers their region-tailored selections for natural plantings, and to Pat Hayward, who orchestrated their efforts.

Scott Whittle's contribution to this book cannot be overstated. His very excellent images and graphic array figure in the appeal and usefulness of this effort.

It should surprise no one who understands writers and writing that elements of this book have previously surfaced as articles or essays in assorted other publications. Many of the thoughts and words that were the basis for columns in Birding's "Tools of the Trade" and "Building Birding Skills" as well as "Pete Dunne's Birding Tip of the Month" (written for *WildBird*) are born again, here. Elements of columns from *New Jersey Audubon* magazine also figure in the text.

Special thanks and acknowledgment is extended to Swarovski Optik of North America, which allowed me to incorporate elements of a brochure first written for it, on choosing optics, in chapter 2; and to Nikon Sports Optics for like graciousness and like-mindedness with regard to the identification section found in chapter 3.

Thanks also to Jeff Gordon of the American Birding Association for permission to include the ABA Code of Ethics.

Re: chapter 1, much credit and thanks go to Scott Edwards, who offered primary insight, reflective review, and, most of all, his expertise.

Introduction

This is not a self-help book. It is not an avenue to spiritual enlightenment or a blueprint to a better you. It is not intended to save your marriage, confer an affirming identity in an indifferent universe, or promote harmony between nations.

These are merely by-products of birding. This book's objective is more modest. All it purports to do is tell you how to find, identify, and enjoy birds. Everything else is a bonus.

Must you read this book to go look for birds? No. You can do what I did at the age of seven. Grab binoculars. Run out the back door. Start peering into the trees.

But you will soon discover, if you have not already, that there is a vast difference between looking for birds and finding them. While looking is fun, finding is more fun (and being able to identify what you find is the most fun of all). If I knew 56 years ago what I know today about birds and their habits, I would have found a good many more and been frustrated a good deal less.

I also would have devoured this book. Because it answers the questions all beginning birders face. Like where to go. When to go. What to bring. And how to tell the difference between a female Purple Finch and a female Rose-breasted Grosbeak (here's a hint: look at the calendar).

The adventure, and this book, begin in your own backyard, with birds anyone can engage and enjoy. Suburbia, it turns out, is a bird-rich environment. The adventure, and the book, go on to jump the fence, conferring page by page the guidance and the skills to enable you to explore what is literally a bird-filled world. There are approximately 10,000 bird species apportioned across the planet. No single individual has yet to see them all.

The author once again peering into the trees in the woodlands behind his boyhood home.

Collect all 10,000 and you win the journey of a lifetime.

Something that has long frustrated me about how-to books is their tendency to delve into too many topics. In their well-intended effort to be thorough and comprehensive, the books allow fundamental information to get lost in the clutter. In writing this book I tried always to keep objective and audience in mind—focusing only on challenges that beginning birders need to address, presenting them in the order in which they are likely to be confronted.

For example, birders who are just learning how to find their way around a field guide don't really need to read about courtship displays or how birds care for their feathers. These subjects are fascinating. But beginning birders are better served learning how to select the right binocular and field guide than engaging in principles of ornithology.

In the same vein, people whose frontier is their first organized field trip need not confront subjects like bird banding, breeding

There are approximately 10,000 bird species on the planet—one of them is Rockhopper Penguin. Collect all 10,000 and you win a lifetime of travel.
LINDA DUNNE

bird atlas projects, or how to plan a "Big Day" (a 24-hour bird-finding marathon). These facets of birding may be interesting, even important or fun, but they are not topics beginning birders need to deal with, yet.

What is important to beginners is getting the right equipment and getting off on the right foot when it comes to finding, studying, and identifying birds. These are the elements of *Pete Dunne on Bird Watching*.

The book is divided into seven chapters: Backyard Birding, Front-Seat Adventure; The Tools of the Trade—Binoculars and a Field Guide; The Fundamentals of Birding; Resources—Dipping into the Pool of Knowledge; Expanding Horizons—Finding and Facing New Challenges; Tips to Better Birding; and Ethics and Responsibilities.

Each chapter is subdivided into relevant subtopics designated by headings and subheadings. For reference, subject areas are listed at the beginning of each chapter. For review, key points raised in each chapter are summarized at the end. New and unfamiliar terms used by birders are defined in a glossary at the end of the book.

If you are beginning to grow suspicious that this book is (dare I say) a textbook—well, it is. To a point. The information it houses has been organized to facilitate learning and later referral (just like a textbook).

It was written in part to serve as the text for "Beginning Birder" classes (as well as a blueprint for those who are discovering birds on their own).

But I never had much love for textbooks myself, and while I truly tried to write this book in a clear, concise, fashion, I'm afraid the sheer pleasure of birding kept breaking through. As a further check against too much starch in the text, sidebars—some informational ("Wing Bars"), others anecdotal ("Tale Spots")—are liberally scattered throughout. These tangential offerings serve to support key points, introduce related topics, and, all in all, keep the book lively.

Many of these sidebars were written by leaders in the birding community. People it is my privilege to know, people whose talents I admire. Their willingness to contribute their knowledge to this book is not only a bonus for me (as I could not have presented their thoughts near so well) but an asset for you. Via Wing Bars and Tale Spots you will make the acquaintance of many of the architects of bird watching, people who share your interest and who have helped make birding the engaging avocation we know today.

And what is that? That, my birding friend, is what you are about to discover. Lucky you.

December 2014

Backyard Birding, Front-Seat Adventure

Stefancik's Corollary

Mr. Stefancik was standing at the blackboard, expounding upon the wonders of decimal points and fractions. I was watching the clock, sweating out the closing seconds of math class.

Why (I demanded of an unsympathetic universe) did 2 + 2 *always* have to equal 4? It rigged the universe. It stifled creativity. It made everything so predictably *boring*.

And *why* (I wailed in my mind) would anyone want to take a perfectly fine number like 1 and divide it by a nice number like 3 to get a product that was less than either? It made about as much sense as taking quality sunflower seed and diluting it with a cheap mix to attract fewer birds to a feeder.

Which is what I lived for. The time spent with nose pressed to window glass, watching feathered minions coming to my feeders. All I knew (or cared) about fractions was that fifty cents on the

1

dollar would buy one whole bag of seed. One whole bag divided into coffee-can-sized portions equaled hours of in-your-face visits by . . .

Nuthatches, Mourning Doves, and *Tree Sparrows! White-throated Sparrows, Goldfinches,* and *Song Sparrows! Blue Jays!* (of the haughty demeanor). *Titmice!* (with their baleful eyes). *Chickadees!* (of the quicksilver reflexes). And every once in a (hold-your-breath, don't-move-a-muscle) while, an adult male . . .

CARDINAL! WOW!

What (I demanded of Mr. Stefancik's back) was some stupid universal mathematical principle next to something as incredible as a cardinal?

That's what *I* wanted to know.

The second hand met the two already joined at 12. I was halfway to the door before being stopped by the voice of Mr. Stefancik.

"Mr. Dunne, can I see you for a moment, please?"

Wondering what homework assignment I'd failed to complete *this* time, I approached the instructor's desk. Instead of the expected

An adult male Northern Cardinal is WOW wrapped in feathers and a feeder favorite within its range.

admonishment, Mr. Stefancik produced a corner-thumbed note-book—one emblazoned across the front with the handwritten legend "Bird Sightings." My notebook. I'd given it up for lost. "I'm only guessing this is yours," he said. "There's no name in it. But I found it under your desk."

I didn't know what to do. It wasn't cool to admit that you were a bird watcher—not in seventh grade, not in 1964. Watching birds was the kind of thing that could get you branded a "nature boy," and get you picked last when they divvied up sides for softball.

Still, I wanted that book. All my sightings were in it. All my observations. Notes about the kind of seed Blue Jays preferred and written sketches of all my feeder regulars.

"That's top-secret stuff," I told him.

"I understand," he said, lowering his voice but not his eyes (which seemed strangely friendly for a math teacher's). "I like birds, too."

"Oh," I said, startled by the disclosure. Then, taking my book, mumbling my thanks, I headed for the door, marveling that an adult (and a math teacher!) could have the same interest I did. It made me wonder whether bird watching wasn't perhaps more popular than I'd imagined.

America's Second Most Popular Outdoor Activity

If you are reading these words, it can mean only one thing. You, like me, like Mr. Stefancik, enjoy watching birds *and* you want to compound that enjoyment by seeing more and knowing more about birds. You stand in good company. There are, in the estimates of the U.S. Fish and Wildlife Service, 47 million bird watchers in the United States (and an equally representative number in Canada)—people who in the course of their lives make time to enjoy birds.

Some are very dedicated in this regard—traveling widely and frequently to view new species to add to their life lists. These are birders.

The adventure of birding begins in your own backyard. After all, the birds there do everything birds in the Antarctic do, and more—penguins can't fly, a feat backyard birds handle adroitly. PAT SUTTON

Most people who enjoy birds are more tempered in scope, if not in their enthusiasm. *Most* people are *most* fascinated by the birds they find in their own neighborhood and yard. There are several reasons for this.

First, depending upon the season, there are between 5 to 20 *billion* birds occupying the land mass dominated by Canada and the United States, a seasonally apportioned average of about 700 to 2,700 birds per square mile. No matter where you live in North America, and no matter when you choose to look, it is almost certain that you are within sight or sound of one or more birds. With birds so common, there is little need to travel to see a rich sampling.

Second, people have an affinity for living in homes that are surrounded by vegetation—lawns, trees, hedges, gardens, wood-lots, fields—the kind of habitat that typifies suburbia. Birds as a group are versatile creatures. A growing number are acclimating

Birds have integrated into our world. Many species, Black Vultures among them, are comfortable in urban and suburban environments.

themselves to highly urbanized areas. These pioneers include Wild Turkeys, Cooper's Hawks, Red-tailed Hawks, Peregrine Falcons . . . to name just a few.

Third, the ownership of property confers a proprietary interest among home owners. People who might never look at a bird someplace else are intensely interested in the wild creatures they find in that place where their respective worlds overlap—"their" yard.

Fourth, people spend much of their time at home and so take pains to make it a place they want to be. Birds are animate, colorful, and vocal. They entertain us, amuse us, add to the pleasure of each day. Just as home owners decorate the insides of their homes with things that give them pleasure, attracting birds to the yard offers pleasure too. In fact, if you are not careful, birds can turn your sense of home inside out. You may find yourself spending more time looking at the beautiful wild things you lured into your yard than the fixtures gracing the inside of your home.

White-breasted Nuthatch. Because of its gravity-defying antics, this widespread species quickly becomes a welcome guest at the feeder.

WING BAR

Birder or Bird Watcher?

People who watch birds have worn many labels; some we've donned ourselves, others have been applied to us. These include: ornithologist, bird student, nature lover, and bird lover. But the two terms most commonly applied today are "birder" and "bird watcher." While they are often used interchangeably, the names denote a differing focus.

"Bird watcher" is all inclusive. It refers to everyone who enjoys watching birds. And this excludes very few people. Most people take pleasure in watching birds.

"Birder" is more specific. It refers to someone who makes watching birds a defining focus of their lives. People who actively pursue birds for pleasure and gratification. The defining characteristic is pursuit, which implies mobility, and a compulsion to seek birds and engage them wherever they are found and keep track of these encounters (or sightings) on various lists.

There are other distinctions, traits more characteristic of one group or the other. Bird watchers focus most commonly on the birds that appear in their yards; birders are keenly interested in birds that lie beyond their property lines and are particularly interested in species they have yet to see. Bird watchers engage birds for pleasure or entertainment; birders often regard birds as a challenge and the act of engaging birds a sport. Bird watchers think of birds as an element that enriches their lives; birders may think of birds as prizes.

But there is no sharp distinction between a birder and a bird watcher—since all birders are bird watchers, and bird watchers differ in terms of how much, or little, birds mean to them. In a 1994 survey of American Birding Association members (ABA is the organization that caters to North America's most avid and travel-minded birders), 82 percent said that they feed birds in their yards—for no other reason than the pleasure it brings. ■

For the Pleasure It Brings

The Four Pillars of a Bird-filled Yard

There is much that home owners can do to attract birds to their yards, and that is the focus of this chapter. The trick is to offer birds what they need—and their needs are fundamentally simple: *food, water, shelter,* and, during the breeding season, *a place to rear their young.*

Setting the Table for Birds

The Myth of Seed and Need

One of my earliest memories involves a paralyzing snowfall and my mom throwing bread into the yard to "help" the hungry birds. It was a typical human gesture, but it was also unnecessary. First, bread (particularly the nutritionally bankrupt stuff that used to be the support base for PB&J sandwiches when I was a kid) isn't

White-throated Sparrow is partial to woodland edges but can be lured to backyard feeders with the right mix of seed.

particularly good for birds. It provides calories but little nutrition. Second, birds do not *need* handouts to survive. If your sole motivation for feeding birds is "to help them survive the winter," STOP. Save your money—or donate it to an organization whose focus is bird conservation and habitat protection. The best reason to feed birds is because you want to attract birds for pleasure and enjoyment. A bird-feeding station is, at most, supplemental to meeting the nutritional needs of birds. Birds will take advantage of your generosity. They will rely more heavily on your offerings when snow or ice covers natural food stocks or when temperatures fall and their energy needs rise. But wild birds are far from dependent on our handouts—even if you are offering what they need. That's why they are called *wild* birds.

What They Need . . .

Differs from species to species. Most birds, after all, are not seed-eating birds. Many, even most species that feed primarily upon seed or berries during the winter are insectivorous. But when cold temperatures enfold much of North America, most insect-dependent species such as warblers and swallows have withdrawn to warmer climates, leaving seed-eating species to dominate the North American landscape. Seed, because it is easy to keep, readily available, and eaten by a variety of species, is key to attracting birds to your yard in winter.

Not Just Any Ol' Seed Will Do

So you go to the local food store. You buy a bag of "mixed birdseed." You figure you are a sophisticated step ahead of the bread-flinging crowd. And you are—if the types of seed in the bag are the sort that birds want. In many cases, however, they are not.

The primary ingredient of any birdseed mix should be black-oil sunflower seed. As with human food items, the components of mixed seed are listed (or should be listed) on the bag, ranked on the basis of percent per volume. Smaller and darker than striped sunflower seed, black-oil is a favorite of Chickadees, Evening Grosbeaks, Purple Finches, and Northern Cardinals—that favorite

Preferred Foods of Some Common Seed-eating Backyard Birds

Bird Species	Preferred Seed(s)
Flickers and other woodpeckers	hulled sunflower, peanut kernels
Jays	peanut kernels, sunflower seed of all types
Black-billed Magpie	peanuts in the shell, peanut kernels
Titmice	peanut kernels, black-stripped and black oil sunflower
Chickadees	black oil and striped sunflower, peanut kernels
White-breasted Nuthatch	striped sunflower, peanuts
Red-breasted Nuthatch	striped sunflower, black oil sunflower
Brown Thrasher	hulled and striped sunflower
European Starling	peanut hearts, hulled oats, cracked corn
Northern Cardinal	sunflower seed of all types
Towhees	white proso millet
Sparrows: Song, Tree, Field, Chipping, Fox	white proso millet
Juncos	white proso millet
White-crowned/Golden-crowned Sparrow	black oil and hulled sunflower, white proso millet, peanuts, thistle
Red-winged Blackbird	white proso millet
Brown-headed Cowbird	white proso millet
Common Grackle and other blackbirds	striped sunflower, hulled sunflower, cracked corn
House Sparrow	white proso millet and canary seed
Pine Siskin	sunflower seed, thistle
Goldfinches	hulled sunflower, thistle, black oil sunflower
Crossbills	black-oil and striped sunflower

continued

Preferred Foods of Some Common Seed-eating Backyard Birds *continued*

Bird Species	Preferred Seed(s)
Redpolls	thistle, hulled sunflower bits
Rosy Finch	hulled and black oil sunflower, white proso milled, cracked corn
Purple Finch	sunflower seed of all types
Cassins Finch	hulled and black oil sunflower
House Finch	sunflower seed of all types, thistle
Grosbeaks	sunflower seed of all types

Selections courtesy of Wild Bird Centers of America, Inc. and Scott Edwards
Note: Not all of these species are found where you live, and even if you put out the right seed, there is no guarantee that target species will flock to your feeder. There is more to bird feeding than seed.

feeder bird of my youth. It also rates high in the esteem of House Finches and Mourning Doves.

Other favored seeds include striped sunflower (the grosbeak delight), peanut kernels (a perennial favorite of jays and titmice), and white proso millet (top rated by doves and assorted sparrow species). Any seed mix that offers a high percentage of these seed types is a blend that will attract a variety of species.

Mixed seed that contains a high percentage of milo, flax, rape-seed, cracked corn, or canary seed is considerably less attractive to most birds. Sometimes referred to as "filler seeds," these types, and the mixes dominated by them, have the advantage of being generally less expensive than mixes featuring "quality" seed. But these discount blends hardly represent a savings. Here's why.

Birds vote with their beaks. The stuff they don't want, they bill-sweep aside to get to the quality items. All that seed piled beneath the bird feeder (now the nutritional support base for rats and mice) is the cheap "filler" you paid for. You'll not fail to notice this waste every time you go to refill your feeder—which is something you will do often, since most of your bargain seed is getting tossed.

Black-oil sunflower seed is a near universal favorite among seed-eating birds at backyard feeding stations.

WING BAR

Bird-feeding Myths

Birding, like most avocations, has its share of myths and misconceptions—things that are widely believed even though they are unsupported by evidence (a polite way of saying *wrong*). Here are a few of the most common misconceptions.

You shouldn't feed birds during warmer weather.

There is no sound scientific data to support this notion. In fact, breeding season is a time of great stress for birds, and during this time feeders are the place for overworked parents to get a quick bite to eat. Also, if you suspend bird feeding outside of winter, you miss migratory visitors as they pass through your area, as well as young birds that come to learn that your yard is a good place to visit.

Birds won't migrate when they are supposed to if there is food available.

While some species shift their populations in response to the absence or presence of food, most do not. Many migratory birds begin their migrations while there are still ample food supplies on their breeding grounds. A few pounds of sunflower seed is not going to derail thousands of years of evolution. Besides, many of the birds that visit feeders are year-round residents that do not migrate.

Hummingbird "juice" must be red to be effective.

This is one that just won't go away. If you could milk a flower that a hummingbird was visiting you would find the nectar quite clear. A mixture of four or five parts water to one part ordinary table sugar, boiled well and cooled, is the appropriate recipe. Hummingbirds *are* very attracted to the color red, but any hummingbird feeder worth using will be more than red enough to be attractive.

Birds' feet will freeze to metal perches.

Birds' feet are dry and scaly, more like bone than skin. They are not inherently moist and therefore will not freeze on contact with cold metal. Imagine how long you would have to leave a chicken bone on a piece of metal to get it to freeze there. ■

—Scott Edwards

Scott Edwards is the former owner and operator of the Wild Bird Center store in Aston, Pennsylvania, and author of several books on birds and bird feeding.

Bird Feeder?

Bird feeder! A device constructed of wood, plastic, or metal that holds and dispenses birdseed. While some bird species, such as juncos, towhees, and assorted sparrows, will readily forage on the ground, other species prefer an elevated platform.

There are different types of feeders offering different advantages, thus catering to different species. The basic feeder types are: platform feeder, hopper feeder, and tube feeder.

Platform Feeder

The simplest feeder is a platform feeder—an elevated, flat, square or rectangular surface with a raised lip to keep the seed on board. Platform feeders are usually affixed to a pole or attached to a

Platform feeders are the most basic feeder type and readily used by a variety of species, including Pine Siskin, an irruptive species (at center), and Dark-eyed Junco, a common winter resident across much of North America.

windowsill; less often, they are suspended from a branch, hook, or wire. They are also effective resting on or very close to the ground (4 to 8 inches up)—where they are most appealing to ground-feeding species (such as towhees).

Advantages: Offer free and open access to all bird species, particularly larger species such as magpies and jays. They also offer optimum viewing opportunity, because there is nothing to block your view. Platform feeders can also be used to hold all manner of attractive (and difficult to dispense) food offerings—assorted large seeds, fruit, mealworms.

Disadvantages: One large species can monopolize the entire feeder, preventing smaller birds from feeding. Seed is unprotected and, when wet, turns into mush. Since there is no seed reservoir, the feeder must also be refilled often and cleaned frequently.

Features to look for: A strong, tight wire-mesh bottom for drainage and to facilitate cleaning or, in wooden feeders, drainage ports.

Hopper Feeder

A modified platform feeder, commonly made of wood, offering a seed-dispensing reservoir with a roof that protects the seed from rain. Hoppers can be mounted on a pole or suspended from a hook or wire. Reservoirs can hold from 2 to 25 pounds of seed (depending, of course, upon size), making them maintenance friendly. Well-designed hoppers offering large landing platforms (not perches, which are shunned by some species) and ample room for birds to dip and feed without bumping their heads against the food reservoir are almost as bird friendly as open platform feeders.

Advantages: Less maintenance than platform feeders. Attractive to a large number of species.

Disadvantages: Depending upon your position, the hopper may block your view. Dispenses seed only. Is more expensive than a simple platform.

Features to look for: Sturdy construction. Large landing area. Generous seed-dispensing slot. Metal-screen feeding surfaces or drainage openings at the corners.

Tube Feeder

A long cylindrical feeder, most often plastic, outfitted with two to ten perches that allow birds to draw seed from openings in the tube. This is an "exclusionary feeder" designed to dispense specific types of seed and cater to smaller and more acrobatic species (although large tube feeders can be fitted with base trays that collect seed and can accommodate larger birds).

Advantages: Attractive to smaller, easily displaced bird species. Easy to hang, maintain, fill.

Disadvantages: Not attractive to many larger species. Poor designs sometimes cause birds to strangle in the seed ports or allow unused seed and hulls to jam lower ports. Fairly expensive.

Features to look for: Openings that offer unencumbered access to seed. Interior baffles that funnel seed to the lower ports and

Tube feeders are exclusionary feeders most attractive to many smaller, more nimble species, including, quite apparently, male and female Blue Grosbeak, which might stop by for a quick bite during spring migration—if you leave your feeder up after winter ends.

prevent it from collecting at the bottom of the tube (tempting birds to reach too deep, get their heads caught, and strangle).

Specialty Feeders

Thistle Feeders

Thistle feeders are modified tube feeders that dispense niger (pronounced NYE-jur) seed, or thistle seed—tiny caraway-like seed that goldfinches, siskins, and redpolls treat like opium (and vendors price like platinum). Perches are sometimes placed above the tiny openings, a refinement that favors smaller acrobatic species and discourages House Finches (which in some places, by dint of sheer numbers, crowd out other species). Thistle socks, nylon mesh dispensers, are inexpensive and effective but vulnerable to the maraudings of squirrels and starlings, which, caught in the grip of thistle lust, will rip a sock to shreds.

Thistle feeders are magnets for Pine Siskin (left) and American Goldfinch (right).

Peanut Feeders

Many bird species love peanuts, among them jays, nuthatches, magpies, starlings, and grackles. Shelled peanuts can be placed on platform feeders or in large hoppers to accommodate larger species or served up in special peanut feeders that feature a coarse wire mesh fashioned in a tube that caters to smaller clinging species.

Suet Feeders

Rubber- or plastic-coated wire-mesh feeders that hold beef suet, the energy-rich fat that surrounds beef kidneys. Woodpeckers (in particular) as well as chickadees, nuthatches, magpies, and other species love suet. These feeders are most effective affixed to the trunk of a tree. Barring this, they can be fastened to a post or the support ends of a hopper feeder. Suet feeders can also be free hanging, but models offering a wooden "tail prop" board will be most favored by woodpeckers (who plant their specially designed tails for stability when feeding). *Note:* Suet is not synonymous with ordinary beef fat, which has a high water content and usually contains pieces of meat. Beef fat freezes in cold temperatures and quickly goes rancid when it's warm. Suet, which has had all impurities boiled out, doesn't freeze and doesn't go bad; in fact, it has a shelf life of two years. While beef fat works, suet works better.

This suet feeder might not be active right now, but by the looks of that well-worked suet cake, it's hosted plenty of hungry diners.

This Broad-billed Hummingbird found an offering of sugar water irresistible. Note how clear the water is—a sure sign of a well-maintained hummingbird feeder.

Hummingbird Feeders

Highly specialized feeders that hold a sugar-water solution that hummingbirds draw from openings surrounding the feeder's base. A solution of 4 (or 5) parts water to 1 part white granulated (ordinary table) sugar is ideal. The standard formula is 1 cup water and ¹/₄ cup sugar. *Do not use honey.* Birds cannot metabolize it. *Do not use artificial sweeteners.* Any bird whose heart rate can reach 1,200 beats per minute and whose wings move at 50 beats per second doesn't need to diet. *Do not add red dye* as a hummingbird attractant. Most feeders are hummingbird-attracting red, and this is sufficient. Whether food coloring is or isn't harmful to hummingbirds is debatable, but it is also unnecessary. Be safe. Do not add food coloring to your sugar water.

Do clean hummingbird feeders frequently. Sugar water ferments quickly, forming alcohol. Feeders should be emptied and cleaned every other day in warm temperatures, every few (three to four) days otherwise. Fill feeders with only as much sugar water as you know birds will consume between cleanings. Clean with a 50/50 solution of warm water and white vinegar and refill. (Rather than mix a sugar solution for every refilling, a premixed batch can be refrigerated and used as needed). Be responsible. *If you are not willing to go to the necessary effort of maintaining hummingbird feeders properly, don't put them up in the first place.*

Incidentally, hummingbirds are not the only birds attracted to sugar water. Orioles and other species will come in for a drink, especially in hot desert climates. Since hummingbird feeders are specialized for birds that hover, a shallow saucer filled with sugar water and placed where birds can perch and drink will serve other species.

Specialty Foods

Seed is widely but not universally accepted among bird species. Other food items, besides suet and sugar water, can help subsidize a bird's diet and make your feeding station attractive to non-seed-eating species.

Fruit is avidly sought by some species and easy to come by. In winter, grapes or raisins or banana, orange, or apple slices placed on a tray feeder will gain favor with robins, mockingbirds, and, where temperatures are more moderate, other half-hardy species, too. In summer, or year round in the extreme southern reaches of the U.S., orange halves affixed to trees or set on trays will attract jays, some woodpeckers, and orioles.

A food item that is not quite as easy to come by as fruit (but is, if anything, even more attractive to some winter birds) is mealworms, the larval form of the Yellow Mealworm Beetle, *Tenebrio molitar.* These small amber-colored protein packages will make seed-shunning birds (wrens, bluebirds) swear allegiance to your feeder, and benefit other birds by augmenting their diet with the protein they need.

Mealworms are not exactly stock items on the grocery store shelf (and are frequently missing from the specialty food section of stores as well). They can, however, be found in pet stores, bird-watching specialty stores, and sporting goods stores that cater to the ice-fishing crowd. They can also be raised at home—a pastime that will certainly be a conversation stopper at the next social you host.

WING BAR

Distribution (Why Birds Are Where They Are)

Wherever you live, you know that bird life changes throughout the year. The power of flight allows birds to move freely over great distances, and migration allows them to move north to raise their young where food is abundant and competition low, and then return to regions that provide food and cover during winter.

To better appreciate why the birds at your feeders vary during the year, you need to understand bird distribution and relate it to where you live. Consider your backyard as a reference point. Birds observed in your part of the country can be classified in the following ways. Some birds, called permanent residents, live in your area year round. As winter winds down,

Irruptive species such as these Red Crossbills stage periodic incursions when their food supply in northern regions is low, forcing flocks to range farther south than is normal.

waves of spring migrants wing their way north. Those that stop off to breed in your area are called summer residents. The migrants that may stop for a while but continue north are called transients. As summer winds down, birds begin their fall migration. Once again, the transients may stop for a while to rest but will continue on to wintering sites farther south. The migrants that stop in your area to spend the winter are appropriately called winter residents. The term vagrant refers to birds that are far away from their normal range. They are sometimes storm driven and can be of any age, but vagrants are often immature birds, which have a tendency to wander more widely in their hatching year. Vagrancy usually involves a single bird, or a small number of birds.

For the most part, the birds that come to your backyard fit one of the categories defined above. But occasionally, birds that normally winter in Canada and the extreme northern United States come south in tremendous numbers, sometimes reaching southern states. Examples include Evening and Pine Grosbeaks, Common Redpolls, Pine Siskins, and White-winged and Red Crossbills. These periodic flights, called irruptions, are actually irregular migrations that typically occur every few years and are associated with a failure of seed crops on which the birds depend. A number of predators, including Northern Goshawks, Snowy and Great Gray Owls, and Northern Shrikes, are also irruptive species that fly south in great numbers during some winters when their populations are high and populations of their regular prey species are low. ■

—Eldon Greij

Eldon Greij began his adventure with birds as a college professor and then became the founding editor of Birder's World, *now* BirdWatching *magazine.*

So Where Do You Get All This Stuff?

Bird-feeding accessories are widely available. One of the advantages of being part of a block of 67 million consumers is that people are eager to sell you things. Commercial bird feeders and seed are seasonably available at most large retail outlets, shopping centers, garden centers, and many general or hardware stores. For the most part, the best information and bird-feeding products are going to be available from stores that cater specifically to the needs of bird watchers—privately owned shops and owner-operated stores in chains such as Wild Bird Centers and Wild Birds Unlimited and nature centers and Audubon Society stores that specialize in equipment and seed. Some garden centers and hardware stores also offer an array of quality bird-feeding equipment and supplies.

Go online and search "bird-feeding supplies" for your area. Or go to the yellow pages and look under "Bird Feeders and Houses." Or you can call your local nature center and ask where they get their bird-feeding products and supplies. They may also tip you off to the food items that work best in your region.

Want Diversity? Mix Feeders, Not Just Seed

Mixed seed has one advantage. It caters to the greatest number of species simply and easily. If you have just one feeder, a mix of black-oil sunflower seed, peanut pieces, and white proso millet will serve best over most of North America. If you *really* want to increase the number and diversity of birds coming to your backyard, however, add feeders that cater to the specific feeding habits of different birds and fill them with the specific seed those species favor. You cannot go wrong having one feeder dedicated to black-oil sunflower seed and another containing mixed seed. By reducing competition for perch space and increasing feeding opportunities you will get more visitors, more often—and that is what feeding birds is all about.

When to Feed

Most people feed birds during the winter months primarily because that is when birds, particularly seed-eating birds, are most easily attracted by artificial feeding. Over most of North America, seed-eating birds begin migrating south in October. Having feeders up then will encourage migrant birds to remain in your area; keeping them filled will hold the migrants until March and April, when most depart.

Do feeding stations tempt birds to remain farther north than is good for them? There is no evidence supporting this, and for those who anguish over the possibility, take this wisdom to heart: *These are professional wild birds. They know what they are doing.* Similar concern has been expressed regarding hummingbird feeders and whether their presence encourages hummingbirds to linger as cold weather approaches. Again, these are professional birds—every one the product of a long line of survivors. Hummingbirds that turn up at feeders above the year-round blossom belt (Florida, the Gulf Coast states, the extreme Southwest, Southern and Coastal California) are pioneers. Some exploratory twist in their genetic blueprint has prompted them to fly a path less traveled. This is the cornerstone of evolution. Feeders that are maintained in marginally temperate places (such as Massachusetts) sometimes attract hummingbird species hundreds of miles outside of their normal geographic and temporal range. While these feeders don't draw these pioneers, they may sustain (at least for a time) what will very probably be an evolutionary dead end.

Since feeding birds is rooted in entertainment, not altruism, there is no reason not to continue to feed birds during warm-weather months (if you so desire). You'll probably want to change your mix to suit the nutritional interests of the summer crowd (for instance, the departure of northern breeding sparrows and juncos will reduce the demand for millet). But other offerings (such as fruit) will draw minions who will stop in, now and again, to grab a quick bite during a busy day of defending their territory, sporting with the neighbor's mate, and feeding young.

All the things wild birds do.

Where to Feed Birds

There are two key considerations that must be balanced when placing feeders: *convenience* and *cover.* The optimally placed feeder is one that can be seen easily—from the kitchen window, from the office, from the porch—wherever you spend the most time and want to be enchanted by the mosaic of color and movement you have created. Feeders should be close enough so that birds can be easily identified and the nuances of their behavior can be observed—the spatial defensiveness of juncos, the grab-and-go style of nuthatches, the alert assertiveness of jays.

A brush pile strategically located near feeders offers birds a safe place to wait until dining space opens up. PAT SUTTON

You'll also want feeders placed so that keeping them filled, particularly when the weather is bad, isn't a daunting chore. Empty feeders don't attract birds, and harsh weather is precisely when your regulars will be counting on you.

The second major consideration when choosing the location of your feeders relates to cover. Birds need shelter—from the elements, from predators. Feeders should be located so that birds can feed in comfort with minimal risk. A feeder sitting in the middle of a yard, open to the elements and far from protective vegetation, isn't going to be as attractive to birds as a feeder properly placed.

Ideally, a feeder should stand on the lee (and sunny) side of something that blocks the wind—a tree, bush, hedge, overgrown garden, outbuilding, fence, or your home. A location that gets warming sunlight during the day gets high marks from birds. The location should be close enough to vegetation so that birds can bolt for cover if a hawk is approaching, *but not so close that squirrels can use limbs as launch points to gain access to your feeders or cats can stalk close enough to ambush a bird.* (Domestic cats rank as one of the primary threats to birds. Be responsible: Keep your cat indoors.)

Ten feet from the nearest branch crosses the launch threshold for most squirrels; four and a half feet above the ground is above the leap-limit of the average tabby. Thirty to forty feet from cover seems to make some bird species hesitant.

If existing cover is at a premium, plan for the future and put in some sheltering plants. In the meantime, you can build one or more brush piles from fallen branches, cornstalks, even the discarded Christmas tree—anything that will offer birds a place to hide when a hawk is closing in, or just to sit while waiting for their turn at the feeder.

A brush pile sitting in the middle of a backyard might not be in the landscaping style of Martha Stewart, but your birds will overlook that, and you'll probably find (maybe to your chagrin) that the pile will be the most bird-active place around.

WING BAR

Glass and Tragedy

Sheet glass is very arguably the most underappreciated lethal threat to birds in general, and to some species far more than others. Birds act as if they do not see it, and most often the consequences are instantaneous death or debilitating injury for countless numbers. My investigations have found that lethal collisions take place wherever birds and glass mutually occur, and the victims of sheet glass have been recorded the world over at windows of all sizes in residential homes as well as single or multistory buildings with entire walls of glass.

There is more than one type of bird-glass collision. One is rarely, if ever, harmful, whereas the other results in a fatality one out of every two strikes. Harmless strikes occur when backyard birds, such as American Robin or Northern Cardinal, repeatedly bang into and flutter against windows in the spring and summer. This action is often of concern to home owners and, for some, no small annoyance, but except for an occasional bloodied face, the birds seem only to exhaust themselves for a few weeks during the breeding season. These types of strikes are the result of birds defending their territories against their reflected image. By contrast, birds that strike glass as if they are unaware of its presence are so totally deceived and vulnerable that they kill themselves flying into it (either outright or over the course of several hours as brain hemorrhages manifest themselves). These birds are attempting to reach habitat visible on the other side of the clear panes or the perfect illusion of habitat and sky reflected by the glass surface. Glass is an indiscriminate killer, taking the fit as well as the unfit of a species population.

For more than 25 years I have been studying the glass hazard by conducting extensive observations and experiments at actual collision sites, at homes and various building types. To put the magnitude of this problem in perspective, by assuming one to ten birds are killed at one building over a one-year period, I estimate that between 100 million and one billion birds are killed striking sheet glass in the United States alone. Some of the most informed scientists consider even the upper limit of this range to be excessively conservative, given the amount of sheet glass in almost every human structure; some buildings are known to kill hundreds of birds in a single day. The death toll worldwide is certainly in the billions. I am frequently asked "If birds are killed at windows to the extent believed, why don't we find them heaped below and in front of the offending panes?" The mounds of bodies never pile up because strike victims are part of and disappear with the 10 billion individuals that are estimated to die from one year to the next in the overall bird population of North America. The billions that perish by any number of means are simply carried off and eaten by predators and scavengers, or lie hidden, decaying.

Approximately 25 percent or 225 species of birds in the United States and Canada have been documented striking windows. The species not recorded as window-kills are those that usually do not occur near human dwellings. The sex, age, or resident status of a bird in any locality has little influence on its vulnerability to windows. There is no season or time of day, and almost no weather conditions, during which birds elude glass. Transparent or reflective windows of various colors are equally lethal to birds. Strikes occur at windows of various sizes, heights, and orientations in urban, suburban, and rural environments—but birds are more vulnerable to large (greater than 2 square meters) panes near ground level and at heights above 3 meters in suburban and rural areas. Continuous monitoring at single-family homes reveals that bird strikes are more frequent during winter than any other time of the year, including the temperate spring and fall migratory periods, when this type of mortality typically attracts the most human attention because victims are often more visible on the sidewalks or around their workplaces. Winter strikes are more numerous because more birds are attracted to the vicinity of glass by first being attracted to bird feeders placed near windows.

Currently, there are many solutions that effectively reduce or eliminate bird strikes, but none that are universally applicable or readily acceptable for all human structures. Protective measures range from physical barriers that keep birds from striking the unyielding surface to detractants that protect by transforming the area occupied by glass into an uninviting space or recognizable obstacle to be avoided. Fortunately, an offending window in a home is easily rendered safe for birds by covering it with netting on the outside surface. Detractants including awnings, beads, bamboo, or fabric strips hung on the outside and in front of windows, or stickers, such as silhouettes of any shape, size, or color—as long as they are placed on the outside, contrast with the glass, and are uniformly separated by 5 to 10 centimeters (2 to 4 inches) over the entire surface. My experiments reveal that a single silhouette, a falcon or other shape, will not significantly deter strikes any more than a window without a silhouette. Covering the window uniformly so that whatever stickers are used are separated by 5 to 10 centimeters will eliminate strikes completely. As long as more than one outside window covering is used, the strike rate will be reduced, and the more there are the better the strike prevention.

Strike prevention measures appropriate for remodeled or new buildings are required if we are to make them safe for birds. Currently, nonreflective glass that gives an opaque appearance is available, but I am told it is rarely recommended by architects because it is inefficient in conserving energy. I have proposed the manufacture of a new product, sheet glass that externally shows creative patterns separated by the 5-to-10-centimeter distance; internally, the glass would have the same unaltered view as contemporary panes. A glass of this type would be especially functional for sunroom additions to homes. My studies indicate that these see-through extensions are death traps for resident as well as migratory birds.

Long ago, I noted that a good deal of protection for birds attracted to feeders occurred when the feeder was moved *closer* to a window. My students and I were able to quantify this protection by conducting experiments that revealed that feeders placed within 1 meter or less eliminated all harmful strikes at the nearby window. Alternatively, a feeder placed at 4 meters (about 13 feet) resulted in significantly more strike deaths than one closer or farther from the offending window.

The closer the feeder is to a window, the safer it is for visiting birds because they focus on landing on the feeder. If when leaving the feeder they do strike glass, they do not build up enough momentum to kill or injure themselves.

Whatever means are used to reduce this unintended killing will be appreciated by those of us concerned about the health of bird populations and biodiverisity in general. Most solutions will require humans to tolerate some aesthetic changes to their dwellings, or more bird species will have to tolerate continued losses. ■

—Dr. Daniel Klem, Jr.

Daniel Klem, professor of biology at Muhlenberg College, in Muhlenberg, Pennsylvania, has studied and written about the subject of glass and bird strikes for more than two decades.

One easy partial remedy for many windows is to keep exterior mosquito screen up all year. Also, for birds attacking their reflections in windows, try soaping up the window from the outside, creating a grid pattern.   —PD

Speaking of Gardening, How About . . .

Landscaping for Birds
Artificial feeding stations encourage birds to frequent your yard and direct them to places where they are easily viewed. But if you really want to make your yard attractive to a number and variety of birds, particularly during warmer months, you'll have to landscape

Landscaping with native plants that are attractive to birds will greatly enhance your property's appeal year round. Pictured here are the gardens of Clay and Pat Sutton, in Goshen, New Jersey. PAT SUTTON

for them. This can be done with a great deal of effort, or through benign neglect.

Many trees, plants, shrubs, and grasses are attractive to birds, providing food, shelter, protection, or nest sites. Most favored are food-bearing plants that offer birds seed, berries, or fruit. Examples include mountain ash, juniper, sumac, Black Cherry, American Holly, mulberry, Little Bluestem, Desert Olive, and Wax Myrtle. These plants are not only sought out by birds coming to your feeder; many are also attractive to reluctant feeder species, such as waxwings and thrushes.

Some plants that are attractive to birds are not direct sources of food. In April and May, flowering oaks support a host of nectar-feeding insects. These in turn draw hordes of migrating (and highly insectivorous) warblers—a colorful seasonal bonus for any backyard.

Flowers, of course, are a food source for hummingbirds. When favorites such as Cardinal Flower, Penstemon, Trumpet Vine, and Spotted Touch-Me-Not are in bloom, hummingbirds may ignore sugar water entirely. Finding some of these plant species may be challenging—although more and more garden centers and bird-watching specialty stores are becoming attuned to the importance and attractiveness of natural plantings. But nature is perfectly capable of decorating her own house if left to do so. One of the best things home owners can do to make their yards attractive to birds is, literally, nothing. Birds are important dispensers of seed. Plants have made their fruiting seed bodies attractive to birds specifically so birds will consume them and distribute seeds to other locations through defecation. If you have a brush pile, you will see plants growing up between the branches in the spring. These "volunteers" come from the seeds birds consumed and defecated. Leaving them, and favorite local food types as selected by the birds themselves, alone will add to your yard's attractiveness to birds.

WING BAR

Planting to Attract Backyard Birds—The Experts' Choice

The best way to attract backyard birds through landscaping is to choose a diverse mix of trees, shrubs, and flowers. Select plants for their flowers and fruits, but also consider them for nest sites and protective cover as well. Experts from around the country have provided lists of their favorite plants to help you get started selecting plants tailored to your region. When in doubt, "go native." Native plants are well adapted to your soil and climate and well suited to meet the needs of native birds. ■

Benign Neglect

Our species likes to impose our peculiar sense of neatness and order upon the world—flat, grassy plains (called lawns) that are

Select Bird Attracting Plants for Assorted North American Regions

NORTHEAST
Selections by Wayne Peterson, Massachusetts Audubon Society, Lincoln Massachusetts

Birch (Betula)	Dogwood (Cornus)
American Mountain Ash (Sorbun americana)	Virburnum (Viburnum)
	Hawthorn (Crataegus)
Eastern Red Cedar (Juniperus virginiana)	Crabapple (Malus)
	Bittersweet (Celastrus)
Cherry (Prunus)	

MIDATLANTIC
Selections by Karen Williams, Proprietor. Flora for Fauna, Woodbine, New Jersey

American Holly (Ilex opeca)	Arrowood Viburnum (Viburnum dentatum)
Eastern Red Cedar (Juniperus virginiana)	Coral Honeysuckle (Lonicera sempervirens)
Oaks (Quercus spp.)	Black Cherry (Prunus serotina)
Eastern Dogwood (Cornus florida)	Elderberry (Sambuccus canadensis)
Hackberry (Celtis occidentalis)	Bayberry (Myrica pennsylvanica)

SOUTH
Selections by Reese Partridge and Tom Barnes

Pine (Pinus)	Hawthorn (Crataegus)
Oak (Quercus)	Honeysuckle (Lonicera)
Holly (Ilex)	Grape (Vitis)
Hackberry (Celtis)	Trumpet Vine (Campsis)
Rough-leaf Dogwood (Cornus drummondii)	Beardtongue (Penstemon)

EAST-CENTRAL/MIDWEST
Selections by Alicia Craig-Lich and Greg Oskay

Oak (Quercus)	Serviceberry (Amelanchier)
Holly (Ilex)	Viburnum (Viburnum)
Pine (Pinus)	Coral Bells (Heuchera)
Hickory (Carya)	Purple Coneflower (Echinacea)
Black Cherry (Prunus serotina)	
Elderberry (Sambucus)	

continued

Select Bird Attracting Plants for Assorted North American Regions

GREAT PLAINS/PRAIRIES
Selections by Chuck Otte

Eastern Red Cedar (Juniperus virginiana)
Crabapple (Malus)
Hawthorn (Crataegus)
Rough-leaf Dogwood (Cornus drummondii)
Sumac (Rhus)

Elderberry (Sambucus canadensis)
Wild Plum (Prunus americana)
Trumpet Vine (Campsis radicans)
Virginia Creeper (Parthenocissus quinquefolia)
Sunflower (Helianthus)

NORTHERN BORDER STATES AND CANADA
Selections by Bucky Dennerlein, Minnesota Department of Natural Resources

Spruce (Picea)
Hackberry (Celtis)
Oak (Quercus)
Cherry (Prunus)
Hazelnut (Corylus)
Snowberry, Coralberry (Symphoricarpos)

Sumac (Rhus)
Virginia Creeper (Parthenocissus quinquefolia)
Trumpet Creeper (Campsis radicans)
Purple Coneflower (Echinacea)

ROCKY MOUNTAINS
Selections by Pat Hayward and Susan Lenard

Colorado Spruce (Picea pungens)
Rocky Mountain Juniper (Juniperus scopulorum)
Cottonwood (Populus)
Hawthorn (Crataegus)
Chokecherry (Prunus virginiana)

Serviceberry (Amelanchier)
Currant (Ribes)
Trumpet Vine (Campsis radicans)
Columbine (Aquilegia)
Beardtongue (Penstemon)

NORTHWEST
Selections by Patty Van Vlack and Carol Pollard

Douglas Fir (Pseudotsuga menziesii)
Pacific Dogwood (Cornus nuttalli)
Birch (Betula)
Elderberry (Sambucus)
Red Currant (Ribes sanguineum)

Raspberry, Blackberry (Rubus)
Virginia Creeper (Parthenocissus quinquefolia)
Aster (Aster)
Columbine (Aquilegia)

continued

Select Bird Attracting Plants for Assorted North American Regions

SOUTHWEST
Selections by Lynn Hassler

Desert Marigold (Baileya multiradiata)	Brittle Bush (Encelia farinosa)
Baja Fairy Duster (Calliandra californica)	Chuparoso (Justicia californica)
Saguaro, Desert (Carnegiea gigantea)	Wolfberry (Lycium)
Desert Hackberry (Celtis pallida)	Penstemon (Penstemon)
New Mexico Thistle (Cirsium neomexicanum)	Red Sage (Salvia greggii)

SOUTH-CENTRAL CALIFORNIA
Selections from New Western Sunset Garden Book, National Audubon Society

California Bayberry (Myrica californica)	Currant (Ribes)
Coffeeberry (Rhamnus californica)	Chuparosa (Justicia)
Strawberry Tree (Arbutus unedo)	Honeysuckle (Lonicera)
California Holly (Heteromeles arbutifolia)	Salvia (Salvia)
Cestrum (Cestrum)	California Fuchsia (Zauschneria californica)

to species diversity what white bread is to nutrition. Woodlots stripped down to a sterile, park-like appearance are less attractive than woodlots where the understory is allowed to flourish and leaf litter left to accumulate.

Nature is different. Nature likes diversity, and she likes clutter. So do most bird species.

If you have a woodlot on your property, or a wooded edge, *resist the temptation to clear out the understory.* A denuded landscape is a bird-free landscape. Many understory trees and vines, shrubs, and plants (dogwood, holly, wintergreen, even poison ivy) are fruiting, and the branches in this strata of the forest are prime nesting places for birds.

If you have a fence, don't trim grass to the edge. Let it grow up as a buffer and food source for birds. If you have a flower garden, don't cut back the dead plants in the winter. Let them tangle and blow down into natural, sheltering pockets. You'll have more birds if you do.

If you build a few strategic brush piles, you'll soon find a wealth of seed-bearing plants sprouting up through the latticework of branches—the product of seeds that have passed through the digestive systems of host bird species and found fertile footing in your yard. This is one of the ways nature spreads her wealth and says thank you for your benign neglect.

Bird-feeding Problems

In an ideal world, birds would come into your yard, offer hours of entertainment, and leave you lighthearted. The world is not ideal—not their world, not ours, and not where two imperfect worlds overlap. Engaging the natural world courts risk and challenge. Here are some common problems backyard birders face and some methods to redress them.

Hawks

Feeding stations create concentrations of birds, which is a natural attractant to bird-eating hawks—most commonly accipiters such as the robin-sized Sharp-shinned Hawk or the crow-sized Cooper's Hawk, but also, in open country, falcons such as the American Kestrel, Merlin, Peregrine and western Prairie Falcon, as well as Northern Harrier. In some parts of the country, some buteo species are bird-hunting specialists, too. Cover is a bird's best defense, but cover is also a two-edged sword. The same vegetative cover birds flee to for shelter may also cloak a hawk's approach.

All hawks are justly protected by law, so destroying them is not an option.

The solution to the problem of hawks picking off birds in your yard is simple. Stop thinking of it as a problem. Start thinking of the hawk as just one more bird coming to your feeder—one that doesn't eat seed. The relationship between predators and prey is one of the natural world's most ecologically important interactions. While we may not like it, we also lack the wisdom or standing to judge or interfere. And for whatever consolation it is worth, when you attract birds to your yard, you are not causing them to be killed. You are only causing them to be killed where you will see them.

If you elect to feed birds in your backyard you can expect visits from bird-catching raptors, like this young Cooper's Hawk. Just learn to accept it.

There is an old adage that applies here: If you can't stand the heat, stay out of the kitchen. If you don't want to engage the natural world, don't feed birds.

House Cats

House cats are different. Small bird-catching feline predators are native only to the American Southwest. Over most of North America, birds are not well attuned to this threat, with the result that an estimated three quarters of a *billion* birds per year are killed by domestic cats that are allowed to roam free. Feeders should be placed so that cats cannot approach or hide undetected. They should be elevated at least $4^{1}/_{2}$ feet, the limit of a cat's leap.

The only effective means of keeping house cats from killing birds, however, is to *keep cats indoors*. Don't let them roam during daylight hours in a yard filled with birds. Don't even think for a moment that your gentle, well-fed, bell-collar-wearing tabby isn't capable of killing birds. It is. It will. If you choose to feed birds and let your cat roam, you have elected to slaughter birds needlessly.

Disease

In any population of birds (and other living things) a small percentage will carry diseases that can be transmitted to other birds. Sometimes disease organisms are transmitted by direct physical contact, sometimes through fecal matter deposited in and around feeding stations. Rarely do diseases common to birds pose a health threat to humans (unless, of course, you are eating out of the feeder too), but in a situation where many birds are concentrated, bird-to-bird infection is facilitated. The solution is just that—a good cleansing solution involving white wine vinegar and hot water—and a periodic cleaning, particularly in warm weather. A thorough vinegar-and-water cleaning is warranted every three months or so. But even a periodic rinse with concentrated spray from a garden hose will help keep feeding stations the healthy environments you want them to be.

Squirrels

Squirrels are animals backyard bird watchers love to hate. They hog the seed. They chew up expensive feeders. They can, through pure esophageal zeal, bankrupt a modest seed budget. Feeders should be positioned away from overhangs or launch points. Poles that support feeders can be fitted with squirrel guards of PVC pipe or galvanized steel. There are "squirrel-proof" feeders that are effective (to a point) at excluding squirrels. Once squirrel security measures are in place, you can try luring squirrels away from feeders by making offerings of whole unshelled corncobs. The squirrels will accept the tribute and go off to enjoy the corn in some private corner so another squirrel won't usurp their prize.

Squirrel deterrents, such as cayenne pepper additives to be mixed with seed, sometimes discourage squirrels—but concerns have been raised as to the effect these irritants have on both the digestive tracts of birds and their eyes. They may also pose a health risk to pets and children. Do not use them.

Squirrels are the animal backyard birders love to hate. This Gray Squirrel very apparently has bird feeders all figured out.

Perhaps the best solution is, simply, acceptance. Squirrels might not be birds, but they are no less envoys of nature, and they like to eat, too. In fact, some squirrels are much akin to birds. Nocturnal and widely distributed flying squirrels are easily attracted to open feeders that offer a surfeit of sunflower seed. To see how common these winsome animals really are, leave the seed out (and the porch light on).

Rats

Passive resistance need not extend to less socially acceptable members of the rodent tribe. Norway Rats are drawn to both stored seed and waste seed that falls below feeders. Store seed in metal canisters—such as galvanized garbage containers—and avoid spillage. Using high-quality seed will reduce waste. Periodic raking of dropped seed will help keep the area rodent free.

If you keep feeding stations free of debris, you should never see a rat beneath your feeders. But if you do see one, know that rats are not the product of spontaneous creation. If they appear in your yard, it is from somewhere else, and that somewhere is probably not far away. One place to look is your or your neighbor's compost pile, one of the planet's most efficient rat factories.

Neighbors

Birds are not universally esteemed. Some people are truly phobic about them; others are simply indifferent. While you can choose friends who share your interests, you cannot always choose your neighbors, and you cannot make birds understand the significance of property lines.

Rarely does a neighbor object to birds coming to someone else's feeders. What draws their ire is an unkempt yard. Letting a yard go natural is not the same as letting it go to hell. Native plantings to attract birds can be orderly; areas left natural can be part of a larger landscaping scheme. *Your yard does not have to look like a cross between a junk heap and a poultry farm to be attractive to birds.*

By far the biggest complaint leveled at those who feed birds has little to do with native species. It has to do with individuals with an obsessive interest in pigeons and who have attracted nuisance-level numbers to the neighborhood. The solution is: *don't*. Rock Pigeons are large birds and ground feeders. Seed dispensed from exclusionary feeders will discourage them. Special prehulled seed can be used that results in almost no spillage (and no reason for pigeons to gather).

The key to avoiding problems with neighbors is not to start one. If your yard or your feathered minions do not bring down property values, you will probably encounter little animosity. In fact, you are far more likely to encounter rivalry.

WING BAR

How to Steal the Cardinal from Your Neighbor's Feeder

Cardinals, like justice, like cell-phone service, are not evenly apportioned. In many western states, the bird does not occur. But where this rakish red-dressed bird is found it quickly becomes one that backyard birders covet. Unfortunately, the Northern Cardinal is one of the most finicky of feeder birds. Here are a few simple guidelines for attracting them.

First, cardinals prefer large, open feeders with a surfeit of landing and feeding areas. Feeders with small perches are not as successful as those that offer lots of room. Fly-through and platform feeders enjoy the most success.

What you put in that feeder is important, too. Cardinals have large, strong beaks designed for shucking sunflower seeds. Black-oil sunflower seed is, again, the food of choice. Cardinals are also fond of striped sunflower seed.

They can also learn to like safflower seed. By initially mixing safflower with your sunflower, you can introduce this food to cardinals, allowing them to develop a taste for it. This is desirable because cardinals tend to shy away from crowded feeders. While safflower is relished by cardinals, it is not attractive to most other birds that might run cardinals off. By filling a feeder with only safflower seed, you can create a spot specifically for cardinals.

Another important characteristic to note about cardinals' feeding habits is that they are among the first up in the morning and the last to visit feeders at dusk. This may be an adaptation born of their dislike for crowds.

So if you want to see your cardinal(s), be prepared to rise early and post-pone dinner. ■

—Scott Edwards

Attracting Birds with Water

Some bird species get all the water they need from the food they eat. Virtually all backyard birds, however, need to drink water to remain healthy (and hardly a bird exists that does not like to bathe now and again). What this means to backyard bird watchers is that *water is a powerful attractant to birds*—whether it is standing, moving, misting, or dripping. In fact, in desert areas, and during summer heat, water will prove more attractive to birds than any amount of seed.

Commercial birdbaths, most typically a basin mounted on a pedestal, are readily available. Placed in a sheltered, shady place,

American Robin, a strong candidate for the title America's Favorite Bird, is a compulsive bather.

they will attract birds that will drink from the rim or step in to take a cooling, cleansing dip. (Hanging birdbaths lose their contents to wind, which accelerates evaporation. Birds don't accept them as readily as baths that offer a stable platform.)

The American Robin—widespread and a perennial candidate for the title of America's Favorite Bird—is a compulsive bather. Yet even for birds as large as a robin, *$1/2$ to $1^1/2$ inches of water in a birdbath is all they want, or need.* Keep your bath filled to this level. Change the water frequently. More water than this in your bath and you defeat your purpose. Also, try placing a large, flat stone in the middle of your bird bath. The most success can be had by putting basins directly on the ground, where birds are used to finding water.

If water attracts birds, moving water is like a siren's call—in fact, just the sound of water running or dripping is an attractant. Drip lines, used for irrigating plants in very dry areas, are a splendid source of water for birds. A hanging dripper can be any vessel that lets water droplets fall at a regulated rate. Birds are drawn to the falling droplets and enjoy standing beneath them. Bird photographers have understood the magnetic properties of drips for years. Many of the most exquisite photographs gracing natural history magazines owe their existence to a cheap, plastic, water-filled bottle with a hole poked in the bottom left to dangle over a shallow tray in some vegetated place.

Commercial misters, devices that send a fine spray of water into the air, are especially effective in vegetated areas where water can collect on leaves. Birds drawn to the spray will leaf bathe, the avian equivalent of sponge bathing among humans.

TALE SPOT

Chiricahua Mountains Morning

I recall an early July morning spent at Rustler Park, a forest island in Arizona's Chiricahua Mountains. The 9,000-foot elevation offers Canadian Zone habitat and a generous mix of Rocky Mountain and Southwestern bird species—at least it did until mid morning, when a hot, dry summer sun brought bird activity to a standstill.

Sitting by a shady stream, more interested in resting than birding, I was delighted when a Hermit Thrush came out of the shadows and proceeded to bathe. It was joined by a House Wren, a Yellow-eyed Junco (a regional specialty), and a Black-headed Grosbeak. Then a Western Tanager dropped out of the canopy, followed by a Hepatic Tanager. They were joined by a family group of Mexican Chickadees, a Plumbeous Vireo, a Grace's Warbler, an Olive Warbler, several Painted Redstarts, even the Red-faced Warbler that had eluded me all morning. For over an hour, I had many of these forest and treetop species at my feet in full view. It was a perfect example of how magnetic water is to birds. ■

Making Water

If you are lucky enough to have a stream or natural spring on your property, you can easily dam a section to create a small pool. Fit it out with rocks for perches and shallows for bathing and nature could hardly do better herself. (*Caution:* In some places, in these litigation-prone times, an area that holds water in an unfenced or otherwise accessible yard could be construed to be what prosecuting attorneys call an "attractive nuisance." When establishing a bird-bathing area, do not make it so attractive or so deep that it might constitute a hazard to children or pets.)

If you do not have a natural water source, there are commercial basins you can buy, complete with recirculating pumps, or you can construct a pool using a plastic liner and rainwater directed from a downspout. The same rules governing shallow depth and ample perching places apply. Naturally growing vegetation will disguise the artificial nature of the place and, in time, make it even more attractive to birds (and other living things).

Birds need water in winter as well as summer, but winter poses problems in places where daytime temperatures remain below freezing. Commercial water heaters are available that run on electricity and will keep birdbaths and pools ice free. In more

Birds need water, and a properly filled and maintained birdbath will attract birds year round, perhaps even Pine Siskin.

temperate areas, ice that forms at night can be replaced with water during the day.

Do not under any circumstances put antifreeze in your birdbath water. The mixture is toxic. The results will be tragic.

Nest Boxes

Many species of birds are cavity nesters—birds that use the defensive confines of tree cavities to protect themselves and their young. Included among the ranks of cavity nesters are several species of waterfowl, some falcons and owls, as well as chickadees, titmice, nuthatches, some flycatchers, Tree Swallows, and, of course, Purple Martins and bluebirds.

Modular Cavities

At some point in the overlapping lives of humans and birds it was discovered that cavity-nesting birds will quickly adopt artificial cavities or nest boxes. Note the use of the term "nest box" not

Properly situated nest boxes are often quickly used by cavity-nesting birds. Wouldn't you love to attract a male Mountain Bluebird to your yard? You need to start by living where this stunning Western species breeds. (Don't despair if you don't; there are lots of other cavity-nesters.) LINDA DUNNE

"house"—a house is something creatures live in, and living in houses is something birds do not do. Cavity-nesting birds use boxes to rear young. Some will roost in them at night. But they don't live in them the way people live in houses.

Semantics governing use and labels aside, properly sized and properly placed, nest boxes will attract cavity-using species as readily as any other hole surrounded by wood.

Properly Sized
Cavity-nesting birds come in all sizes, from House Wrens to Spotted Owls. All have at least these generalities in common: they choose or, in some cases, excavate cavities customized to fit, and they have nesting requirements relating to elevation, cavity depth and size, hole size, and habitat that should be met.

Summary of Bird Box Specifications for Select Species

Species	Interior Size	Ht. hole from ground	Hole	Mounting Ht.
Eastern Bluebird	4x4x10"	6"	$1^1/_2$"	4–10'
Western/Mountain Bluebird	5x5x11"	6"	$1^9/_{16}$"	4–10'
Chickadees	4x4x10"	6"	$1^1/_8$"	5–15'
Titmouse	4x4x10"	6"	$1^1/_4$"	5–15'
Nuthatch	4x4x10"	6"	$1^1/_4$"	5–15'
Finch	4x4x9"	5"	$1^3/_8$"	4–10'
House Wren	4x4x9"	6"	1"	4–10'
Bewicks Wren	4x4x9"	6"	1"	4–10'
Carolina Wren	4x4x10"	6"	$1^1/_2$"	4–10'
Prothonotary Warbler	4x4x10"	6"	$1^1/_2$"	4–6' 2' water
Purple Martin	6x6x6"	1"	$2^1/_2$"	8–10'
Barn Swallow	4x4"	shelf	--	4–15'
Tree/Violet-Green Swallow	5x5x10"	6"	$1^1/_2$"	4–15'
American Robin	6x6"	shelf	--	6–15'
Phoebe	6x6"	shelf	--	6–15'
Downy Woodpecker	4x4x12"	6"	$1^1/_4$"	6–20'
Hairy Woodpecker	5x5x13"	9"	$1^1/_2$"	6–20'
Flickers	6x6x16"	14"	2"	6–20'
Other Woodpecker Sp.	5x5x14"	9"	2"	6–20'
Ash-throated Flycatcher	5x5x9"	9"	$1^1/_2$"	8–20'
Great-crested Flycatcher	6x6x10"	7"	$1^3/_4$"	8–20'
Wood Duck	10x10x22"	17"	3x4" oblong	4' water 12' land
Screech/Saw-whet Owl	6x6x15"	9"	3"	8–30'
Boreal Owl	8x8x16"	10"	4"	8–30'

continued

Summary of Bird Box Specifications for Select Species

Species	Interior Size	Ht. hole from ground	Hole	Mounting Ht.
American Kestrel	7x7x16"	11"	3"	15–30'
Barn Owl	18x20x16"	4"	8"	10–20'
Barred Owl	14x14x26"	16"	8"	20–30'

Most measurements provided by Robin E. Clark, owner of Robin's Wood Ltd., specializing in quality nest boxes.

Having the right-sized opening will help exclude larger and less desirable species (such as starlings and House Sparrows). Having the right dimensions for your box will ensure that young birds have enough room to grow and be able to reach the opening when it's time to fledge.

Things to Look For in a Commercial Nest Box

Most, and arguably all, nest boxes should be constructed of wood. The arguments against other substances such as plastic or aluminum (nestling overheating, injury to nestlings caused by unnaturally slippery surfaces) are contestable. One thing only seems clear: The histories of both cavity-nesting birds and cavities made out of wood have been long and successful. You can't go wrong with wood. Plain, unpainted, unstained, untreated wood. Pine and cedar are durable and popular (and from a resource standpoint, environmentally acceptable). Exterior plywood is durable but not as easy to work with. Old planking, recycled lumber, and sawmill discards are ideally suited for constructing nest boxes if you are the do-it-yourself type.

Well-constructed nest boxes are sturdy in construction with boards at least 1 inch thick. Thicker wood insulates better than

thinner slabs, keeping interiors cooler in the summer and better insulated for birds (such as bluebirds) who use boxes as roost sites in the winter.

Exteriors should be unpainted. Interiors should be left rough and unfinished to offer nestlings traction when they evacuate.

Boxes should have ventilation slots near the slanted, rain-shedding top and drainage points at the bottom to vent any water that does enter the box.

No nest box should *ever* come with a perch. It is an open invitation to predators—akin to leaving the key in the front door. In nature, cavity-nesting species do without perches. They are at best superfluous and at worst life threatening to brooding adults and young.

As an added defense against the hole-widening incisors of squirrels and the chiseling bills of nest-box usurpers like starlings, nest-box openings can be

Cavity-nesting birds like this Black-backed Woodpecker excavate cavities that are subsequently used by other species. Nest boxes are merely man-made cavities and are as readily accepted as the real thing.
LINDA DUNNE

fitted with a surrounding predator-proof plate made of slate or metal or, barring this, a double-thick layer of wood.

All nest boxes should provide easy access to the interior—through a hinged or removable top or side—so that old nest material can be removed at the end of a nesting cycle. Some species that do not build nests per se like to have a thin ($1/2$ inch) layer of wood shavings cushioning the bottom of the box. Don't let your tidy inclinations overstep their natural proclivities.

Properly Timed

Winter (January through February) is the best time to place nest boxes. Many species start prospecting for good sites early, even if occupation is still weeks away. Bluebirds, Tree Swallows, and even Purple Martins are very early migrants, establishing themselves over much of North America by March.

Some species (bluebirds and wrens) double or even triple clutch (i.e., raise two or three broods during the breeding season). Nest boxes put up late, in May or June, may catch these species the second time around.

Properly Placed

Different species have different requirements. What attracts one discourages another. Ideally, boxes should be placed so that they receive some shade during midday heat, as a nest cavity in a tree trunk would.

Boxes attached directly to the trunks of trees come closest to replicating nature. Fence posts make suitable substitutes for some species, most notably bluebirds. With human-tolerant species, such as wrens and House Finches, boxes may be affixed to homes, even to well-trafficked outbuildings.

Many species, including some open-country birds, like a tree or perching surface within 10 or 20 feet of the front of the box (a notable exception is the Purple Martin, which likes unencumbered airspace). Adults use this as a launch site to gain access, and on their inaugural flight, fledgling birds have a "safe point" to target that will help keep them out of harm's way.

One thing that does not seem to matter a great deal is the direction the opening faces. Let other considerations dictate this concern—one of the most significant being where you are most likely to enjoy the view.

Properly Elevated

Most species are fairly tolerant regarding the height of a nest site. There is an acceptable range, but an "ideal" height is something established more for our benefit than theirs. Accordingly, boxes placed an easy-to-reach 4 to 6 feet above the ground are acceptable to most species, including bluebirds, chickadees, titmice, nuthatches, Tree Swallows, House Finches, and wrens. Woodpeckers, Purple Martin, and *Myiarchus* flycatchers like their cavities at stepladder height: 8 to 10 feet. Cavity-nesting ducks, owls, and American Kestrels fall in the extension-ladder range: 15 to 20 feet.

Properly Protected

Nesting in a cavity offers a good defense but does not impart immunity from predation. Rat snakes, bull snakes, and pine snakes are very adept at finding and entering cavities to consume both eggs and young. Raccoons and house cats are deft enough to reach into boxes and remove nests and young. Three and a half feet of seamless metal flashing or PVC pipe affixed around and above the base of the pole will discourage most terrestrial-based predators from climbing to a box. A 3-foot-wide metal "skirt" placed several feet above the ground will accomplish the same thing.

There are many other problems cavity-nesting birds face besides predators: competitive species like House Sparrow; infestations of ants, wasps, and parasites; hypothermia; and starvation. There are things that backyard birders can do to combat these problems birds face, but there is nothing that can be done to stop them.

Something every person should know, understand, and accept before engaging with the lives of other living things: in most songbird species, 90 percent of the birds hatched in any given year fail to see the next. Nest failure is the first major cut on the way to maintaining the environmental status quo.

It might not seem right. It might not seem fair. It might not be to our liking. But it is natural.

Birding the Other Side of the Fence

No matter how many feeders you place, no matter how many nest boxes you erect, no matter how bird friendly you make your yard, there is a finite number of species you will be able to attract—only a fraction of the species that occur in North America.

No loon has ever come to a feeder, yet five species of loons occur in North America, three of which are common in coastal areas all winter long. No Black-crowned Night-Heron or Golden Eagle or Yellow Warbler has ever been coaxed into a nest box. But these species are widespread and easy to find—so long as you know how and don't narrow the scope of your interest to the confines of your yard.

Whether you travel and casually encounter birds that are exciting and new, or travel with the expressed objective of finding

No matter how many feeders you hang or boxes you erect, there are just some birds you will never attract to your yard. Words never uttered:"Look, dear, there's a Red-throated Loon in our birdbath." LINDA DUNNE

species that you have never seen before, you will face one fundamental challenge: getting a feeder-close look at birds that are not habituated to flying in for you to view.

For this kind of look, you will need binoculars—an instrument that makes distant objects appear close. You are also going to discover that many of the birds you see are very unlike the familiar birds of your yard. To learn what they are requires a field guide, a book or app with images and supporting text that guides you to an identification. Learning a bird's name is the first step toward forming a bonding relationship—a relationship akin to that which exists between you and the birds in your yard.

SUMMARY

Birding is immensely popular, enjoyed by 67 million people in the United States alone. Yes, most bird watchers are most interested in the birds they find and attract to their yards. Birds are drawn to food, water, shelter, and suitable nesting sites. The primary tool of backyard bird watching is the bird feeder. Black-oil sunflower seed is attractive to the most species of birds, but other seeds—striped sunflower, peanuts, and white proso millet—are highly esteemed by birds. Using a combination of basic seed-dispensing feeders and specialty feeders will appeal to a greater diversity of species. Birds can be safely attracted all year with targeted food offerings. While the job of a bird feeder is to get birds close, landscaping for birds (using plants they need for food and cover) will greatly increase numbers and diversity.

Water is a powerful attractant to birds—in some places and at some times better than seed. Nest boxes are also attractive to a number of cavity-nesting species. But the overwhelming majority of bird species cannot be found in a typical yard no matter where you call home. To engage most of the birds found in North America, you will have to go where they are, and you will need to go properly equipped. ∎

CHAPTER 2

The Tools of the Trade—Binoculars and a Field Guide

IN THIS CHAPTER

Of Chimney Swifts and Larceny

The phone was ringing as I gained the door to New Jersey Audubon's Cape May Bird Observatory. It continued to ring as I won passage past the temperamental old lock. It persisted as I switched on the lights . . . crossed the room . . . threw my jacket over a chair . . . and stood, hand poised over the receiver, considering.

It was (after all) only 7:30 A.M., a Saturday, and my first day back as CMBO director following a six-year post elsewhere within the New Jersey Audubon hierarchy. I'd come in early to gain time to collect my thoughts before opening the door to visiting birders at

9—and I really wanted that time. Cape May is one of the planet's most celebrated bird-watching locations, and CMBO was the focal point for information.

The phone kept ringing.

"Cape May Bird Observatory," I said, answering the ring, and surrendering (as naturalists the world over typically do) to someone else's need.

"OH!" a voice intoned. A beautiful voice. A voice whose notes rose and fell like a Warbling Vireo but in timbre and pitch was as musical as an oriole. "So early I thought I would get a machine" (she pronounced it mah-sheen).

"No," I replied through a smile, "just a person this mor . . . "

"Good," she replied so fast her pronouncement broadsided my response. "I saw a program on the television about Cape May and that it was a good place to see birds, especially hawks, and is it true? Because if it is then I want to come and can you send me information? And tell me when is the best time to be there?"

Near as I could tell, she said this all in one breath. Near as I could tell, my answer to the conjoined elements of her question was a blanket "yes." But before I could reply the effervescent caller landed one last incongruous inquiry.

"And do you know about Chimney Swifts?"

"A . . . little," I stammered, which is true. I'm not an ornithologist, one who studies birds as a scientific pursuit. I'm a birder, one whose interest in birds is steeped in fun, challenge, discovery, and adventure. But as someone who has watched and studied birds for 56 of my 60-plus years, and as one who has observed some 20 species of swifts on 6 continents (including the Chimney Swift of eastern North America), I estimated I could claim to be, at least, swift conversant.

"Well do you know that Chimney Swifts live in the Bronx? And that they fly to South America in the winter? And that they come back again?" She said this with tones suggesting incredulity and, was it my imagination, or were her words tinged with longing, too?

In fact, I did know this principle of Chimney Swift behavior. Chimney Swifts are insect-eating birds, one of four swift species that nest in North America, and as insect-dependant birds, they must leave the Northern Hemisphere in winter. What interested me more than Chimney Swift distribution were the circumstances that had brought a 60-year-old Latino grandmother living in the Bronx to become fascinated with swifts in the first place.

"I saw them in a big cloud that disappeared into a chimney outside my window," she explained. "So I went to the bird people at the Bronx Zoo who told me that they were Chimney Swifts and that they were migrating and that if I went to Central Park I would see other birds so I did and met a lady with binoculars who told me that if I waited by this pond a 'black night-heron' would come and . . . and . . . IT DID!

Chimney Swifts are nimble birds that forage for insects in the open air—they are at home in the uncluttered skies above cities.

The lady let me see it through binoculars," she added. "It was beautiful."

I didn't respond at first. I was too *enchanted* by her story. And while I'm no stranger to people who have become fascinated by birds, having taught courses and led field trips and workshops for most of my adult life, I found it wonderfully affirming that even in a place as environmentally estranged as the Bronx, birds have the power to touch human lives.

"Do you have binoculars of your own?" I asked. "No," she admitted, "but my grandchildren are saving to buy me some."

"Do you have a field guide?" I inquired.

"What is that?" she wanted to know.

"A book with pictures that helps you identify the birds you see."

There was silence for a time—silence that was the echo of suspended breath. Then a voice that approached the thought the way shy desert birds approach water asked, "There are such things?"

"Yes," I said, glancing at the hundreds of titles sitting on the shelves of CMBO's bookstore—all of them filled with information about birds, all of them available to people who know such resources exist. "There are such books," I promised. "Can I have your name and address, please?"

She gave me the information I requested. We concluded our conversation. I placed a standard visitor-information packet into a padded envelope. Before sealing it, I crossed the room, lifted a Peterson Field Guide, *Eastern Birds,* off the rack, and slipped it into the envelope, too.

"They'll never miss it on inventory," I explained to my conscience.

So I'm pleased to say that my first act as the returning director of the Cape May Bird Observatory was ushering a new birder into a world of discovery. I'm embarrassed to say it was also larceny.

Keys to the Kingdom

Binoculars and a field guide—birding's tools of the trade. One vaults distance, offering supernatural intimacy. The other is a blueprint to discovery, a Rosetta stone to the birds. Together, they buy a person passage on a lifelong treasure hunt . . .

Binoculars and a field guide—the keys to the kingdom of birds. Together, they open the door to a world of discovery.

Unless the optics in your hands are unsuited for birding, making it impossible to find birds quickly and easily. Unless your field guide is poorly conceived, or abridged to simplify the selection process, thus building a conceptual barrier between you and a correct identification.

As for binoculars, there are, literally, hundreds of makes and models on the market, ranging in price from less than $100 to more than $3000. That's the good news. The bad news is that most are ill suited for bird study. They do not focus fast enough, do not focus close enough, are not waterproof, do not offer a generous field of view, or come with a distorting color bias.

As for field guides, there are more than a dozen popular general field guides to birds, all with strengths and weaknesses. The balance of this chapter will explain what you should look for in birding binoculars and a basic field guide to the birds.

Make the right choice and a world of discovery and wonder awaits, one vivid encounter at a time. Arm yourself with ill-suited optics or a poorly conceived field guide and frustration will be your birding companion—until you fix the problem, or give up birding.

Choosing the right binoculars is the single most important decision you will make as a new birder. Take your time. Do it right. And if you remember nothing else, remember this guiding principle: There is only one real test of binoculars—*you bring them to your eyes and you see things quickly and easily.*

Quality has a price. There is a reason why people buy premium binoculars. Even if you can't afford one, I encourage you to look through a premium instrument and see what puts the good in good glass. It will take your breath away.

The Defining Tool of Birding

Just as the bird feeder is the defining tool of backyard bird watching, a pair of binoculars is the primary tool of active field birding. They makes distant birds appear close, allowing detailed study of birds behaving naturally because you are far enough away not to be perceived as a threat, thus not prompting them to fly away or hide.

Binoculars are the defining tool of birding. Note the position of this birder's left hand—a placement that confers optimal stability and restful long-term viewing.

Before optics were refined and widely available, the study of birds was almost exclusively a scientific pursuit called ornithology. The primary tool of the early ornithologist was the shotgun—a tool that, like binoculars, vaulted distance, permitting close study of birds. Ornithologists such as Alexander Wilson (the "Father of Ornithology") and John James Audubon (America's pioneering bird painter) "collected" bird specimens, identified them, and, in the case of species new to science, described them, then rendered them into study skins and stored the specimen in their bird collections.

Shotgun ornithology had several advantages: close scrutiny, unlimited opportunity for later study, positive proof relating to the identification of a species. But it had obvious disadvantages, too. Shortly after the American Civil War, the quality of optical instruments improved markedly, finally reaching a point at which the characteristics that distinguished one bird species from another could often be seen in the field, eliminating the need to collect birds for identification purposes. By the early twentieth century, "field glass" ornithology was augmenting, even supplanting, "shotgun" ornithology, making it possible for scientists to expand the scope of their studies into the behavioral aspects of birds. Improved optics did another thing. They opened the door to bird study to broader segments of the population—people whose interest in birds was, in the conservation spirit of John Burrows, John Muir, and Teddy Roosevelt, enhanced by an aesthetic appreciation of birds and concern for their well-being. These hybrid individuals—a cross between the shotgun ornithologist and the turn-of-the-century "nature lover"— were the first bird watchers, although the term was not widely used until the last half of the twentieth century. The primary tool of the bird-watching crowd was, and remains, binoculars.

Binocular Basics

A binocular is a handheld, twin-barreled telescope whose barrels are aligned to fall upon the same spot. Each barrel contains glass elements called lenses and prisms. These catch, magnify, and direct an image down the length of the tubes to fall as shafts of light through exit pupils upon the binocular user's eyes.

Binoculars are more useful than telescopes insofar as they are lighter, more portable, more versatile, and designed to be operated with both eyes open, making them generally easier to use. Telescopes, more commonly referred to as spotting scopes, offer higher magnification than binoculars and are useful for more specialized forms of birding (spotting scopes are discussed in chapter 5).

Not Just Any Old Binoculars Will Do

Binoculars, like cars, like clothing, are designed with specific uses in mind and so have qualities that match the instrument to need. Some user groups, such as hunters, demand binoculars that are kick-around rugged. Others, such as sailors, demand instruments that are impervious to weather. Still others, such as backpackers, want instruments that are light and portable.

Birders demand all of these qualities, and more. For binoculars to be birder worthy they must be light, rugged, portable, *and* waterproof. They must also offer a wide field of view (to facilitate finding birds quickly), exceptional depth of field (to aid in finding birds in a maze of branches), close focus (so that birds can be viewed in tight woodland confines), fast focus, good balance, an intelligent and comfortable and stable design . . .

In short and in sum, binoculars suited for birding must meet more stringent demands than those of any other user group. There are indeed such birder-worthy instruments on the market. Don't settle for less.

Attributes of the Birding Binocular

The most important consideration when choosing binoculars is: Does the instrument fit—your hands, your face, your eyes? There is no one-size-fits-all binocular, and this truism is not something that can be canceled out by simply spending more money. Many people have spent in excess of $1000 for binoculars only to discover that for assorted or compounded reasons they don't work for them. Don't make their mistake.

TALE SPOT

The Binoculars with Arms and Legs

The participants of my birding workshop group were mustering. I was eyeing up their binoculars, assessing who might benefit from one of the loaner instruments in my trunk.

One young woman stood out, and not because of her size, which was petite. What made her conspicuous were the large 10x50 Night Owl binoculars suspended from her neck.

The Night Owl was a fine glass but not one designed for ballerinas. Burdened as she was, the woman looked like a binocular with arms and legs.

Without asking I could guess precisely how such a mismatch had happened. Knowing nothing about optics, this new birder concluded the best solution was to throw money at the problem. Going online she'd looked at a dealer's catalog and simply bought the most expensive instrument they carried—heedless of any other consideration, and concluding, as many consumers do, that most expensive is synonymous with best.

It was a very costly mistake because now she was armed with expensive binoculars so large she couldn't wrap her hands around them. In fact, I wasn't even confident she could lift them. ■

Doesn't the Quality of the Glass Matter?

Of course it matters. But optical quality, measured in terms of an instrument's ability to produce a bright, sharp, color-accurate image, pretty much stops being a concern as soon as you start thinking in terms of buying a well-designed $200 to $500 instrument—because (with few exceptions) this is the very least you should expect to pay for decent, durable, birder-worthy binoculars. Since manufacturers of lower-end instruments don't necessarily advertise the quality of the glass they use, buyers must often make this determination obliquely, by looking at the sticker price, and directly, by looking through the instruments. Trust your eyes. When the image makes you say "WOW!" that's what you are looking for. "Oh" is fine, but nothing beats "WOW!"

The trick is finding WOW at a price point that doesn't also make you say "OUCH!"

All things said and done, there really is only one way to test binoculars: You bring them to your eyes and you find things quickly and easily. Really, it is (or should be) that simple.

As with electronics, the emergence of Asia as a center for optics production has brought the price of very commendable binoculars down, and more and more optics manufactured in China are being built to birding specs.

But performance and durability have a price. Meeting the performance demands of birding increases production costs. But once you start paying $200 and up for binoculars, you can pretty much stop worrying about the quality of the glass and its ability to resolve detail (the image may not be superlative, but it will most probably be serviceable) and start assessing other considerations. The performance difference between $300 binoculars and $1000 binoculars may be considerable, but it often has less to do with the quality of the image than it does with durability and quality control.

Porro Prism versus Roof Prism

Wide-bodied versus Sleek

Binoculars come in two basic design patterns: porro prism and roof prism. Both have advantages and disadvantages that relate directly to price and performance.

Porro prism binoculars are classically shaped, wide-bodied instruments. The big lenses in the front (the objective lenses) and the smaller lenses close to your eyes (the ocular lenses) are offset— not lined up along a linear axis. Advantages: Porro prism binoculars are generally less expensive than roof prisms and by the nature of their internal design inherently brighter and sharper. But, because of this design, which forces users to bring arms and elbows away from the body, porro prism binoculars are generally more difficult to hold steady than roof prisms and are generally less rugged (and typically less waterproof, too).

Two basic binocular designs: porro prism (left) and roof prism (right).

Roof prism binoculars are sleeker and generally more favored among skilled birders. Advantages: The sleeker design is inherently more ergonomic, fitting most hands better and allowing users to keep elbows closer to their sides—factors that contribute to a more-stable viewing platform. A stable binocular contributes to better overall image quality, particularly with higher (10x) magnifications. Also, the roof prism system is better anchored inside the barrels, so it's inherently more rugged. Disadvantages: Roof prisms are modestly more expensive than porro prism instruments because the internal glass elements must be more perfectly aligned and the antireflective coatings that reduce light loss as image strikes glass must be more sophisticated. Lenses must also be "phase coated" to compensate for light-wave distortion inherent in the roof prism design. Yet and still, and as said, most experienced birders prefer roof prisms to porro prisms because of their ruggedness and more stable image. The optical shortfalls of the roof design can be mitigated by improving the quality of the glass, using superior reflecting materials (silver versus aluminum) and treating all glass surfaces (inside and out) with multiple coatings of antireflective material.

In short, by spending more money.

Key words to look for when buying binoculars are *waterproof,* *FULLY multicoated,* and, for roof prism binoculars, *phase corrected* or *phase coated.* Another sign of quality is the warranty. Many superior optics, even some in the mid-price range, come with unconditional no-fault warranties. Only manufacturers confident in the durability of their products would offer such a generous option.

Magnification, or Power

Most new binocular buyers are fixated on binocular magnification, or "power," which is printed on the binoculars as part of a two-number formula: 7x42 or 8x32 or 10x50, for example. The first number relates to the binoculars' power. A 7x pair of binoculars will magnify an object so that it appears seven times larger, or only 1/7th the actual distance away. Higher magnifications make the image appear even larger or closer.

And isn't bigger better? Only to a point.

Remember, binoculars are hand held. The higher the magnification, the harder they are to hold steady. Increased hand-shake degrades image quality, nullifying the advantage of higher magnification. Yes, you have a bigger image, but the detail you perceive (and need for identification) is diminished because of vibration. "But," you say, "I have steady hands, so I can hold a 10x steady." I'm sure you do, but I am equally certain that if you can hold a 10x steady, you will hold a 7x steadier. (To see how hand-shake affects image quality, and how unstable your hands are, train your binoculars on a star. The target will dance in your glass.)

But the biggest problem with increased magnification is that many of the performance qualities that make binoculars easy to use are diminished as magnification increases.

For example, as power goes up, the field of view goes down—the chunk of tree or sky you see is reduced. And a wide field of view is important to birding. A wide field (one that offers at least 320 feet at 1,000 yards) is particularly important for inexperienced birders—for whom birding's greatest challenge is often *finding* the bird in their binocular, not necessarily *identifying* it. The more generous the field, the easier it is to get on target because your aim doesn't

Magnification is usually shown on binoculars as part of a two-part formula. Shown here is one barrel of 7x (or seven-power) Leica binoculars.

need to be precise. Higher magnification also reduces depth of field, making it harder to locate birds in a three-dimensional world. Higher magnification also results in a darker image because the shaft of light passing through the binocular is narrower. And it also becomes more difficult to quickly align the exit pupils of the binocular to the pupils of your eyes.

So by choosing 10x binoculars instead of a 7x or 8x, you have thrown away many of the performance qualities that make a glass user friendly. You've given up field of view, depth of field, ease of focus, and image brightness—all for a larger image that offers little to no appreciable boost in your ability to note distinguishing details. What you have gained by magnification you have lost to hand-shake.

That's a lot to sacrifice for nothing more than a bigger image.

Please, please, please heed this advice: *Buy a 7x or 8x.* You'll be a happier, less frustrated birder who gets on target while others are spinning their focus wheels.

Objective Lens Size

While we are discussing basic binocular standards we might as well demystify the rest of the binomial formula etched on the instrument.

The second number in the formula 7x42 or 8x32 relates to the size, or diameter, of the objective lens as represented in millimeters. So a 7x42 binocular is a seven-power binocular with an objective lens 42 millimeters wide. A 7x50 binocular is a seven-power binocular with an objective lens 50 millimeters wide.

The number has nothing to do with field of view—a performance quality that is commonly printed elsewhere on your binoculars or in the literature and expressed as XX feet at 1,000 yards or XX meters at 1,000 meters. Field of view might also be expressed as degrees of arc.

But the second number in the binomial formula does have a great deal to do with how bright your binoculars will be in low-light conditions. Bigger objective lenses increase the diameter of the shaft of light passing through the instrument as well as the diameter of the exit pupil. The destination of this shaft of light is the pupil of your eye, the portal through which light passes to your optical nerve. In adults, the human eye pupil expands in low light to about 5 millimeters and contracts in bright light to about 2 millimeters. The width of the shaft of light (or diameter of your binoculars' exit pupil) can be calculated by dividing the first number in the binoculars binomial (power) into the second (objective lens diameter) Thus, a 7x42 binocular will have an exit pupil 6 millimeters in diameter—a diameter that corresponds well to the maximum expansion of the human pupil in low-light conditions. An 8x32 binocular has an exit pupil of 4 millimeters. In low-light conditions, when the human pupil is fully expanded, a larger objective lens is a desirable thing, but in average light, a 8x32 provides the eye with enough light to perform perfectly well, and with less weight around your neck. (Glass is heavy stuff; smaller objective lenses contribute to lighter binoculars.)

In real-world terms, the performance difference between binoculars with 42mm lenses as opposed to 32mm lenses is about the first 15 and last 15 minutes of daylight. It is only when your eyes' pupils are wide enough to accommodate wider shafts of light that the advantage of larger objective lenses can be appreciated.

This is not to say that binoculars with 32mm objective lenses don't work in low-light conditions. They do. It's just in low light when binoculars with wider objective lenses and bigger exit pupils will be noticeably brighter than comparably powered instruments with smaller objective lenses.

So Which Is Better, Roof or Porro?

Neither, if the qualifying standard is overall image quality (what you see). Porro prisms offer superior optical performance for less money; roof prisms offer greater stability. Image quality is the sum of both. If you plan to spend less than $300 for binoculars, a porro prism design will probably offer the best optical package for the money. On the other hand, if you don't mind spending a little more, the inherent advantages of phase-corrected roof prism binoculars become manifest.

More fundamental than design is . . .

How Does the Instrument Fit You?

If you grasp binoculars and your index finger does not fall easily upon the focus wheel, or if you must raise an elbow or shift your grip to reach the focus wheel, put them down. The instrument is too large for your hands or poorly designed. When you raise your elbow up and away from your body you destabilize the platform, increasing hand-shake, thus reducing image quality.

If you bring the binoculars up to your eyes and find that you cannot adjust the ocular lenses close enough or wide enough to allow you to see a single image effortlessly, or you are constantly plagued by black flashes or vignetting, put them down. The interpupillary distance does not fit your face and eyes. Check first to see if the twist-up eyecups are comparably adjusted—that both cups are equally up or down. If the interpupillary distance cannot be brought close enough or wide enough to fit your eyes easily, the shaft of light will fall to the side of one or both of your pupils, causing your eye to see the image only in snatches.

On well-fitted binoculars your fingers should fall easily on the focus wheel.

Size and shape directly affect how easily and steadily a binocular can be held. Light, pocket-sized, mini-binoculars favored by backpackers offer little to anchor your grip, so hand-shake is exacerbated. For this reason, and because mini-binoculars trade off optical performance for size, birders generally avoid them. Marine and military binoculars are bulky and heavy, causing muscle fatigue, which also increases hand-shake and reduces image quality. Birders should avoid these, too.

Binocular Weight

For people who have neck or back problems, weight may rank as a determining factor governing the choice of binoculars. The most popular birding binoculars on the market range from 16 to 38 ounces—a very wide range. Binocular manufacturers are conscious of weight and so will house instruments in polycarb bodies and lightweight metal alloys, shaving ounces. The fact remains that most of the weight in high-quality binoculars is in the optical glass. The denser glass, the better it is, but the more it weighs and costs.

The best-performing birding binoculars on the planet weigh between 16 and 38 ounces, with most premium instruments weighing about 28. That is the weight and price of quality.

Note: If binocular weight is a concern, there are ways to redress it short of compromising the performance of your instrument. Wide, spongy neoprene neck straps help distribute the weight across your neck. Lengthening the strap and wearing binoculars bandolier fashion (over the shoulder and across the chest, with the binoculars resting under one arm) also help some people. There are also harness systems available that distribute the weight to the shoulders and off the neck entirely. Some of these systems are hard to get in and out of, but they do work, and many also keep binoculars from bouncing against the chest, which some people find annoying.

Focusing

Birding requires constant focusing—from active shorebirds foraging close at hand to a bird of prey fast disappearing over the horizon to that pop-up, point-blank sparrow that is going to disappear in about 0.05 second. All birding binoculars must focus quickly, easily, and responsively via a center-focus system.

Center-focus binoculars should feature a single wheel that falls where your index finger can easily find it. When this wheel is turned, both barrels of your binoculars are focused simultaneously. Center-focus binoculars should come with either an individual eyepiece adjustment ring located near one of the oculars or an adjustment knob fitted to the barrel bridge. This adjustment control compensates for the small differences between your two eyes. You set it once then never again (unless, of course, your eyesight changes). Directions for finding your personal ocular adjustment are included in your binoculars' owner's manual. For the purposes of test-driving multiple binoculars in the store, try setting the ocular ring setting on 0. Unless your eyes are markedly different, this should work and save time.

Some military or marine binoculars have individual eyepiece focus systems, rings on each ocular that must be focused separately. This system is slow, cumbersome, and has no place in birding.

Some instruments feature focus levers or bars instead of wheels and are touted for their ability to "fast focus" or "instant focus." The reality is quite different. Lever-focus systems are undermined by a too-small range of focus. The instrument's capacity to resolve detail from near to infinity is controlled by what amounts to an abbreviated wheel—a wheel with only a 90-degree arc (or, looked at another way, a wheel that is 270 degrees short of being a wheel). Also, the lever usually requires a two-hand grip and a great deal of back-and-forth micro-adjusting to create a sharp image. It is easy to get *almost* focused quickly but time consuming to get the image *sharp* (if it's possible at all).

To be functional, focus wheels should cover the range of focus (from close as possible to infinity), something between $3/4$ to $1^1/2$ turns of the wheel. In my opinion, the optimal range is one full revolution to go the full range of focus—accomplished with three quick pulls of a finger.

Some manufacturers offer low-priced "permanent" or "no-focus" binoculars—instruments prefocused on a set distance, which is a predetermined "average" that corresponds only to moderately distant objects. With these, the user's eye, not the binocular, does the focusing when the object isn't where the average says it should be, the result being that eyes tire quickly and the ability to resolve detail at close quarters (like less than 70 feet!) is lost. Instruments like these might be fine for the theater or sporting events but are not acceptable for birding.

All birding binoculars should be able to focus clearly down to at least 10 feet. Superior instruments allow birders to focus down to 6 feet, even 5 feet. This is the range you should aim for. Close-focusing instruments are particularly useful for birding in woodlands, where birds may be very close and in confines or situations that preclude your moving farther back to get a sharp image—e.g., off the trail in a chigger-infested rain forest. *Note:* There is a functional limit to close focus. Some instruments are designed to focus down to 4 feet or less, but to accomplish this they typically sacrifice the glass's capacity to maintain a single sharp image at less than 25 feet. *Beware:* Many super-close-focusing binoculars are subject to parallax or image separation; the images in your barrels are no longer superimposed and your eyes will strain to bring them together.

TALE SPOT

Single-Eye Solution

I once knew the sales rep for a company that boasted of creating binoculars that focused down to 4 feet. They did indeed, but this very expensive and highly touted instrument also suffered from an acute parallax issue. I asked the rep how he dealt with the problem. His response: "I close one eye." That's a workable solution, but it negates the advantages of using a binocular. Also, it is my opinion that equipment is supposed to compensate for our shortcomings. I look askance at instruments that force me to compensate for their performance failings. ■

TALE SPOT

Less Power, More Performance

In 1987, five years after I'd switched from 8x binoculars to 10x, I was given oblique insight into the functional limits of higher magnification via a test conducted by representatives of Carl Zeiss Optics, a German manufacturer of premium instruments. Several birding-equipment reviewers and I were flown to a resort on the West Coast of Florida, where we were introduced to the new Zeiss 20x60 binocular—a very sophisticated instrument that featured an internal stabilizing mechanism and a $4750 price tag. The engineers set up an eye chart across the parking lot, distributed production model Zeiss 7x, 8x, 10x, and 15x instruments (all superlative binoculars), and invited us to study the chart and read the smallest line of type.

We could not—7x, 8x, 10x, 15x . . . it made no difference. My ability to read the print stopped at line 6 or 7 no matter what magnification I was using. Higher magnification made the letters larger but increased handshake, rendering them no more readable.

Then the Zeiss engineers gave us the new 20x60 and directed us to try again. If anything, the results were worse. Twenty-power was simply too difficult to hold steady. The letters danced. Then we were instructed to push the button that kicked the internal stabilizer online. The result was magic. The dancing letters froze. Line 10 was perfectly readable.

But as impressive as the new product was, what impressed me more was the performance parity evidenced by the other instruments. As noted, no matter what the power, my ability to resolve detail stopped at the same lines. In terms of seeing details, a 15x Zeiss held no advantage over a 10x, or a 10x over an 8x, or an 8x over a 7x. At higher magnification, the letters were bigger, but because of increased image distortion caused by hand-shake, they were no easier to read. No matter what the power, image quality remained essentially unchanged.

At that time I was using a 10x40 as my primary glass, and the test begged the question: Why was I using binoculars that offered a much smaller field of view than the 7x, a much shallower depth of field, a very critical focus, a darker image, and a marginally acceptable close focus of 16 feet (as compared to the 7x Zeiss' 11 feet) when I was not getting any appreciable advantage in return?

There was no reason I could see to use a 10x. Shortly thereafter, I retired my 10x40s, started using a 7x42, and was a much happier birder who was finding and appreciating more birds more quickly.

There are stabilized binoculars on the market today that are considerably less than $4000, and some are optically fine. But most require batteries, and their ergonomics leave much to be desired. But the fact remains: With 7x or 8x binoculars, there is little need for stabilization unless you suffer from a pronounced hand tremor. ■

Last Thoughts on Power

Most experienced birders choose binoculars between 7x and 10x—with 8x binoculars being most favored, particularly among birders who spend a great deal of time in woodlands or rain forests or who want a versatile instrument. Ten-power instruments are sometimes preferred by birders who habitually bird in open country or specialize in the study of very distant birds in flight (hawk watchers).

If you cannot decide between a 7x or 10x, consider a compromise—an 8x or 8.5x. *But never buy zoom binoculars!* They are a gimmick whose theoretical appeal is an adjustable power setting but whose practical usefulness falls flat. Even at the lowest power setting, zoom binoculars offer a narrow field of view (making it difficult to find birds). As power is increased, the field diminishes even more, and image quality deteriorates so dramatically on most models that users find they rarely exceed the lowest power setting anyway. Virtually all zoom binoculars are heavier than fixed-power instruments of comparable quality, their optical quality is generally poor, they are mechanically inferior, and they're usually priced higher.

I say again, *never buy zoom binoculars.* If you look at the lines offered by the three companies that specialize in superior-quality, high-performance binoculars—Zeiss, Leica, and Swarovski—you will not see zoom binoculars at all. Also, I know of no professional bird-tour guide who uses zoom binoculars. This should send a clear message to the discerning consumer.

More on Light and Brightness

A bright image is important to birding since it directly relates to the ability of the eye to discern color and detail. Binocular brightness is the product of several things, including the size of the objective lens, the power of the instrument, and the number of glass surfaces the shaft of light must pass through or reflect off of before it reaches your eye. Brightness is often rated by formulas that measure twilight factor, relative brightness, and relative light efficiency. It sounds confusing, and it can be made confusing—but unnecessarily so. Virtually all binoculars (and certainly all quality binoculars) feature antireflective coatings that greatly reduce light loss (and have bent the old rules governing light and brightness). To be confident that the binoculars you buy are adequately bright, all you have to concern yourself with are two considerations: the quality of the instrument's antireflective coating system and the size of a binocular's exit pupil.

Here's the problem: Every time light strikes an uncoated glass surface (such as an uncoated binocular lens), approximately 5 percent is lost, either reflected away or absorbed by the glass. Since the

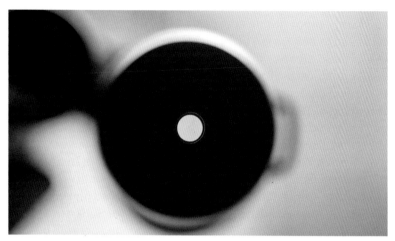

The exit pupil is the end of the straw that is the shaft of light passing through binoculars; it looks like a silver bubble floating in the ocular lens.

average pair of binoculars has 14 to 16 glass elements, approximately half of the light entering the instrument would be lost before it reaches the eye. The result: a dark image. What you are looking for is an instrument with glass elements that are *fully multicoated.* Not just coated, but *fully multicoated.*

A large exit pupil provides sufficient light in low-light conditions, and it has another advantage. Exit pupils are like the paired ends of straws that users must look through. The wider the straw, the easier it is to get eyes aligned quickly and easily. The smaller the exit pupils, the more precise the alignment between your eyes and the shaft of light must be.

Lens Coatings—Bending the Rules of Light Gathering
At the onset of World War II, German scientists discovered that a coating of reflection-reducing material applied to the surface of glass reduced light loss caused by reflection from 5 percent to almost 1 percent. These coated lenses, most often treated with magnesium fluoride, appeared blue, purple, or green. Later it was discovered that the application of several thin layers instead of a single layer would reduce light loss even more. Some multilayer

coatings can cut light loss to less than $^1/_2$ of 1 percent per reflecting surface, with the result that light transmission through quality fully multicoated binoculars can be as much as 95 percent! Some superior-quality instruments boast no light loss whatsoever.

As mentioned earlier, roof prism binoculars have an inherent shortfall—diminished contrast caused by a modest light-wave shift as light passes through glass. The application of a *phase coating* will correct this problem, with the result that phase-coated or phase-corrected roof prisms will offer the same sharp image contrasts offered by porro prism binoculars.

The take-home is this: To ensure that the binoculars you buy will be at least adequately bright, be certain that they have an exit pupil of at least 3.75mm diameter and that all glass elements (not just the outside ones you can see) are *fully multicoated.* Not just "coated," not just "multicoated," but "fully multicoated." Without this express promise there is no guarantee that a less exacting coating process was not used on some (most or all) glass elements.

A larger exit pupil (such as the 6mm exit pupil offered by a 7x42 binocular) will offer a brighter image in low-light conditions—conditions you might encounter on a dark, overcast day or beneath a woodland canopy or at dawn or dusk—and will facilitate finding birds quickly and easily.

But under most conditions, and for most people, a fully multicoated 8x30 (exit pupil of 3.75) will serve just fine.

Field of View and Depth of Field

Looking through binoculars magnifies the size but diminishes perspective, or field of view—that chunk of the world seen through stationary binoculars measured from one edge of the field to the opposite edge. The field of view is often etched on the instrument and should be included in the support material found in or written on the box. It may be described in terms of degrees of arc (example: 6.6 or 5.7), or feet at 1,000 yards (example 415ft/1,000 yards) or meters at 1,000 meters.

However it is measured, a wide field of view—one that offers a minimum of 320 feet/1,000 yards (or 120 meters/1,000 meters, or

6.3 degrees of arc)—is essential. A field of view in excess of 350 feet is not unusual and very desirable; 400 feet or more is prized.

Having a wide field makes it easier to find birds quickly and easily. It makes it easier to get onto fast-flying birds. It makes it easier to map a search by scanning a wide area.

A wide field of view is particularly helpful to inexperienced birders whose greatest challenge lies in finding birds while looking through unfamiliar instruments.

Birding binoculars should also offer a generous depth of field, which is the ability of a pair of binoculars to resolve detail short of and beyond the point of focus. A forgiving depth of field makes it easier to find birds in woodland situations, where outside the point of focus the view becomes a blurry maze of branches. It also eliminates the need to make constant focusing adjustments every time a bird moves a little closer or farther away.

Both field of view and depth of field are closely related to magnification. In general, the higher the magnification, the smaller the field of view, the shallower the depth of field, and the less user friendly the instrument will be.

Eye Relief

Eye relief is the measure of distance between the ocular lens and the point where the human eye comfortably perceives a full field of view. This ideal distance, the eye point, is measured in millimeters. The extended length of binoculars' eyecups should automatically set the user's eyes to this ideal.

Eye relief is not an important concern for many birders, but it is critical for eyeglass-wearers, whose eyes are necessarily set 15 to 20 millimeters behind a glass plate. Unless binoculars offer a high eye point (15 to 20 millimeters), most eyeglass-wearers using binoculars with poor eye relief will find their field of view considerably reduced—the functional equivalent of trying to look through a keyhole when your eye is some distance from the door. With eyecups retracted (or rolled down) binoculars with a high eye point offer eyeglass wearers the same field of view non–eyeglass wearers enjoy.

Note: Just because binoculars feature adjustable eyecups does not mean they provide sufficient eye relief. The proof is in the

With eyecups twisted down, eyeglass wearers should enjoy the same wide field of view that non–eyeglass wearers enjoy.

length of the cups. Unless eye relief is at least 15 millimeters, many eyeglass wearers are getting shortchanged.

Water and Gravity

By far the most common challenge to the integrity of binoculars is levied by water and gravity. Combating these two enemies of optical performance accounts for much of the production cost that distinguishes $1000 binoculars from $300 ones.

Binoculars need not be immersed in water to be rendered dysfunctional in the field. Something as innocuous as taking poorly sealed binoculars out of an air-conditioned car into a steamy Florida afternoon can cause moisture, sucked in by working the focus mechanism, to condense on internal glass surfaces, fogging them up entirely.

Even binoculars that are well cared for are not immune to accidents. One fall from the kitchen table to the average linoleum floor is enough to put the average pair out of alignment (a condition in which the twin barrels no longer focus on the same point). Even binoculars that are moderately out of alignment will tire your eyes

Never, ever rest your binoculars on the roof of your car, NOT EVEN FOR A
MOMENT!

and make birding burdensome. Binoculars that are severely out of
alignment will make you see double and never present a single
sharp image.

The best birding binoculars are waterproof—meaning immers-
ible—and shock resistant. Many instruments are armored with a
hard rubber or polyurethane outer shell. But the best way to keep
your binoculars in proper shape is to not drop them. Never place
your binoculars on the roof of your car. Not even for a moment.
Even the most durable binoculars on the planet are not impervious
to a 6-foot fall onto macadam at high speed.

The Sum of Its Parts

Engineering binoculars is an exercise in compromise. Higher magnification reduces field of view. Resolution can be absolutely sharp
at the center of the field but distorted at the edge or averaged out
across the field. Binoculars can be made waterproof—but for a
higher price.

Different people will put an emphasis on different attributes, but here, for reference and quick summary, are the standards that are acceptable for a birding binocular.

Size: Large enough to be grasped firmly, small enough for your index finger to find the focus wheel quickly and easily without compromising your grip.

Weight: No more than you care to bear.

Shape: Most roof prisms are easier to hold steady, but any size or design that allows a firm, strain-free, shift-free grasp is fine.

Interpupillary distance: To fit your eyes.

Design: Porro prisms are inherently optically superior, until you start spending $300 and up for phase-corrected roof prism instruments.

Focus system: Center-focus system with a wheel that goes the range of focus in fewer than one and a half turns of the wheel (or three quick pulls of your finger).

Magnification: 7x or 8x is best for beginners and all-around and woodland birding. Some high-quality 10x instruments perform very well in open country and for hawk and seabird watching (from land). Never buy zoom binoculars or binoculars that feature permanent or fixed focus.

Exit pupil size. No less than 3.75mm; 5mm to 6mm is preferred.

Optics: BAK-4 glass or denser ED, or HD (High Density), glass.

Coatings: Fully multicoated optics only. Color bias minimal. All quality roof prism binoculars also have phase-corrected coatings.

Close focus: Down to at least 10 feet, preferably less than 8. *Note:* There is a functional limit to close focusing binoculars. Some binoculars designed to appeal to butterfly watchers focus down to 4 feet or less. But to accomplish this, some manufacturers accept a degree of parallax (image separation) that becomes most apparent at less than 30 feet and may be so pronounced that users of super-close-focusing binoculars must close one eye to get a distortion-free image when looking at subjects less than 25 feet away.

Field of view: No less than 320 feet/1,000 yards (for conversion purposes: 1 degree of arc = 52.5 feet at 1,000 yards; 1 meter = 3.28 feet and 1.09 yards).

Eye relief: For eyeglass wearers, no less than 15mm, unless your eyes are not deeply recessed.

Water resistance/durability: Rugged, waterproof binoculars are desirable—but expensive. If you bird in the tropics, or offshore (pelagic birding), waterproof instruments are essential.

Performance's Bottom Line

There is, after all is said and done, only one test of a pair of binoculars. When you bring them to your eyes, you see what you want to see quickly and easily. That is all. If the engineers had birding in mind, if the instrument fits you, if it's properly adjusted, that is truly all there is to it.

If you go into a store and find that you are having difficulty with the instrument you are testing, put it down. Reach for another model. There is an array of quality instruments that meet birding specs. One is almost certain to fit you.

How to Buy Binoculars

Forewarned Is Forearmed

When you go shopping for birding binoculars there are several things you should know. First, as a birder, you represent the largest consumer block in the binocular industry. Over 30 percent of *all* binoculars are purchased for birding.

Second, binocular manufacturers understand your needs as a birder. The average salesperson may not. Don't let them confuse you with jargon and formulas. Having read this chapter you probably know as much and perhaps more than the person on the other side of the counter about your optical needs as a birder.

Third, the only way to be certain that the binoculars you purchase truly work for you is to test a number of different makes and models first. Most stores don't offer a selection that includes multiple manufacturers. They may carry an assortment of instruments, but the selection is intended to appeal to a number of potential user groups—backpackers, boaters, hunters, vacationers . . . To keep inventory down, stores typically limit the manufacturing lines they carry. Store purchasing-agents commonly choose one or two instruments from these select lines that should appeal to birders.

They have a vested interest in selling the product they carry, not necessarily in selling you the binoculars that are absolutely right for you (which might be in a line they don't carry).

I repeat: *The best way to choose binoculars that work for you is to test a number of makes and models.* If there is a store in your area geared to meeting the needs of birders and offering a wide selection, go there. Play with the whole array. If a store is not convenient to you, go to a popular birding spot in your area. Find out what instruments experienced birders are using. Ask to try them (birders will be only too pleased to help) and ask them where they made their purchase. Another good way to test a number of binoculars is to attend a birding festival. Dealers and company reps commonly attend major festivals, and they often offer loaner instruments that you can try in the field.

Fourth, not only are there performance differences between makes and models, there are differences between individual instruments of the same make and model. Be certain you examine the instrument you buy and ask the salesperson to check it, too—for proper alignment, for optical performance, for any dust or debris in the barrels, for any mechanical problem. If you are a very particular individual, and if the store you are dealing with has the inventory, you can ask to test two or more instruments of the same make and model and select the one that out performs the others—the one that seems brighter or sharper or focuses more smoothly or whose hinged bridge is not already loose.

TALE SPOT

Good Glass and the Quality Gradient

"Let me check these out for you, sir," I said, addressing the imminent owner of a pair of Zeiss 7x42 Classic binoculars—at the time one of the alpha optics of birding (and now one of the industry's all-time greats).

Mine was an automatic reaction, something we do routinely (and usually unnecessarily). You pay $1000 for the privilege of owning a superior instrument, you feel confident that you are getting your money's worth.

At least that's what is assumed.

Bringing the binoculars to my eyes, I trained them on the eye chart across the hall. Line 10, at the bottom of the chart, was set in teeny-weeny 6-point type. Nevertheless, I expected to read it with ease. I was wrong. The letters were indecipherable.

"That's odd," I thought. An hour earlier I'd sold a pair of Swift Audubons, a glass that retailed for $700 less than the Zeiss, and I had been able to read the bottom line with ease!

"Hold up on that credit card," I said to the cashier. "Let me try something," I said to the customer. Reaching into the display case I extracted the display model Zeiss 7x42 and trained it on the eye chart. Line 10 was perfectly readable. I tried the suspect pair again and got the same blurred results.

"Hmmmm," I said, "let's try something else."

Delving into our stock, I brought out multiple 7x42s and tested them all. The results were illuminating.

One instrument offered resolution that was clearly superior to all the others. Another was obviously brighter than the rest. Three were functionally fine. One, the instrument that had initiated the test, was simply not up to the optical caliber of the others.

So the point is that Zeiss' quality control is poor? No. Zeiss' quality control is very good—as someone who has visited the Zeiss factory, I can assure you. Plus, the quality of the instruments that find their way into the hands of consumers attest to Zeiss' high-quality standards. The point is that there is a range of quality and performance inherent in all mass-produced products, including the very best German optics.

Or, look at it this way: Companies set minimum quality standards for instruments coming off their assembly lines. But nobody has a *maximum* standard (they don't kick an instrument off-line because it is so much better than the average glass).

Since this eye-opening experience, I have found other examples of how much variation there is between individual optical instruments—even noticeable and disconcerting differences between the images offered by the barrels of the same instrument.

The point is you want to avoid binoculars that are performing at the bottom of the quality threshold. If you want to buy a glass that beats the field, you had better test the binoculars you buy before you buy them—in fact, you might want to test several. ■

Testing Instruments Before You Buy

Testing the performance of binoculars in the store does not take a degree in engineering. It takes about three minutes. Things to check for are: optical performance (resolution/field), brightness, color bias, close focus, internal dust, and alignment.

Resolution

Some retailers offer consumers an eye chart to test an instrument's ability to resolve fine details. If not, find (or bring) a printed page of type (a newspaper featuring different size type works well; some people use a dollar bill or business card). It becomes a simple matter of finding the instrument that lets you see the most detail, as defined by being able to read the finest print.

Field Quality

Low-cost instruments often show considerable distortion across the visual field—the image is blurred in patches. To test for this, focus the instrument on an open newspaper set approximately 30 feet away and determine whether the print is uniformly sharp across the field, blurred in patches, or blurred toward the edges of the field. Instruments that blur at the extreme edge are fine. Those that show random, patchy distortion across the field, or are sharp only at the center of the field are not instruments you want to own.

Field of View

Find a target that offers a number of reference points, such as a multivolume book rack, a row of photos on a wall, or a bulletin board plastered with notices. Train the left edge of the field onto a fixed reference point. Note where the right edge falls. What you are looking for is the instrument that reaches the farthest to the right—the one that has the largest field of view.

Color Bias

Few binoculars offer a totally unbiased image. And while some biases are subtle, some are horrible (amber- or ruby-coated instruments, for example, that claim to offer better contrast turn the world a ghastly green). Many people find that some instruments from Asia have a red color bias, turning the world pink. The best way to test the color bias is to train binoculars on a white background. A subtle shift to red, yellow, or brown may be acceptable, but if the bias is enough to affect your perception of natural colors, that is too much. Bird study, after all, is very much a matter of seeing colors.

Close Focus

Simply a matter of dialing down to see how close an instrument can focus. Tiles on a floor or patterns in a carpet offer good reference points. Anything under 10 feet works for most birding situations, but 5 to 8 feet is excellent, and many instruments offer close focus to 6 feet. But close focus has a functional limit and trade-offs . . .

Parallax or Image Separation

After adjusting the individual eyepiece setting to fit your eyes, focus on an object 20 to 25 feet away that has no surrounding visual clutter. Determine that you are seeing a single, clear, distortion-free image. If you see a problem (a double image or two shadowy images that are not superimposed) that's no good. In time, and with concentration, your eyes will bring the image together. But why should they need to? Binoculars should offer a clear image without causing eye fatigue. Don't settle for less. Remember that many binoculars that offer close focus under 5 feet also show pronounced image separation.

Dust in the Barrel

This is more common than you think. To check for it, turn the binoculars upside down. Look through the objective lenses, focusing on the ceiling, the palm of your hand, or, optimally, a clear blue sky. Internal dust or debris seated on a lens or prism will appear as gray or black specks. Note that dust (or debris) on the exterior surface of the ocular lens will also show up in this examination. If you find a dust spot, be sure it is not just debris on the outside of a lens. If you suspect that the exterior surface has a dust speck, ask the salesclerk to clean the instrument with a brush or soft lens-cloth. Retest.

Alignment

Focus the binoculars on a horizontal line—a windowsill or the point where the wall and ceiling meet. Keeping the barrels level, draw the binoculars away from your eyes until the single image splits into two, leaving the left eye to look through the left barrel and the right eye through the right. If the line is broken in the center but remains horizontal, no problem. If one line is higher or lower than the other, the binoculars are out of alignment—the barrels are not focused on the same point, as they are supposed to be. Many instruments, particularly those retailing for less than $100, are out of alignment right off the shelf. In some shipments, "many" means one out of every three. Buyer beware.

Barrel Parity

Check to make sure the two barrels are offering nearly identical images. Go back to your resolution target. Using just one eye, focus on the image and note the resolution, size, and brightness. Now, turning the glass sideways, look through the other barrel using the same eye (you'll probably need to refocus). If one barrel seems noticeably sharper or brighter than the other, try another instrument. What you are seeking is two barrels that are nearly identical so your eyes will not strain to strike an average. I once tested an instrument whose barrels offered different magnifications. I was suspicious because when I looked through them, I felt an uncomfortable and unaccountable tug, or strain, on my eyes.

It took me a few days to diagnose the problem. Who ever heard of two barrels on the same instrument offering differing magnifications? There is no way to get a single sharp image with a glass so compromised.

Should I Buy Premium Binoculars Now?

If money is no object, absolutely. Beginning birders even more than accomplished birders need the advantages of superior equipment. But for most of us, money is a consideration, so I will repeat what I said earlier: Expect to pay no less than $200 for an instrument that works well for birding.

Either that or you can buy a less-expensive instrument that doesn't work (and replace it) or you can get lucky and buy a less-expensive instrument that does work but won't last as long as a premium instrument would (in which case you will replace it, too).

The rule of thumb: Buy the best binoculars you can afford, and buy them as soon as you can afford them. If you have a pair that works (but doesn't excel and doesn't thrill you) tolerate them and save for the one you really want. If you have no binoculars at all and cannot borrow a pair, buy the best you can afford now. Save for the ones you want.

I urge all new birders to at least look through a superior pair of binoculars (something in the $2000 to $3000 range) even if you have no intention of spending that kind of money. See where the optical performance ceiling lies. See what WOW looks like. See what the people who write the field guides see.

Binocular Use and Care

Making Your Binoculars Yours

The first thing to do after purchasing your binoculars is to throw away the stupid plastic lens covers, should they be included. (Rain guards, which come with some instruments and fit over the ocular lenses, are not the same as lens covers and do indeed serve a purpose; they should *not* be discarded.)

I recommend not sending in the warranty card until you take your binoculars into the field. Give them a test-drive. If you have a problem or are not thrilled, take them back to the point of purchase. Let the dealer deal with the problem (don't forget to ask about the return policy at the time of purchase). And don't forget to send in the warranty card once you and your binoculars are securely wedded.

Binoculars come (or should come) with adjustable neck straps. The length you use is a matter of choice. Most people adjust the strap so that the binoculars ride on the chest or just below the chin. Some people (such as those with neck problems) prefer to lengthen the strap so it cuts across the chest bandolier fashion, with the binoculars riding under the arm.

Your choice is governed by two concerns: comfort and quick access. Only you can decide what is best for you.

Adjust the eyecups. Fully extended for non–eyeglass users. Down if you wear glasses—but not necessarily all the way down. Find a length or setting that is comfortable for your eyes. If the eye relief is not right, your image will be plagued by vignetting or disconcerting, shadowy flashes that obscure the image.

Adjust the interpupillary distance to fit the distance between your eyes by bringing the binocular up to your eyes and spacing the barrels so you see a single image. Customize the instrument for your eyes by adjusting the ocular adjustment ring or knob. Instructions should come with your binocular. If not, for most binoculars, look at a detailed object with just your left eye. Turn the center focus wheel until the image is sharp. Then close your left eye, open your right, and without turning the center focus wheel move the individual eyepiece adjustment ring (located on the right ocular or in some cases on a separate adjustment knob) until the image in the right eye is sharp. Now look down and see where the adjustment is set—this is the setting that is calibrated for your eyes on these binoculars. Remember this setting (in case the adjustment ring shifts). If the setting slips frequently (as sometimes happens) you can affix a piece of black electrical tape over the adjustment ring to prevent it from moving.

Don't labor over this process. Once the image looks sharp, it is sharp. From here on in, all focusing will be done with the center focus wheel alone. There should be no reason to change the individual eyepiece adjustment unless your vision changes.

The key to using binoculars is practice. The best way to practice is to go outside and find birds. It's no more complicated than this.

Make Caution a Mind-Set

Binoculars are tubes filled with glass, and glass is not the most durable stuff on the planet. High-quality binoculars require less care than less expensive ones—because they are generally more rugged, better sealed, and designed with long years of service in mind. No matter how rugged the design, however, binoculars should not be dropped or banged about. Mistreat them and you will soon find out how good the manufacturer's warranty really is.

Caution: Binocular straps wear and fray; connection points break. Check your strap frequently and replace it at the first sign of wear.

If they are not being used for long periods it doesn't hurt to keep binoculars in a case to prevent dust or corrosives from collecting on the lenses.

Cleaning Lenses

Unless they malfunction, the only maintenance binoculars require is a periodic cleaning of the ocular and objective lenses to remove dust, oil deposited by eyelashes (and sandwich drippings, salt spray, apple juice . . .). Improper cleaning, however, can really undermine the performance of the instrument.

Coatings are just that: thin, baked-on layers of a chemical substance that can be scratched, abraded, even polished off. In an ideal world, the way to clean binoculars is: (1) Use canned air, purchased from a camera store, to blow the lens surfaces clean. (2) Work lens surfaces lightly with a camel-hair brush to remove macro-gritties. (3) Breathe onto the glass to "fog the lenses" then, using a clean chamois cloth or soft optical cleaning cloth, dry the lenses by polishing them using a circular motion without bearing down. Never use lens tissue treated with silicone. If lenses are severely fouled, try applying a small amount of distilled water to a cloth and wiping the lens surface first; commercial lens cleaners work well, too. But spray the solution onto a cloth to moisten it. Do not spray directly onto the lens.

But this is the real world, and you will generally find that lenses are most often in need of cleaning while you are in the field, fully engaged in that real world.

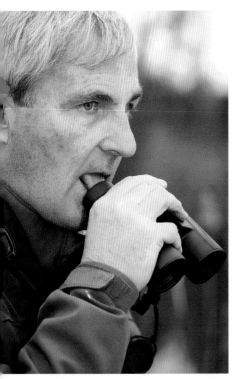 

My favorite binocular-cleaning method: lick and wipe. For obvious reasons, it's not recommended in subfreezing temperatures.

Real-World Scenario A: Dirty lenses. Seated in car between birding stops. What you do is: (1) blow on the lens, (2) breathe on the lens to fog it, (3) reach for a soft cotton handkerchief and wipe the lens clean.

No handkerchief? Try the corner of a clean 100-percent-cotton T-shirt.

Real-World Scenario B: On deck of boat with salt-spray-marred lenses and North America's first record for Magenta Petrel heading for the horizon. What you do is: (1) lick lenses, (2) wipe with whatever absorbent material is handy (wool and pile jackets do not work). It's not hygienic. But it is a Magenta Petrel.

And you are going to miss it.

Actually, I use the lick-and-wipe method routinely. You can taste when the lenses are clean. They stop feeling rough and gritty on your tongue.

Field Guides—the Rosetta Stone to Birds

If binoculars are the defining instrument of birding, field guides are the key that unlocks each bird's most closely guarded secret— its identity. The challenge in birding is simple: Match a feathered Rumpelstiltskin with its name and you make it yours—a credit to your skill, a token of your encounter with one of nature's most magnificent creations.

Field guides are precisely that—books or apps compact and portable enough to be carried into the field and whose illustrations and descriptive content guide users toward a correct identification. How well a field guide manages this ambition can mean the difference between a challenging encounter and a frustrating one. It also defines the difference between a useful guide and one that does not serve as well.

Broad in Scope and Basic

There are, literally, scores of field guides. Some are very simplistic, the number of birds contained in their pages limited or abridged to cater to casual or backyard birders. These simplified books have their place. But if you are reading this book, you are already beyond what these guides can offer.

There are hundreds of bird-identification guides on the planet. Here is a small sampling at the Cape May Bird Observatory shop.

Some field guides are very involved and very detailed, focusing narrowly on specific groups of birds that show an array of plumages (such as gulls) or are, as a group, very difficult to differentiate (such as shorebirds and distant birds of prey in flight). These are specialty guides and are discussed in chapter 5.

This section of this chapter deals only with the basic, or general, field guide. The scope is North American birds, all that regularly occur north of Mexico and that you as a resident of the United States or Canada can aspire to find.

The Naming and Ordering of Birds

Systema Naturae
Every field guide attempts to impose a logical organization and order on the natural world to make it easier for users to quickly narrow down options and focus on candidates that most closely resemble what they see in the field. The foundation upon which all field guides rest incorporates two articles of faith: (1) that at some biological level all living things relate only to one of their own kind or species, (2) that each species has traits that both distinguish it from, and relate it to, similar species—i.e., they are grouped in the same family or genus.

The system of naming and ordering birds and other living things, called taxonomy, can be traced to the work of a Swedish botanist, Carolus Linnaeus. In 1758, Linnaeus devised a system that assigned two Latin-based (or Greek-based) names to each distinct species. The first name, called the genus, grouped living things with very similar traits. The second name denotes species. Together, they confer a unique identity—a sort of scientific last name, first name.

A Swift Review
Take, for example, the species *Chaetura pelagica*, the scientific name for the bird that captivated my caller from the Bronx and whose common name is Chimney Swift. The scientific name is not only unique to this species, it is also descriptive (as scientific names tend to be). *Chaetura* comes from the Greek words *chaite,*

"a bristle," and *oura,* "tail"—an obvious reference to the short, stiff tail that helps swifts anchor themselves to the walls of chimneys (and, before chimneys, cliffs). *Pelagica* (according to Ernest Choate, author of *The Dictionary of American Bird Names*) derives from the Greek *pealgios,* meaning "marine"—a reference not to any presumed association with oceans (swifts are not ocean birds) but, perhaps, to the wayfaring habits of this long-distance migrant (in Linnaeus's time, all great voyagers were sailors). I have a different hypothesis. I believe that *pealgios* relates to the bird's tippy, gliding flight, which easily calls to mind a tacking sailing ship.

There are other species of swifts in North America, including the western Vaux's Swift, *Chaetura vauxi* (named in honor of scientist William S. Vaux), and White-throated Swift, *Aeronautes saxatalis* (*aeronautes:* Gr. *aer,* "air"; Gr. *nautes,* "a sailor"; L. *saxitalis,* "rock dweller"—an apt name for this western cliff-dwelling speedster).

Chimney Swift and Vaux's Swift are very similar—so similar that they share the same genus. White-throated Swift, on the other hand, has traits that distinguish it from the other two and so is placed in a separate genus.

All three swifts are found in the same scientific family, Apodidae, and fall in the same order, Apodiformes. This larger grouping includes both the swifts (Apodidae) and the hummingbird family (Trochilidae).

All birds, of course, share a common class: Aves. This class relates to the large scientific grouping that distinguishes birds from other living creatures: mammals, reptiles, insects, and fish.

In a schematic diagram, the breakdown of the three swifts looks like this:

	Chimney Swift	Vaux's Swift	White-throated Swift
Class	Aves	Aves	Aves
Order	Apodiformes	Apodiformes	Apodiformes
Family	Apodidae	Apodidae	Apodidae
Genus	*Chaetura*	*Chaetura*	*Aeronautes*
Species	*pelagica*	*vauxi*	*saxatalis*

There is a level of differentiation below the species level called, appropriately, subspecies. These regional forms are sometimes different enough in appearance to be distinguished in the field by plumage (or voice) but are not (at least not currently) thought to be genetically dissimilar enough to be regarded as distinct species. Subspecies, too, are often represented in field guides.

Here's the Take-Home

Avian systematics are really very simple. Birds that have traits in common get grouped together. The more birds have in common, the more closely allied they are, and the more closely they fall in the ordering of birds in your guide. The more dissimilar they are, the more space and other species lie between them. The taxonomic ordering of birds is summarized and defined by the American Ornithologists' Union Checklist of North American Birds.

While birders typically refer to birds using their common names instead of their scientific names, they have generally accepted both the species differentiations established by ornithologists and the taxonomic grouping and ordering of species as presented in the AOU Checklist, which is updated periodically.

The problem is, and has long been, that from the standpoint of identifying birds, what makes sense in the hand and in the lab does not always play out in the field.

So What Does All This Taxonomy Stuff Have to do With Field Guides?

Back when Linnaeus began grouping and ordering the natural world the traits he used to relate, distinguish, and order species were anatomical. Some of these traits were easy to see—like the xygodactylous feet of woodpeckers (most birds have three toes in front, one in back; woodpeckers have two toes in front, two in back). But some were not—like the fused vertebrae that help distinguish falcons from other birds of prey. Today, scientists are looking even closer in their efforts to distinguish species, comparing the very genetic makeup of birds and rearranging the taxonomic order of birds accordingly.

Field guides order and group birds too. As with ornithological tradition, this arrangement is made on the basis of shared traits, frequently the same anatomical traits used by scientists. But the tradition of ornithological taxonomy hinges on traits that can be distinguished *in the hand or in the lab.* The objective of field guides is to establish relationships and differences between species that help distinguish them *in the field.* So where practicality dictates, the order and groupings in many field guides strays somewhat from the strict AOU order in favor of one that is more comparative in the field.

Evolution of Field Guides

Books about North America's birds have a long tradition. Notables include works by English naturalist/painter Mark Catesby, who explored the American Southeast in the first half of the 1700s; Alexander Wilson, author of *American Ornithology;* and John James Audubon, whose *Birds of America* is a visual masterpiece.

But these were ornithological and artistic treatments. None of these works even pretended to be a "field guide," a term that was not even coined until the twentieth century. The very nature of bird study at the time, conducted over the barrels of fowling pieces, precluded the very notion (much less need) to carry reference books into the field. The approach to bird identification then was *shoot first, identify later.*

In 1895, Frank M. Chapman, curator of the New York Museum of Natural History, published the first edition of his *Birds of Eastern North America,* a compact accounting of bird species that he called a "handbook." It was expressly written (as his 1926 third edition states) to meet the needs of the "bird student . . . who demands, primarily, information concerning the bird *in nature* [italics mine]." His approach—involving a dichotomous key to distinguish species backed up by painfully detailed descriptions—probably broke more hearts among aspiring "bird students" than it did new ground. Take, for example, this species description:

Top and sides of head black, a white spot above and below the eye; rest of upper parts grayish slate-color; margins of wings slightly lighter; tail blackish, the outer feathers with white spots at their tips; throat white, streaked with black; rest of the underparts rufus (tipped with white in the fall), becoming white on the middle of the lower belly; bill yellow, brownish in fall.

Few readers would recognize the bird described here as the common American Robin.

The first field guide worthy of the name was Chester Reed's famous *Bird Guide: Land Birds East of the Rockies,* published in 1906 (a western version was published in 1913). It was pocket sized ($3^1/_2$ by $5^1/_2$ inches), featuring thumbnail portrayals of birds and descriptive text.

The painted illustrations were surprisingly good—showing birds as they might naturally appear at a distance, with details muted. The text fell short of today's field guide standards but was a revolutionary leap ahead of the laborious, beak-to-tail descriptions by Chapman. Reed's descriptions were terse, intended mainly to

Chester Reed's light and portable field guides ushered in a new age of bird study.

guide readers to an identification. Illustrations and text appeared on the same page for easy reference.

Many millions of copies of Reed's guides were purchased, one by a 13-year-old "student of birds" living in Jamestown, New York, who carried it into the field along with his 4x LeMaire binoculars. His name was Roger Tory Peterson. Twelve years later, he would publish *A Field Guide to the Birds*—a true field guide. The first 2,000 copies would sell out within three weeks. Now in its fifth revision, Peterson's revolutionary guide has sold many millions of copies.

New Guide, New Age

Roger Tory Peterson (1908-96), the once and forever "Grand Master" of North American birding, never claimed proprietary rights to the breakthrough that made his *Field Guide to the Birds* the right idea for the times. In the first line of the preface, in his first edition, Peterson acknowledges the catalytic influence of writer Ernest Thompson Seton's *Two Little Savages* and the "pattern charts" drawn by Seton (attributed to one of the book's characters) that depicted ducks seen from a distance. What the illustration shows are the plumage patterns distant ducks project that distinguish them—these plumage traits Seton called *uniforms* and birders today call *field marks*; Peterson initially called them *trademarks of nature.*

The very few illustrations found in Chapman were too detailed, showing the marks that might be seen on hand-held birds, in the tradition of ornithology. And while Chester Reed depicted birds at a distance, he failed to fully appreciate how distance affects plumage appearance.

Details disappear, but through binoculars, the subjects do not blur. Quite the contrary, contrasts sharpen and patterns not evident at close quarters emerge. These patterns are the "trademarks of nature" that were, and are, the cornerstone of Peterson's identification system. In his guide, he points them out with arrows that quickly direct the reader's attention.

What Peterson did was take the field-mark approach pioneered by Seton and apply it to all eastern birds, later western birds, codifying in his depictions and text the characteristics that distinguished

In 1934, 24-year-old Roger Tory Peterson published the first true field guide to birds. It's now in its fifth edition. Shown here is a first-edition Peterson Guide opened to the warblers plate. Also shown: LeMaire binoculars similar to those use by the young RTP. LINDA DUNNE

one species from another in the field that are visible through binoculars. He arranged and portrayed his subjects to facilitate comparison. Peterson did not, by any means, discover and disclose all the distinguishing field marks in his book all by himself. There were a number of eager minds trying to solve the riddle of bird identification in the field during the last decades of the nineteenth century and the first decades of the twentieth—among them the members of the Bronx Bird Club (Roger's birding "chums").

What Peterson brought to the challenge was a winning blend of artistic talent and a comparative design sense, communication skill, a cutting-edge understanding of his subject, and a utilitarian vision of purpose that to this day others have merely refined.

The last time we spoke I asked Dr. Peterson how he wanted to be remembered. His reply: "as an educator." In this, and in so many other endeavors, he succeeded.

Systema Natura Revisited

Most field guides to North American birds, including Peterson's *Eastern Birds* and *Western Birds,* follow, at least nominally, the order established by the AOU. These guides use an anatomical approach to grouping similar species and diverge from the taxonomic order only where the primary focus of a field guide—differentiation between similar or confusing species—dictates reordering birds (most often based on plumage characteristics rather than anatomy).

For example, in the Peterson Guide the sections that discuss vireos and warblers, two songbird groups that are similarly sized and shaped and sometimes plumaged, are adjacent to each other. By AOU standards, warblers and vireos are not closely related; many bird groups lie between them, including crows, jays, chickadees, nuthatches, and thrushes (to name but a few).

A few field guides have attempted grouping and ordering systems that depart radically from the AOU taxonomic order (and from other guides, too), and while no field guide is without merit and no system is perfect, some guides are simply more useful and user friendly than others.

My favorite guides for beginning birders, listed in no particular order, are:

- *Peterson Field Guide to Birds of North America,* by Roger Tory Peterson (aka the Peterson Guide)
- *Kaufman Field Guide to Birds of North America,* by Kenn Kaufman (aka the Kaufman Guide)
- *The Sibley Guide to Birds,* by David Allen Sibley (aka the Sibley Guide or Big Sibley)
- *Birds of North America: A Guide to Field Identification,* by Chandler S. Robbins, Bertel Bruun, and Herbert S. Zim (aka the Golden Guide or Robbins Guide)
- *National Geographic Field Guide to the Birds of North America,* by Jon L. Dunn and Jonathan Alderfer (aka the National Geographic Guide or the Geo Guide)
- Another guide worth owning and commended by its very excellence, and because many species found in Europe have populations in North America, too, is *Birds of Europe,* by Lars Swensson and others.

A sampling of the author's favorite guides.

There are other very commendable general guides to North American birds—field guides that deserve a place on your bookshelf. But the guides listed here enjoy widespread acclaim and have stood the test of time. I personally encourage you to own them all. But one guide is destined to be your primary guide. It will be the book you take into the field. The rest become supportive, but hardly subordinate, insofar as all guides add something to the identification matrix and will either support your initial identification or undermine it.

What Puts the Good in "Good Guide"?

First, *size*. A field guide should be small enough to be carried into the field.

Second, *scope*. A good field guide contains all the birds you are likely to encounter where you are birding.

Third, *focus*. A good field guide has only one aim—to impart key information relating to the identification of birds.

Fourth, *organization*—an intelligent and comparative organization and presentation of material predicated upon the needs of birders who are being challenged in real time in the field.

Fifth, *a consistent, well-conceived layout and design* that imparts key information quickly and easily.

Sixth, *quality depictions* and *useful, concise supporting text.* While field identification and field guides are largely image driven, text is your reality check, supporting your initial determination, or, because of inconsistencies, suggesting you try another candidate—a similar species whose range, habitat, and perhaps behavioral characteristics are more in accord with what you believe you saw in the field.

Seventh, *process projection*—the capacity to impart to readers the "process" of identifying birds (identification "Right Think") as well as a nuts-and-bolts means to that identification. Guides are organized in a way that is consistent with the way the authors themselves approach the identification process.

Size

It has been many years since anyone has been able to squeeze all that is useful to know about bird identification into the format of a Chester Reed field guide. Field-guide apps have solved the size problem without necessarily addressing the issue of volume—i.e., how much information is too much?

But among the most popular guides that offer full, unabridged species treatments, only Peterson, Kaufman, and Robbins might fit into a hip pocket. The others may require a jacket or a vest with big pockets, or a belt-pouch designed to carry larger-sized field guides (or you can try the old slip-it-between-your-belt-and-the-small-of-your-back technique).

Scope

Field guides should be all inclusive, meaning that all the species that regularly occur in the geographic scope of the book are depicted. In an effort to make a guide easier to use, and to reduce pages and variables, some guides have separate eastern and western volumes that exclude species unlikely to occur on opposing

The element that puts the "field" in field guide is portability. For a guide to be truly fieldworthy it must be sized to accompany you in the field.

coasts. Most basic guides, however, elect to include all North American species in a single volume.

There are advantages and disadvantages to both approaches, but the fact remains: For a guide to be useful, and for it to offer the assurance that a bird you find will be reflected in the pages, all birds within the geographic scope of the book should be represented. Guides that try to second-guess nature, editorializing to favor probability, shortchange users in a higher currency—that of possibility.

TALE SPOT

First Guide Frustration

My first field guide was a hip-pocket-sized paperback with robins on the cover and 112 species depicted within. Another 148 species were briefly mentioned in the text, but since they didn't have pictures, it stood to reason (to me at least) that they were birds that weren't likely to be seen, otherwise they'd be illustrated. Right?

Right.

Don't get me wrong. I treasured this truncated little book, but several things still irritated me. First, there were birds in it that I knew I'd never see, living as I did in the East—western birds such as the Black-billed Magpie. I also grew frustrated trying to find birds such as the Bald Eagle, Red-headed Woodpecker, and Bobolink—birds that seemed easy enough to identify and (according to the range maps) were supposed to be found where I lived.

Except the maps dealt with distribution, not habitat—a fine point of distinction I didn't appreciate then.

But what really frustrated me were the birds I saw that were not illustrated in the pages of the book. And there were lots of them—especially during spring and fall migration. Lots of tiny, brightly colored ones that moved like quicksilver. It occurred to me that maybe these unfamiliar birds were the species whose names were mentioned in association with another species in the text, which was indeed the case, but there was no effective means (or process) to lead me to those identifications short of buying a better, more comprehensive guide. The field-guide process directed me to look at illustrations then changed the rules by redirecting my focus to brief descriptions buried in the text.

What I never appreciated was that my book had been highly simplified (now called "dumbed down")—to reduce possibilities and make it easier for new birders to find the most common species they might encounter every day. Species that found their way into the pages were birds that were usually common nesting species widely distributed across North America. Migrants that could during migration be very common in my local woodlands had been left out.

So even though the book was simple, it didn't save me from frustration. It just substituted one frustration for another, and it held back my development as a birder because it didn't depict all the birds I was finding. It was, in short, a book not directed toward my level of interest, or my needs. ■

Focus

Field guides or, more specifically, the species accounts within a field guide should have one aim: to impart key information relating to the identification of birds. The elements of this include an accurate depiction and concise description summarizing or highlighting distinguishing field marks, as well as information relating to a species' range, seasonal occurrence, and abundance, and additional information relating to habits, habitat, and vocalizations that help distinguish it from similar species. The Peterson Guide, Sibley Guide, Golden Guide, and National Geographic Guide are models of utilitarian brevity.

Accuracy and Timeliness

The need for accuracy is, of course, paramount, and while no guide will ever be above reproach, all those I have mentioned offer a degree of accuracy that users can depend on.

More troublesome for new birders is the battle all guides have with time and change. Books in print are static. Science is not. Species are constantly being reevaluated and reclassified. Sometimes a scientific or common name is changed—and a book becomes dated. For example, the Peregrine Falcon was formerly called Duck Hawk; the Great Egret was once known as the Common Egret and the American Egret.

Sometimes two species are lumped—determined to be genetically similar and "combined" into a single species (example: Baltimore Oriole and Bullock's Oriole were lumped to become Northern Oriole). Sometimes a species is split—recognized, after study and debate (or, in the case of the orioles, more study and debate) to represent two or more distinct species (thus, later, Northern Oriole was "split" back into Baltimore Oriole and Bullock's Oriole). If your field guide is more than five years old, you need a new one, or an updated edition.

Sometimes changes in nomenclature affect the text but not necessarily the illustrations. For example, in the second edition of the National Geographic Guide, the Rufous-sided Towhee is listed and both the very distinctive eastern and western forms are depicted. These two regional forms are now regarded as different species—Eastern Towhee and Spotted Towhee—and are identified as such in the most recent edition.

Since the first Peterson Guide was published in 1934 there have been scores of name changes, and multiple updates of the guide to keep up with them.

When beginning birders say "I can't use the traditional field guides" what they are really saying is "I haven't taken the trouble to familiarize myself with them." There is no quick fix to bird identification. There is only a process of gaining familiarity with birds—learning what knits them together and what sets them apart.

The solution is simple: Take the trouble to get familiar with the birds throughout your guide and how they are presented within its layout. It is an exercise that is illuminating, fun, and exciting in the possibilities it unlocks.

Utilitarian Design

The ideal is simple: all the information you need to make a correct identification—field marks, distribution, relative abundance, seasonal occurrence, vocalizations—presented in an intelligent, systematic order. No two guides are exactly alike, but some standards hold true.

Guides that incorporate all necessary information on one page or facing pages are easier to use than guides that separate text and illustrations, or text and range maps.

Guides whose layout provides direct comparisons between similar species facilitate identification and learning.

Balancing both these objectives in a book designed to be carried into the field is not an easy feat.

The Golden Guide, Sibley Guide, National Geographic Guide, and Kaufman Guide succeed best—offering information, range map, text, and illustration in an easy linear sweep across one page or two. The famous ease of the Peterson Guide is diminished somewhat by the relegation of detailed range maps to the back, but this organizational shortfall is mitigated by the size and excellence of the maps as well as the insertion of small vignette range maps within the text.

Quality of the Depictions

Probably the most important consideration in any field guide—how accurately and intelligently a bird is portrayed—will very likely determine whether it will or will not be properly identified. Some field guides use painted illustrations to depict species. Some use photographs. For the most part, illustrations have generally worked better than photographic images.

Why? First, illustrations are idealized depictions, composites that draw upon the illustrator's multiple experiences with the species and show a species and its field marks to best effect in order to convey this essential information to the user. A photo shows only what *one* individual bird looked like at one frozen moment in time, under a certain light, in a particular plumage, at one angle and pose (which may or may not be typical). Also, owing to the excellence of digital cameras and the effort photographers make to get exceptionally bright and sharp images, what the photos typically show are supernatural renderings, not the less-than-perfect images of birds in motion birders often get in the field.

Second, an illustrator can easily portray and arrange birds to show relative sizes between species as well as distinguishing traits. Illustrators also have the latitude to portray birds in typical, sometimes idiosyncratic, postures. Most photo guides do not meet these objectives as well. Having said this, the revolution in image capture and white-room modification has greatly improved the way images can be arranged and depicted on a page, as evidenced by the Kaufman Guide, which features photos.

Fifth, as determined by Roger Peterson and affirmed by many field-guide authors and illustrators since, the background that best illustrates a subject for the purpose of identification is no background at all. In the Kaufman Guide, the birds are digitally isolated from the photo background and arranged comparatively on a blank, visually neutral page.

My partiality to illustrated guides should not be construed to mean that photographic guides are without merit, or that the information they contain is not good, or that photos inaccurately depict birds. I'm only saying that illustrations generally depict birds better when the objective is identification and that the placement and depiction of birds follows a calculated approach, designed by an expert whose overall objective is to guide you to an identification in a calculated comparative fashion.

But Bird Photography Changes the Game

Increasingly, a number of birders are finding their way into the avocation not through the ocular lenses of binoculars but through the viewfinders of cameras. Birds are enticing but challenging subjects—challenging to shoot and challenging to identify. Yes, you can email your images to experienced birders for identification. But this is the lazy way, and it will not help you develop your own identification skills.

Also increasingly, many accomplished birders are making fast-shooting digital cameras outfitted with 300–400mm lenses part of their basic field equipment. The cameras are used as tools to document rare birds and help to identify challenging species or birds in flight. Identifications are made by studying the image on the camera's viewing screen.

It's ironic, actually, that after a century of emphasizing field-identification skills, bird study might well be heading back to the shotgun school: Collect the bird/image in the field. Identify after the fact.

If you are a photographer trying to identify bird images rather than birds in the field, a photo-driven guide may serve you better than an illustrated guide because it may more closely approximate the image of the bird you have "collected." Few would disagree with the assertion that bird identifications are image driven and that field guides should be, too. Having said this, I also maintain that it is precisely the synergy that exists between the descriptive text and the images that make guides excel, or not. A picture may indeed be worth a thousand words, but it can be enhanced, even trumped, by a few well-chosen words. For example:

Description: A common, plump, blackish-backed, rusty-breasted thrush that walks, stops, probes for earthworms across suburban lawns.

What do you think of that, Mr. Chapman?

In my opinion, two field guides out of the many distinguish themselves by the sympathetic accord that exists between illustration and text. They are the Peterson Guide and the Sibley Guide. In

Anybody have a problem with calling this one American Robin? LINDA DUNNE

both, the writer and illustrator are one. What they say and what they want to show are in perfect accord. You need to buy both these books. Don't second-guess this. Just do it. And buy the Kaufman Guide and National Geographic Guide, too (and as many other guides as your credit limit will allow).

Process

This is a subjective consideration. It has little to do with the identification of a single unknown bird. It has everything to do with how a birder learns the mechanics of bird identification—the process of seeing and assimilating detail that is the foundation of making an ID.

In part, this process is linked to how the author of a field guide imparts information—the order of significance they assign key information such as abundance, range, habitat, most prominent feature, size, shape, and supportive field marks. In part, process is projected by the illustrations—how the birds are grouped (facilitating comparison or suggesting possibility). In the Peterson, Sibley, and Golden Guides, there is a comforting consistency of portrayal and style. Birds are depicted, page after page, in a standardized composition that facilitates not only review and comparison but imparts to users a uniform approach to study.

The Sibley Guide broke with tradition by integrating informative text and illustrations so that a user's eyes would not have to stray from the illustrations that lie at the core of bird identification. But Sibley's layout, species to species, is reassuringly consistent.

More recently, Richard Crossley introduced a photo-driven guide, *The Crossley ID Guide,* that is plumage comprehensive; it arranges multiple photographic images of a species against a representative natural setting in much the same way museums arrange specimens in an exhibit that treats a specific bird.

All field guides can be used to help identify a puzzling bird. This is a static approach to bird identification. But bird identification itself is a process. Guides that work best are those with a format not so much anchored in the author's process but effortlessly projecting it—without the user being any the wiser.

The Elements of Bird Identification

How to Pin the Name to the Bird

There is no single correct system. But in time, there will be your system—one that accommodates your strengths, weaknesses, and interest—that in conjunction with the process outlined in your primary guide hybridizes into the analytical template you will bring to bear every time you confront an unfamiliar bird.

Every field guide offers a how-to section at the beginning. It is both a basic introduction to the elements of bird identification and an owner's manual for that guide. Once you have selected a primary guide, you have wedded yourself to the identification process championed and presented by the author.

There are whole books written on the subject of bird identification techniques (one of them mine: *The Art of Bird Identification*). But there are no shortcuts.

TALE SPOT

The Take-Home of Learning to See Critically

For some curious reason, I never discovered real field guides until I was in my late teens. What filled this niche from the age of 11 to 18 was a two-volume set published by the National Geographic Society entitled *Song and Garden Birds of North America* and *Water, Prey, and Game Birds of North America*. The books had an informative (but not very identification-oriented) text and a mix of both photos and illustrations, which too often were not useful for identification purposes. Nevertheless, these served as my field guides, even though they had one big fundamental shortfall. They were too big and too expensive to take into the field.

So instead of looking at a bird and then leafing through the pages of a guide while the bird was still in front of me, I developed the technique of looking critically at each new bird, memorizing the details, and then running home (literally running) with the image fresh in my mind.

Color, shape, size, wing bars, tail spots, eye line . . .

Sometimes I'd get home only to discover that there were two (or more) species that had the features I'd remembered and that the way to tell them apart was to look at the feet or the prominence of the eye ring. So I'd run back again and try to relocate the bird and get the missing information.

Often, I could not find the bird I'd seen reproduced in the books at all (since the books were not field guides, not all plumages were necessarily shown) or sometimes I did absolutely, certifiably find my bird in the pages (only to discover weeks or years later that my identification was dead wrong).

That wasn't the point. The field-guides-that-weren't forced me to see critically and memorize the details I saw. They may have prevented me from identifying some of the birds I found, but the process their shortcoming instilled was the best lesson any guide could hope to convey, and one I have used all my life: Use field time for study. Note everything you can about an unfamiliar bird because you never know what key characteristic will distinguish this species from another.

But like I said, I've written a whole book on the subject of bird identification. No need to be reDunnedant. ■

Choosing and Using Field Guides

What Works for You

There is no single guide that does everything best. They vary in complexity, regional bias, and usefulness. There is also no reason to own just one field guide. They are inexpensive and treasure troves of valuable information.

Having said this, in all likelihood there is one field guide out of the many that is destined to become your primary guide—the one that will, in short order, become as familiar in your hands as your binoculars, the one that will be your proxy mentor.

Many guides come in hard and soft covers. Soft covers seem to work best in the field. Many are wrapped in weather-resistant material. They tend to be a bit more kick-around tough than hardbound books (and they contour more comfortably in a hip pocket, or to the small of your back).

Using Your Field Guide

Don't let the name fool you. Field guides are not just to be used in the field. In fact, in some places, the use of guides in the field is discouraged. Birders coming upon an unfamiliar bird are encouraged to sketch the bird from life, using field time to study the bird in the field, making a depiction of all pertinent details.

But here in North America, and in most places, field guides typically are part of the real-time identification process. You can cut crucial seconds, even minutes, off this process by becoming intimate with your field guide before going into the field.

Read the introductory material—learn how to decode the maps and use the text to best effect.

Learn the order in which groups of birds occur and where species fall on the page. It saves lots of page flipping.

Read the species descriptions, not necessarily to memorize them but to link in your mind key field marks to key birds so that you know, when a sighting is only momentary, what you should be looking for. Peterson's highlighting arrows are an invaluable aid in this regard.

Customizing Your Guide

It is your guide. Anything that makes it more useful and more personal increases its value to the only person that matters. Commercially available quick-key indexes can be glued inside the covers of books to facilitate finding target species. Also available are commercially attachable index tabs. Or you can design your own. Some guides have a quick-reference system built in.

If the scope of your guide is more far ranging than you are, you can underline or highlight birds that are most likely to occur in your area, or use masking tape to cover birds whose range and yours don't overlap—to reduce variables among look-alike species and optimize study time. As your skills grow or your search for birds expands, the tape can be peeled away.

The best way to customize your guide is to mark each species you find with a check, followed by the date and the place. These particulars relate your first encounter with the species. And this encounter is known among birders everywhere as finding a life bird.

In Praise of Peterson

You might bet that as one of Peterson's "adopted sons," as he referred to a select handful of my generation, I would have a special place in my heart for the guide and the man that ushered in the Age of Birding. I won't disappoint you.

There are several reasons why the Peterson Field Guides continue to serve beginning birders well. First, the text is simple and friendly, written with the beginning birder in mind. Second, the illustrations are very thoughtfully laid out in a fashion that makes undistracted study and comparisons with similar species easy. Third, and very much related to these first considerations, the text

Sometimes Ma Nature throws you a bone. Adult male Harlequin Ducks are all field mark. (At a distance, however, the boldly patterned duck appears mostly dark.)

and illustrations were crafted by a single hand—a single mind—so there is perfect accord between what the author wanted to say and what the illustrator wanted to depict. The only other field guide author to offer this same seamless accord is my friend David Sibley. And the "Peterson System," which relies on tiny arrows to quickly draw the user's eye to key field marks is, for novice birders, an advantage beyond price.

For beginning birders who travel widely but whose birding is conducted primarily in the East, *Birds of North America: A Guide to Field Identification* remains a wonderful choice. While this guide, first published in 1966 and revised in 2001, has fallen somewhat out of favor with some accomplished birders, the number of new birders who continue to be won over by its simple, straightforward, utilitarian ease speaks for itself.

For western birders, and birders who are already grounded in basic birds and are now searching for uncommon and elusive species all across North America, and who are fascinated by regional forms, the *National Geographic Field Guide to the Birds of North America* is a favorite. Owing to its expanded focus on western subspecies, beginning birders living from Texas and the Rocky Mountains west might want to consider the Geo Guide their primary guide—and since it is all-inclusive, you won't need to change to a different guide when you travel to the East Coast on vacation, or vacation in the Rio Grande Valley of Texas in search of Mexican vagrants. Note, too, however, that the Geo Guide also comes in western and eastern versions as well as the original comprehensive format.

But I am also very partial to the Kaufman Guide, a utilitarian and user-friendly guide that integrates digitally modified photos and simple, engaging descriptions to guide users to a proper identification and, just as importantly, warn them when their sleuthing has taken them down the wrong path.

There are other general field guides on the market; several are superlative, and all bring something to the identification matrix. These include the *National Wildlife Federation Field Guide to Birds of North America,* by Edward Brinkley and Craig Tufts; the *Smithsonian Field Guide to Birds of North America,* by Ted Floyd; and the very basic yet compelling Princeton Illustrated Checklist *Birds of North America and Greenland,* by Norman Arlott.

But for most people, for my money, the guide that serves the beginning birder (even the intermediate birder) best is the Peterson. For all the reasons mentioned, and one other.

Roger Peterson grew up, and learned his skills, in the formative age when birding was born. His skills advanced as birding advanced, but his grounding is very much in the age when seeing a bird close and well through binoculars and identifying that bird was the frontier. The very same frontier every beginning birder faces to this day. (Yes, the guide is offered as an app.)

Users don't need to understand why the Peterson Guide works so well, but like the tens of millions of users before them, they cannot help but appreciate it.

Last Page, Bottom Line

One thing every incipient birder should know is that no matter how good your field guide, there are times when you are going to find a bird that looks like nothing depicted in the books.

You lose this round.

Bird wins.

In every species there is variation between individuals. Sometimes those variations in size, shape, and, particularly, plumage are enough to sow confusion. Occasionally, too, birds of two different species will mate and produce hybrid young with characteristics of both parents. Waterfowl hybridize habitually. Or birds may become stained (by tar, paint, pollen, even dyes applied by ornithologists to study bird movement).

And of course guides are limited by a defined range. Birds do sometimes wander far outside their "normal" ranges and perhaps the geographic limits of your guide.

The point is this: A field guide is just that. A guide. It is not the final word. It isn't gospel. There are times when you are going to find birds that just don't look like anything in the field guide. That's one of the reasons there are specialty guides.

WING BAR

Birding Apps and Recordings

Several field guides are available as apps, greatly enhancing their portability and allowing birders to carry a library of guides into the field. One of the greatest advantages of apps is the incorporation of bird vocalizations that can be called up and compared directly to what you are hearing outdoors.

Yes, these recordings can also be used to lure birds into view, but this is never something to be done casually. Playing a species' song in that bird's territory is the biological equivalent of kicking in the front door and shouting, "I'm here to take your home and abduct your wife!"—obviously a stress-inducing situation. Since a concern for birds is fundamental to bird study, the use of playbacks for casual bird watching is not encouraged.

Birding is a leisure pursuit. Birds are not here for our immediate gratification. Relax. Lighten up. Enjoy the moment and the bird in its natural environment. Engaging wild birds in the field was never meant to be as mindless an exercise as using your remote to find a favorite program on television. And watching a thoroughly agitated bird hopping branch to branch deprives you of the opportunity of seeing it behave naturally. ■

Books or Apps?

Whether you use books or apps one thing is universal: field time is a time for study, for noting details relating to a bird's structure, plumage, mannerisms, vocalizations, and habitat. Your field guide or app comes into play after you have exhausted your initial opportunity to study the bird. But having your guide at hand will prove useful when your initial identification efforts draw a blank and you are forced to study the bird anew to note some differentiating trait unappreciated in your initial study.

Portability is the trait that puts the "field" in field guide. I know many birders who use the book version of their guide in the car and at home but carry the app version in the field.

Clothing

Quiet, Cryptic, and Comfortable

The expensive part of gearing up is over. Binoculars and a field guide constitute the greatest outlay of cash at the entry level of birding.

But you have to wear something while birding outdoors, and it might as well be something that fits—both you and the activity. The dress code isn't strict, and a birding wardrobe doesn't have to be expensive. In fact, if you look in your dresser, you'll probably find just the items you need to go birding in comfort and style.

Two Basic Principles: Causal and Comfortable

The guiding standard is: casual. In fact, so casual are birders about their attire that at the annual banquet of the American Birding Association not even the keynote speaker wears a tie.

Regulation garb is quick-drying slacks or jeans, T-shirt or polo shirt or work shirt, and running shoes or light hiking boots. In wet areas, or for walking around in dew-heavy mornings, knee-length rubber boots (Wellies) work well.

North America is climate rich and you need not travel far to appreciate this meteorological diversity. Changing seasons and fast-moving weather systems deliver them to our door. In very hot (but insect-impoverished) areas, shorts supplant long pants. Hats with a brim shade the brain and serve to keep eyes in a squint-free microclimate. In hot and insect-rich environs, a light, long-sleeved, cotton shirt worn loosely over a T-shirt offers some protection.

In cool climates, knee-length or thigh-length jackets are standard, and in cold temperatures, underlying layers of synthetic fleece or wool work well. Wool or synthetic fleece caps (worn so that ears can be at least partially exposed) help keep you warm. Gloves are preferable to mittens, not because they are warmer but because gloves keep index fingers free to focus binoculars.

Waterproof jackets are advisable but fabrics must breathe—i.e., allow perspiration to transpire through the material. The waxed cotton jackets preferred by British birders (and country gentry) work well in cool, wet climates but are too hot, too clammy (and too

The birding dress code is casual and not necessarily coordinated; baseball caps and jeans are fairly typical. Name tags are optional, unless you are on duty, as are these two hawk-watch interpretive interns at Cape May.

heavy) over much of North America much of the time. These jackets do offer two qualities, however, that are important to birding . . .

Two Qualifying Standards: Quiet and Cryptic

Clothing worn by birders should be quiet—rustle and crackle free. Quiet means that you can hear birds while walking with arms swinging at your sides. Quiet means that birds (and other wildlife) will not hear you and beat a premature retreat. Cotton, synthetic fleece, wool, and even some synthetic shell jackets meet (or approach) this standard.

Clothing worn by birders should also be cryptic, not garishly bright or colorful. It doesn't have to be camouflaged, although the camouflage patterns popular among photographers and sports hunters are becoming more popular among birders. But clothing

Camo clothing designed primarily for the hunting market is beginning to become quite popular among birders not only because it is cryptic but also because it's usually waterproof and quiet—i.e., rustle free.

should be a cool, neutral, or natural color such as tan, brown, dull green, or smoky gray—colors that make a figure blend into a landscape, not stand out.

Birds, of course, see colors, and bright colors advertise your presence and may even startle birds should you turn a corner or come upon them quickly. (Imagine, for a moment, being a ground foraging, shadow-loving Hermit Thrush and having a hooded figure in a full-length yellow rain-suit suddenly swing into view).

One color you should absolutely avoid is white. Across much of the animal kingdom, the color white is visual Esperanto for "HEY, LOOKEE HERE! DANGER—TAKE COVER!" Sometimes this message is flashed from a deer's raised tail, sometimes from the underparts of schooling bait fish turning to avoid a predator's rush. Since your objective is to get close to birds, "take cover/fly away" is not a message you want to send.

TALE SPOT

Good Birders Don't Wear White

On October 14, 1991, I spent several hours crouched by the trail in upper Ramsey Canyon monitoring a nest. Most birds in southeastern Arizona had fledged their young months earlier, but these were no ordinary birds. These were Eared Quetzals—a handsome, globally rare species—and this was the first nest ever recorded in the United States.

These Eared Quetzals had arrived in the Huachuca Mountains in early August, among several that crossed the Mexican border that summer. News of this sighting worked its way through the birding grapevine, and soon birders were flooding into Ramsey Canyon from near and far in hopes of spotting this treasure from the Sierra Madre. But the birds were extremely wary, disappearing into the dense forest at the first sign of human intrusion.

On October 10, a group of visitors videotaped the female trogon entering a cavity in a dead maple easily visible from the trail; a member of the same group returned on October 12 and watched as the male carried a caterpillar into the same hole, confirming the presence of nestlings.

The nest was a two-mile hike from where I lived and worked at Ramsey Canyon Preserve, so on October 14, I took a day off to watch the nest and record every detail of this historic event. At 12:44, an hour since the previous feeding, the male signaled its return to the nest with several "squeal-chuck" calls, silencing the six birders patiently awaiting its arrival. After two breathless minutes the male landed at the nest entrance with a caterpillar in its bill, then immediately flew to a nearby tree. There it sat, squeal-chucking in alarm, each call accompanied by a flash of white outer tail-feathers.

On previous feeding visits, the arriving parent had entered the nest almost immediately despite the presence of several observers—so what caused this delay? Over the next eight minutes the male flew back and forth across the clearing, calling constantly, before landing once again at the nest entrance. Through the spotting scope I saw its head turn briefly toward the trail before it flew off again, still squealing in alarm. I followed the direction of the trogon's gaze to a recently arrived birder sitting apart from the rest but in plain view of the nest. The man's white long-sleeved shirt and cap glared against the dark forest background. The problem suddenly became clear.

Though movement might disturb the bird even more, I quickly sidled over to the birder in white and asked him to remove his shirt and cap. Taken aback at first, he quickly complied when I explained the reason for this odd request. I crept back to my spotting scope, and after six tense minutes the male trogon finally entered the cavity. After less than a minute inside it left again, returning to the tree a few minutes later with another insect; this time there was little hesitation as it slipped inside the nest to feed its young.

That evening a colleague and I cut a few yards of camouflage cloth into simple ponchos for loan to inappropriately dressed trogon-seekers, allowing dozens of people to observe the nest with minimal disturbance to the parent birds. The nestlings died in an early storm just two weeks later, but what we learned in that short time has made many birders aware of how something as seemingly innocent as a white shirt can affect the birds we watch.

Though Eared Quetzals are unusually sensitive they are not unique. Most birds are highly visual creatures, and color plays a significant role in their lives and behavior. Elegant Trogons also flash their white tail-feathers to signal alarm. A Northern Cardinal's parental instinct is triggered by the gaping orange mouths of its young. Male Red-winged Blackbirds keep the peace in winter by concealing their provocative red epaulets. Blue-crowned Motmots instinctively recoil from the red, black, and yellow ringed pattern of coral snakes. As sensitive as birds are to such visual cues, is it logical to expect them to ignore white shirts, red hats, and florescent yellow day-packs? Yet unlike hunters and wildlife photographers, the average birder still doesn't give much thought to field wear. Trading in that white birding festival T-shirt for a camo jumpsuit and face paint is a little extreme, but selecting neutral colors that blend with the environment can reduce the impact of birding on birds and other wildlife, and improve birding success for all. ■

—Sheri Williamson

Sheri Williamson, a consummate naturalist, is codirector of the Southeastern Arizona Bird Observatory, in Bisbee, Arizona. Before that, she and husband Tom Wood were stewards of the Nature Conservancy's Ramsey Canyon Preserve.

Other Things You'll Need

Unlike backpackers and photographers, birders like to travel light. Over time, I've pared down needs to a utilitarian minimum.

- Cotton handkerchief or soft lens-cleaning cloth, for cleaning optics (particularly when it's raining).
- Lip balm and sunscreen, for sun protection.
- Insect repellent (when necessary).
- Sunglasses (particularly for hawk or seabird watching).
- Waterproof pocket notepad and two pencils or a ballpoint pen.
- A small day-pack (if I'm going to be off for more than a casual morning's birding at a familiar haunt) to carry a water bottle, field guide, regionally calibrated bird-finding guide, and shed and extra clothing (depending upon conditions and need).

  I never use a day-pack if a fanny pack will do. I never use a fanny pack when what I need will fit comfortably in pockets—which brings up a good point.
- Suitable jacket. When shopping for a birding jacket, select in favor of those offering a good array of pockets—pockets big and diverse enough to accommodate your field guide, hat, gloves, notebook, and other gear. In hot climates, light, tough, multipocketed vests such as those worn by photographers and journalists are popular, but they should not be construed to constitute a birding uniform.

SUMMARY

Binoculars are the defining tools of birding, but not all makes and models meet the demands of birding. These demands include: sharp and bright optics, wide field of view, adequate depth of field, close focus to below 10 feet, responsive focus mechanism, ergonomic design. Lower magnification (7x or 8x) is more versatile and user friendly than higher magnification.

The best place to buy binoculars is a store specializing in meeting the needs of birders. Test a variety of makes and models, and always test the instrument you plan to buy. The rule of thumb is: buy the best binocular you can afford, and buy it as soon as you can afford it. Expect to pay no less than $200 for an adequate birding binocular; $200 to $500 for a commendable entry-level pair; $1,500 to $3,500 for a top-performing instrument. There is really only one true test of binoculars: You bring them to your eyes and see things quickly and easily.

Field guides are key to bird identification. Field guides that follow and group birds by the standard taxonomic order based on the shape and anatomical traits of birds and use comparatively arranged illustrations have traditionally worked best for most people. Field guides should be studied at home as well as taken into the field. All guides have useful information, but for sheer utilitarian ease the Peterson Guide seems to work best for most beginning and novice birders.

Field clothes are casual, loose fitting, comfortable. Fabrics should be quiet so birds can be heard. Colors should be cryptic so you blend in with your environment and birds will not be startled or alarmed. ■

The Fundamentals of Birding

Like Grosbeaks for Purple Finch

It was sunny but cold. Buds, not leaves, were still in season. I was birding the Great Swamp National Wildlife Refuge, a federally designated Wilderness Area smack in the middle of suburban North Jersey. Ahead of me was a birding couple. Their binoculars were functional and new. Their field guide bookstore fresh. Their clothes casual but coordinated.

By all signs, beginning birders.

They were feverishly scanning the branches above them—branches made animate by a vocal flock of Purple Finch, mostly females. Boldly patterned, charcoal brown on white, their single, sharp, call notes filled the air, broadcasting their identity to anyone with experienced ears to hear.

"Seen anything good?" I invited, offering the near universal greeting among birders that lets the respondent set the level of the information exchange.

"Yes," the gentleman said, smiling widely. "A whole flock of Rose-breasted Grosbeaks. All females. We're trying to find a male."

"Huh," I said, trying to decide how to correct an obvious but understandable misidentification. Female Purple Finch and female Rose-breasted Grosbeak do have similar plumage characteristics. And plumage is the characteristic beginning birders tend to focus on, because this is the trait most field guides emphasize and because, as distinguishing characteristics go, it usually works.

Not this time. By relying solely on plumage, the couple had overlooked several other salient clues that might have shifted their sleuthing down a more productive path. For instance, they'd failed to note that the birds they were looking at were sparrow sized, not starling sized, a determination that would have eliminated Rose-breasted Grosbeak from a list of possible candidates. Rose-breasted Grosbeaks are almost twice the length of Purple Finch and overall heftier, more robust.

The couple had also failed to note the less-than-"gross"-sized beak on the birds. Grosbeaks aren't called "gross beaks" for nothing, and while the conical bills of Purple Finch do recall a grosbeak's bill in shape, they fall short in both size and relative proportions.

Less obvious for beginners, but even more determining, was the date. Purple Finch are winter residents over most of New Jersey. Rose-breasted Grosbeaks, on the other hand, are summer breeders and neotropic migrants and so are rarely found in the state after September and before May 1. A whole flock of grosbeaks, in late March, in New Jersey, should have sent up warning flags all over the deductive centers of the couple's brains. As well, the very fact that the birds were flocking at all should have planted suspicion. While Purple Finch typically gather in flocks, Rose-breasted Grosbeaks are almost never found in aggregate numbers—even during migration they tend to be solitary or members of mixed-species flocks (sometimes found with tanagers and orioles).

That the birding couple was troubled by the absence of the rhubarb-bibbed male grosbeak was encouraging. I figured that this undermining concern would eventually lead them to discard their initial identification and get onto the right track. No reason to pre-empt the educational process with a heavy-handed correction.

Female Purple Finch (top) and Rose-breasted Grosbeak (bottom) share some plumage traits, but plumage is only feather deep. Other salient hints and clues help distinguish the two species.

But since the couple was leaning in the right direction, I concluded it wouldn't intrude too much to give them a nudge.

"Nice male Purple Finch singing up there," I remarked, directing them to the wine-stained bird perched in a nearby tree. I felt confident they'd be able to work things out from there.

Where, When, and How to Go Birding

You have your binoculars. You have your field guide. You have a task-free morning, and all your socially suppressed hunter/gatherer instincts are tugging at the leash. Now what?

That's easy. Just go birding. It's not a first date. It's not the oral defense of your thesis. It's an act as simple and engaging as strolling along woodland paths or perusing paintings in a gallery. Except, unlike paintings, birds have free will. They select to be in certain places. Go to the places birds choose to be and your success will be greater.

Almost Any Ol' Natural Place Will Do

You don't have to travel to the Amazon Basin just to see birds. You don't even have to go to a national park or migratory bird refuge (but if there is one nearby, by all means, take advantage of it). As mentioned in chapter 1, birds are common and birds are everywhere—even in habitats modified exclusively to meet our species' needs (i.e., cities) there are birds to be found.

But while some species of birds have acclimated themselves to urban habitats, most birds are more at home in natural, highly vegetated areas. Different species are specialized for, and apportion themselves in, different habitat types. The habitat where you go birding will largely determine what species of birds you are likely to find and what identification challenges you are likely to face. So not only does habitat narrow down your choices, it aids in the identification process.

But Not All Habitats Are Equal in the Eyes of Birds

Here's a basic hint. Birds like trees. Not all birds, and not all birds are partial to all trees, but the largest and most abundant scientific

Many species, including this male Orchard Oriole, are typically found where trees are part of the landscape. When searching for birds, you can't go wrong seeking out trees. Perching birds overwhelmingly favor perches associated with trees.

order of birds in North America is the Passeriformes, aka the "perching birds." Sometimes they perch on wires. Sometimes on weeds. Sometimes they "perch" on the ground. But the overwhelming favorite perches passerines choose to perch on are the branches associated with trees.

So if you are a new birder looking for birds, even (and maybe especially) in places where trees are few and far between, you can hardly go wrong heading for a tree-rich place. In urban or suburban areas this can mean a riverside park, an environmental center's grounds, even a cemetery. In more rural areas choices are broader (although not necessarily better).

In a large park or natural area dominated by mature trees, you are likely to find such representative woodland birds as woodpeckers, nuthatches, jays, and chickadees. These are called permanent residents, and over most of North America these are birds that will be encountered almost any time you walk through woods.

No Trees? Be at Ease

Birds have you covered. They have diversified and are specialized to occupy almost every conceivable habitat. Some species are at home in grasslands, typically different species from those that are specialized to occupy woodlands, but no less at home. A morning afield in one of the prairie states might turn up such grassland and open-country specialists as meadowlark, Horned Lark, or one of several grassland sparrow species. Rivers, lakes, and coasts offer different possibilities—among them loons, grebes, waterfowl, and gulls.

The compelling thing about waterfowl is that they are common denizens of urban parks, and although the ubiquitous Mallard typically constitutes the bulk of park-pond birds, other more unusual species often join the local birds, especially in spring and fall, and when freezing temperatures coat other bodies of water in ice, forcing ducks to find open water. For identification purposes, ducks generally play fair. They are large, and they typically stay in the open, where they are easily observed. The plumage of adult male birds, at least, is generally distinctive. And for much of the year, the more cryptic females are commonly found in direct association with males and thus easily identified. As a beginning birder learning the rudiments of field identification you'll find that ducks make good subjects.

Freshwater marshes, which are a sort of a habitat cross between a meadow and a lake, are home to rails, bitterns, herons, egrets, and assorted waterfowl. Tidal wetlands, which expose their muddy or sandy bottoms at low tide, open the door to a host of sandpipers and other shorebirds.

Desert, tundra, chaparral, sagebrush plains, spruce bogs, open seas, mangrove swamps—each habitat has its own peculiar flavor and habitat-specialized species. So no matter where you are, there is a nearby habitat that is wrapped around a compelling package of birds ideally suited to be there.

WING BAR

The Subject Is Sewage Ponds

Sooner or later (but sooner is better), you will learn that some of the best birding anywhere, at almost any time, is upwind of the local sewage treatment plant or collection site.

These epicenters of effluvium are attractive to birds of many persuasions and divergent feeding habits. Species may vary geographically or seasonally, but there is rarely an ornithological void.

Bird diversity is often indicative of the level of present-day technology in the management of organic waste. For instance, in areas where the cleanup proceeds from pond to pond, eventually to be deposited in adjacent fields via spray heads, and with the natural addition of man-made fresh marsh, or even emergent vegetation, one might find an astounding variety of birds, with virtually all the expected families represented by one or more species. Examples: grebes, cormorants, herons, ducks, terns, gulls, rails, shorebirds, birds of prey, flycatchers, swallows, wrens, warblers, sparrows, blackbirds, and so on.

By whatever name these repositories of sludge are known among birders, be it lagoons, ponds, or even lakes, they are listed in one's telephone directory, under town, city, or county government agencies, with high-sounding names—such as Blank Blank Pollution Control Commission, or Blank Blank Wastewater Management District, or something similar.

Your best bet is to ask another birder, as in, "Take me to your sewage lagoon," or call the proper agency and request permission to bird the area (some have relatively open access; others have locked gates and sign-in sheets).

By virtue of one or more astounding birds, some lagoons are justifiably famous. The humble pond at Starkville, Mississippi, was the site of the first and only record of a Citrine Wagtail in the Western Hemisphere. The Baltimore, Maryland, operation made the newspapers when a Ross's Gull visited for a few days. Some treatment plants, like that in Jackson County, Mississippi, keep a guest book and serve us as well as any official wildlife refuge.

But it isn't really the rarities—it's the season-in, season-out array of birds we expect near water, even if the water is sluggish and the air is foul. These man-made habitats are there before and after all else fails.

While sewage lagoons rank number one on the off-Birdway circuit, there are other suspect habitats birders favor that most others would give a very wide berth. These include: cemeteries, industrial parks, landfills, and impoundments—anywhere a few good birds may be found, even on a bad day. ■

—Judith Toups

The late Judy Toups, formerly of Gulfport, Mississippi, was a writer, field-trip leader, birding instructor, and friend who was for many years the "bird lady" of coastal Mississippi.

When to Go

How about now? There is never a time when birds are not present. Over most of North America the calendar determines what mix of species you will encounter, not whether birds are present. There is a seasonality to bird distribution. In summer, the ranks of permanent residents are augmented by summer residents. These are species that spend most of their lives beyond winter's reach but who return when summer temperatures make the Northern Hemisphere hospitable. They establish territories, find a mate, nest, rear their young, and then retreat before winter closes over the land once again.

The retreat is not necessarily far. Some birds, such as the Prairie Falcon, may simply go from higher elevations to lower ones. Some species go from inland lakes to the ice-free coasts. Some retreat a few hundred or a few thousand miles but still remain in North America. These are also winter residents, and depending upon where you live, the diversity of winter species may equal or even surpass the number of species found in your region in summer.

So it is not a matter of whether birds are present, it is a matter of what species you will see and where they are seasonally apportioned. The best time to see the greatest diversity is while populations are shifting as many species engage in a twice-annual redistribution called migration. While migration is a very protracted phenomenon, the peak migratory periods over much of North

Red-eyed Vireo is a common summer resident in the eastern U.S., but it retreats to the tropics in winter.

America range from March to June in spring, August through November in the fall.

Not all species migrate at the same time. In spring, in some places, waterfowl and birds of prey are migrating north in late January and February; yet the last straggling northbound shorebirds and songbirds may not reach their nesting territories until June.

In "fall," the first southbound shorebirds begin journeying south during the third week in June (yes, June!). The southbound migration of several songbirds actually peaks in early August. Assorted raptors, seabirds, and hardy winter finches anchor the autumn migration, with some birds reaching their winter ranges in January.

Bird populations are dynamic. The seasons determine the mix. There is almost never a time when bird populations are not shifting, which for birders means that every day afield offers the possibility of finding something new.

One of the unsung benefits of being a birder is all the beautiful sunrises you are going to experience.

How Early Is Now?

Active birds are easier to find than quiescent birds. Different species have different daily activity patterns. But for most species, early morning and late afternoon are when they are most active. Everything you might have heard and dreaded about the early bird catching the worm is true. If you are not an early riser but are a newly dedicated birder, then a dramatic change in your daily activity pattern is imminent. Look on the bright side: One of birding's unspoken benefits is the number of extraordinary sunrises you are destined to see.

But if you simply cannot get up with the birds, know that birds usually remain active and vocal until midmorning and that some bird groups (most notably many migrating hawks) don't start soaring until the sun is high and thermals are plentiful.

And in coastal areas, the foraging pattern of many species is governed more by the tide than time of day.

How to Find 'Em

You have seen birds all of your life—by accident. You are about to discover just how challenging it can be to get a look at one once you make it your objective.

First, give yourself every advantage. Pick a birding location that offers good light, the sun at your back, a little room to maneuver, and a vantage to see birds at distances that won't force them to retreat before you can bring your binoculars to bear.

It usually pays to stay out of the deep woods, where shadows mask color and even birds standing still disappear in a blurry maze of branches. Conduct your search along woodland edges, in mixed field and patchy woodlands, or on paths or roadways that offer lots of room on both sides and an avenue of sky above. Windless conditions are generally more productive for most birding insofar as a bird's movements will not be masked by wind-stirred vegetation.

You don't have to stalk. Just walk quietly and naturally, keeping eyes alert for motion and ears attuned to call notes and song. Even if you don't know bird vocalizations enough to identify the bird, they will alert you to the presence of birds.

You don't have to keep your hands on your binoculars at all times. If you see motion, reach deliberately for your binoculars. If you are approaching a place where you suspect or know there are birds, yes, by all means, hold your binoculars at the ready. If you flush a bird, freeze. It may fly a short distance and perch to get a look at the intruder (you). If it disappears, it is very likely to reappear.

The bird has wings but you have the advantage. You are standing where that bird wants to be. You have the strategic edge. Be still. Be patient. You may get the look you want.

Caution: If the bird is behaving in a very agitated manner—calling, moving from branch to branch, doing everything it can to call attention to itself—back off! The bird is telling you that you are too close to its nest or its young. The ethical practice in birding is to respect the bird's territory and retreat to a comfortable distance. The bird, by its actions, will tell you when you reach that spot.

The Common Tern with wings raised is telling you you've gotten close enough. If it flies, so too may many others, perhaps before you've thoroughly studied the flock.

WING BAR

Getting Between the Lines

Birding's battleground is played out between two invisible lines—one defined by the limit of your binocular to resolve detail, the other by the bird's flush point. An identification must be made between these two lines or, unless fortune smiles and the bird makes an identifiable call as it flies away, it isn't made at all.

The way birders have always approached the problem of getting close enough is precisely that—approach. Sometimes it works and you see the detail you need. Sometimes it doesn't and you get too close. The bird determines this distance, and it votes with its wings.

Flush distance is not an absolute point. It differs from species to species and between individuals of a species. (Approach a flock of gulls or shorebirds and you will see one or two birds that raise their wings, preparing to exit, while the others remain unperturbed). But flushing birds also has much to do with how birds are approached. Knowing how not to push a bird's panic button will get you closer, and it might get you the look you need to make an identification.

Rule 1: Pick a birding area where birds are habituated to human motion—a park where people exercise, a beach where people stroll, a refuge with a trail and hide (aka blind) system. Birds become habituated to a normal human traffic pattern, and so long as you don't break the pattern (by leaving the trail and approaching), they will usually be tolerant.

Rule 2: Don't rush. Take it easy. Let the bird or birds get used to you. If they seem agitated, about to flush, wait. Give them time to relax.

Rule 3: When approaching a bird, don't walk directly toward it. Try to approach obliquely so that as you draw closer it is obvious that on your present course, you are not going to intercept it.

Rule 4: Don't get between birds and their escape route. Do not, for example, approach birds resting on a beach from the water's edge. Many of the species that frequent beaches seek safety by flying over open water. If you seem intent on cutting off their escape route, they will flush sooner. Similarly, when approaching a flock of ducks or gulls, approach from the downwind side (thus keeping the wind in your face). Birds like to take off into the wind. If you approach in a fashion that will force them to cut across your path or fly toward you to get airborne, they will flush sooner than if you are respectful of their avenue of retreat. ■

Photographers are always trying to get a little closer for a better shot. Know that flushing desirable birds in popular birding areas before others can get a satisfactory look is not regarded favorably and gives bird photographers a bad name. Consider buying a bigger lens or photographing birds in a more secluded and less-popular birding area.

Now You'll Understand Why You Bought those Birder-Worthy Binoculars

Keep your eye on the bird. You are already looking in the right place. All you need to do is bring the binoculars up so that they fall between you and the target.

Don't be surprised if your aim is off, particularly if the bird is very close. Bringing binoculars up to your eyes and having them fall where you want them takes practice.

If you are not on target, don't swing your binoculars wildly around trying to find the bird. You are probably closer to being on target than you think (and a lot of wild gyrating isn't going to instill confidence in a bird whose suspicions are already aroused).

Remember that the challenge you face is three-dimensional. Move the focus wheel until the bush, or limbs, or wires, or whatever the bird is sitting on or near is clear, then be patient, waiting for the bird to betray its location with movement. If you don't find the bird after a short search (5 or 10 seconds), slowly lower your binoculars. Peer over the top. Confirm that the bird is still there. Fix your gaze on the bird. Try again.

Sometimes, in cases where a bird is perched amid leaves or branches and not visible to the naked eye, there may be an obvious reference you can use to help get on target—an oddly twisted branch or a discolored leaf. Bring your binoculars to bear on this target instead of the bird, focus, and then wait for the bird to betray itself with some subtle motion. We humans are hardwired to detect motion, and birds are animate creatures.

Sometimes, if the bird is near a tree trunk or on a branch, you can focus on this obvious feature and work your binoculars along its length until the bird is found.

But there is no substitute for bringing binoculars up and having them fall precisely where you want them. This skill takes practice, but it is central to the art of birding. The best way to gain proficiency is to go birding and discipline yourself to bring your binoculars to bear every time you spot or flush a bird. Even if you already know what it is.

Basic Bird Identification

I See It!

Congratulations. You've just joined the ranks of birders. Now comes the hard part.

Ten Steps Away from an Identification

Much of the challenge of birding is bound up in identifying birds. For a birder to master the challenge, he or she must pursue an identification based on hints and clues. Birders approach this challenge in much the same way that Socrates sought the essence of truth—by asking a series of questions. Each answer pares away possibilities and builds a case until all the questions are answered, the bird is linked to a name, and another checkmark falls upon the pages of your field guide.

The questions are:

1. How large is the bird?
2. What is the shape of the bird?
3. What are the bird's field marks (plumage patterns, traits)?
4. What are the bird's mannerisms? (Does it walk or hop? Flick its wings? Wag its tail? Does it stab the water with its bill or probe?)
5. How does the bird fly? (Direct or undulating? With rapid wing beats or sluggish? Is the flight even and regular like a crow? Or irregular and halting like Belted Kingfisher or American Robin?)

6. How does the bird sound?
7. What kind of habitat does the bird prefer? (Brushy edge like Song Sparrow or grassy edge, even bare roadside, like Savannah Sparrow?)
8. Where in North America was the bird?
9. When was the bird seen?
10. What is the bird's relative abundance?

The first seven questions are real-time queries, questions to be asked in the field while studying the bird. The last three are reflective qualifiers that serve to eliminate possibilities from consideration and guide an observer to a correct identification—very often eliminating or calling into question an initial hypothesis.

How Large Is the Bird?

This is a very important question, one that has a direct bearing on identification, because species vary greatly in size. For the couple working out the identity of the flock of Purple Finches, a better sense of size would have put them on the short route to a correct identification.

Their failure to appreciate the importance of size in the identification process led them astray, and when you err at the beginning, you typically continue down the wrong path until your identification hits a dead end.

But size is sometimes difficult to determine because distance affects perspective. Distance can make even birds the size of eagles look tiny; close proximity makes smaller birds seem unnaturally large. Misjudge the distance, you misjudge the size. While we begin developing our sense of size, distance, and perspective almost as soon as we open our eyes, few of us come to birding with our sense of perspective finely honed. Practice (and using binoculars that always offer the same magnification) will make you a better judge of both.

A good trick when trying to establish the size of an unfamiliar bird is not to measure it in inches but to compare it to the size of a bird you are familiar with. Is the bird sparrow sized? Starling sized?

Robin sized? Or is it as big or bigger than a pigeon? Size determinations are often best made before binoculars are brought to bear, when you have vegetative reference points to relate to—seed heads, pinecones, leaves, and so on.

Many birds are gregarious, gathering like waterfowl in mixed flocks. Under these ideal circumstances, direct comparisons between familiar and unfamiliar species are often possible. If the bird is alone, or the flock uniform and unfamiliar, try comparing the birds to any known reference. For example: If the bird is perched on a fence post, is it as long as the post is wide or longer? If the bird is perched next to the insulator on a utility line, is it larger or smaller?

A correct assessment of size is the first and often deciding element to be confronted in the identification matrix. Size can often be determined by a bird's surroundings. This Ferruginous Hawk is obviously larger than the wire insulators next to it and so very apparently is a large bird of prey—not eagle sized, perhaps, but larger than a falcon. LINDA DUNNE

A backlit falcon perched on the crossbar of a telephone pole might be an American Kestrel or a Merlin. Or it might be one of the larger falcons—a Peregrine or, in the West, a Prairie Falcon. If the bird is more than twice the length of the average insulator, be assured it is not the diminutive kestrel, and it isn't a Merlin either.

Determining the size of birds in flight can be a real challenge, but even here comparisons are possible. Soaring birds, in particular, often join other species turning circles in the sky. Solo birds are a matter of conjecture, but the way they fly can sometimes offer an oblique reference to size. Large birds turn in wider circles than smaller ones. Their flight is more deliberate, less acrobatic; their wing beats are slower.

Remember: Every day afield is an opportunity to build upon your bird-watching knowledge base. Study common and familiar birds to give you a reference point to compare to unfamiliar species when you encounter them.

TALE SPOT

Bryan and the Red-faced Feeder Bird

As Bryan Bland—birder, tour leader, and resident of Cley, England—tells the story, a call came in to him one day from a local resident who was perplexed about a bird "at her feeder."

"Well, can you describe the bird, madam?" invited the knowledgeable Mr. Bland—which she did, offering assorted details of the bird, the most determining of which was a "red face."

"Well," said Bryan, giving proper weight to this last disclosure. "That's not difficult. You have a goldfinch, madam." The European Goldfinch, *Carduelis carduelis,* is a common resident species in the U.K., similar in many respects to North American goldfinches but distinguished from them (and from all other songbirds commonly found in England) by a bright red face.

"No," the woman apologized, "I don't think it is a goldfinch."

"Well," said Bryan, somewhat perplexed. "There are not many options here. Perhaps if you could describe the bird again."

The woman obliged, saying nothing inconsistent with the identification of goldfinch, which Bryan offered again as the most likely possibility.

"No," the woman asserted, "I am quite certain it is not a goldfinch."

Intrigued, Bryan inquired about the woman's address, concluded it wasn't too far off his daily commute, and resolved to stop by the woman's house on his way home—which he did.

"Excuse me, madam," said Bryan, "but I am the gentleman who spoke with you earlier by phone. Is the bird still at your feeder?"

"Yes," the woman confirmed. "I just saw it there."

And so it was. All four feet of it. Standing beside the woman's feeder was a Sarus Crane, a bird whose normal range doesn't come much closer to England than India but one that does indeed have a bright red head.

As Bryan noted, "She neglected to mention the bird's size." ■

—PD, for Bryan Bland

What Is the Shape of the Bird?

Shape is another key piece in the identification matrix because a bird's shape places it into categories that narrow down the search—categories such as scientific order and family (I told you this *Systema Naturae* stuff was important). Is the bird lanky like a crane or stocky like an owl? Are the legs long like one of the wading shore-birds' or short like a duck's?

Is the tail long like a Mourning Dove's or short like a mead-owlark's; blunt tipped like a gull's or forked like a tern's? How forked? Deeply forked like the tail of Forster's Tern? Modestly forked like a Caspian Tern's? Or hardly forked at all, like a Black Tern's?

Is the wing long, tapered, and pointed like a kestrel's or short and blunt-tipped like a Sharp-shinned Hawk's? Is the bill thin and pointed like a warbler's? Thick and hooked at the tip like a vireo's? Or short and conical like a sparrow's or Purple Finch's?

Remember, birds are grouped largely on the basis of structural similarity. Knowing what those binding traits are—the thin, pointy bills of warblers, the conical bills of sparrows—will help you

Are the legs long like a Great Egret's or short like a Mallard's?

Shape is a very important clue to a bird's identification. Is the bird lanky like a heron or stocky like an owl?

quickly place the bird you are studying into its proper family. From that point it is simply a matter of narrowing down the possibilities, and for this you need to determine . . .

What Are the Bird's Field Marks?

Most birds show conspicuous plumage patterns that are visible at a distance. These patterns are made up of "field marks," the little building blocks of bird identification. They include: eye rings; eye lines (or lines above or through the eye); stripes on the crown; bars or patches on the wings; spots on the tail; and spots, stripes, or bibs on the chest, to name some of the basic few.

Some field marks are most visible or only visible when a bird is in flight. For example, the red epaulets of an adult male Red-winged Blackbird may be partially or totally hidden beneath cover-

Some field marks are visible when birds are flying. For example, the black wing-pits, or auxiliaries, of Black-bellied Plover are most conspicuous in flight.

Orange-crowned Warblers and first fall Tennessee Warblers are similar, but the Orange-crowned (top) has underparts that show blurry streaks. Tennessee (bottom) is clean breasted.

ing feathers when birds are perched. A juvenile Black-bellied Plover can be confused with a juvenile American Golden-Plover—until the bird flies, exposing a white rump and black patches on the "wing pits" (which golden-plovers lack).

Some plumage characteristics are not field marks at all. The orange crown on the Orange-crowned Warbler is not something to look for in the field (it is rarely seen). Better to use the bird's blurry, streaked breast to distinguish it from the similar but cleaner-breasted immature Tennessee Warbler.

How do birders distinguish warblers from other woodland birds—from kinglets or vireos? Part of the answer is shape; part of the answer is . . .

What Are the Bird's Mannerisms?

Have you ever noticed how you can recognize a friend from a distance by the way they walk? Birds can be distinguished this way, too—by their movements, by the way they eat or run.

Sandpipers, for example, feed on the run; plovers walk, stop, pick . . . walk, stop, pick (the way robins do).

Many flycatchers dart from a perch, snapping insects from the air, and return to a perch; swallows and swifts sweep insects out of the air and keep flying. Woodpeckers and Brown Creepers hitch themselves up the trunks of trees; nuthatches clamber up, down, and sideways. Terns dive into the water, head first, or swoop low, snatching prey from the water; gulls plop to the surface and swim.

Orange-crowned Warblers are hyperactive acrobats, darting quickly from twig to twig or weed stalk to weed stalk, *stre-e-e-etching* to reach some insect just out of reach, fluttering their wings

Also compare Orange-crowned Warbler to Red-eyed Vireo, which shows more head pattern and the classic vireo hook-tipped bill. Warblers have pointy bills and, behaviorally, are active feeders, commonly feeding on outer branches or springy weeds. Vireos feed more slowly and methodically, plucking prey from leaves instead of darting out.

Sanderling (top), like other sandpipers, are hyperactive, feeding on the run. Plovers, such as this Semiplamated Plover (bottom), walk, stop, and pick.

to cross those last few centimeters. Kinglets are hyperactive, too—so active that they flick their wings nervously even when perched.

Vireos are typically slower, more methodical, dropping branch to branch like a leaf on a windless day or flying short distances to try another nearby, typically sturdy, branch, pausing to search the foliage around them, reaching up, and deftly plucking caterpillars that unsuccessfully try to pass themselves off as part of a leaf.

A bird's mannerisms can disclose its identity at distances that eclipse other field marks. The Eastern Phoebe, a flycatcher that frequents woodland edges, and the Eastern Wood-Peewee, a forest species, are very similar—distinguished most readily by wing bars (peewees have them; phoebes do not—except in fall, when juveniles will be sporting pale, buffy bars).

But if the bird is pumping its tail up and down, plumage becomes a secondary consideration. Phoebes are tail waggers; peewees are not. With the flick of a tail, phoebes sign their name.

How Does the Bird Fly?
Some birds are soaring birds, able, like gulls, pelicans, and birds of prey, to turn lazy circles in the sky without moving a wing. Other birds, such as loons, ducks, and most shorebirds, are more energetic in their flight—moving quickly and directly with wings constantly moving. Still others, such as rails (a family of marsh birds), fly like the Wright Brothers—their struggling efforts are reed hugging, labored, and usually end with a controlled crash.

Movement projects itself over vast distances. Knowing how a bird flies permits identification well past the point at which color, field marks, even shape are discernible.

Crows fly in the proverbial straight line. The Pileated Woodpecker, a crow-sized bird, usually flies with an undulating, rollercoaster pattern typical of woodpeckers.

Nighthawks are stiff winged, darting, erratic, batlike in flight. The wing beat of a loon is loose, elastic, and continuous, its flight purposeful and direct. Loons don't soar, ever.

Great Blue Herons do soar, and glide and flap with their wings cupped distinctly downward. Bald Eagles soar on flat wings. Golden Eagles soar with their wings slightly raised in a dihedral or V.

Belted Kingfishers fly with a distinctive halting and irregular wing beat—a rapid series interrupted by a pause, followed by another shorter series. Kingfishers can also hover in place—a difficult maneuver few birds can accomplish.

Turkey Vultures hold their wings in a dihedral, too. But Turkey Vultures teeter or rock in flight—like a tightrope walker in the sky. Golden Eagles don't rock.

Some birds, like hummingbirds and most birds of prey, fly solo. Others, like swallows, often fly in loose flocks with other swallows (often mixed species). Still other species fly in large numbers and large, tightly packed groups (e.g., starlings or Cedar Waxwings) or well-ordered chevrons (waterfowl and many shorebird species). All these clues can be used to help clinch an identification, or at least put you on the right track. (Many of these behavioral hints and clues are summarized in my book *Pete Dunne's Essential Field Guide Companion.*)

Of course, not all migrating birds are visible because their migrations are conducted at night. This is just one of the reason birders will want to ask . . .

Turkey Vultures (top) typically hold their wings in a pronounced dihedral. Bald Eagles (bottom) soar and glide with a flat-wing profile.

How Does the Bird Sound?

Bird sounds are a form of communication for them, and an audible fingerprint for us. Everybody recognizes the *caw, caw, caw* call of American Crow or the resonant, two-note *honk* of Canada Goose. If you can identify these calls, you can master all the rest. The rules don't change.

Once you can recognize the song or call of a species, you can identify it as surely as any identification made by visual means—sometimes even more precisely.

For instance, American Crow and Fish Crow are similar in size and shape. Even experienced birders with ample time for study find the species difficult to tell apart. But if the bird calls—and the call is nasal, two noted, and has the quality of a denial *(Uh, uh)*, the bird is telling you it isn't American Crow.

Some birds, such as the *Bob-white* Quail, Black-capped *Chick-a-dee*, Eastern *Pee-wee*, and Long-billed *Curlew*, say their name, or at least an approximation of it. Some birds have songs that can be phonetically rendered into a rhyme or another mnemonic aid (example: the song of Common Yellowthroat is often rendered as *witchity, witchity, witchity*).

Even if you don't recognize the song or call, even if you cannot recall all its elements, just noting the dominant qualities—whether it was a note-blurring trill, a rapid series of distinct chip notes, a single note or phrase repeated over and over, or a complex ensemble of notes and phrases—can serve later to separate similar species.

For example, the two dowitcher species, Long-billed and Short-billed, can pose an identification challenge, particularly when the birds are in basic plumage (nonbreeding plumage). Their calls,

The two dowitchers can be difficult to tell apart. Their vocalizations are great aids: Long-billed (shown here) typically utters a one-note *keek*.

however, aren't shed with the season and are quite different. Long-billed Dowitchers most often utter a sharp, single-note *keek*. The Short-billed Dowitcher's call is a mellow three-note stutter: *tu-tu-tu*. One note versus three. You need not have perfect pitch or the audio recall of Igor Stravinsky to recognize the difference.

What Kind of Habitat Does the Bird Prefer?

Birds are not just creatures of habit, they are creatures of habitat. They fit, hand in glove, within the habitats for which they are specialized. Even in migration, species will seek out habitats that most closely meet their needs.

The widespread Marsh Wren, as the name implies, favors open, wet places festooned with tall reeds. The western Rock Wren prefers rocky slopes and canyons. Both are wrens, but where their ranges overlap, neither is likely to occur in the habitat of the other.

Many species occupy only specific habitats, although few are as particular as Kirtland's Warbler, which nests only in Jack Pine forests. During migration, however, the bird is a bit more eclectic in its foraging habitat choices.

The ranges of Marsh Wren (top) and Rock Wren (bottom) overlap in the West. Neither is likely to be found in the habitat preferred by the other, however. LINDA DUNNE

Some species are very adaptable, able to acclimate themselves to a variety of different habitats. A stellar example is the Red-tailed Hawk, a common raptor with a long list of favorite foods that is at home in marshes, prairies, interstate highway medians, farmland, deserts, open woodlands, roadside suburbia, even urban parks. Some species are very discriminating, found only in habitat that offers specific plants or food items. A prime example is the Kirtland's Warbler, a bird specialized to nest in young Jack Pine forests and whose nesting range, accordingly, is limited primarily to several counties in north-central Michigan where Jack Pines flourish.

Often the habitat preferences of birds can be used as aids to identification. Take, again, the example Long-billed and Short-billed Dowitchers. Short-billed Dowitchers readily forage in salt water; Long-billed Dowitchers prefer fresh.

Another example, one broader but no less determining: People who operate bird-feeding stations are often visited by hawks that feed on songbirds. Momentary glimpses are often not enough to determine whether the hawk is a falcon (maybe a Merlin) or an accipiter (maybe a Sharp-shinned Hawk).

But falcons are birds of open areas; accipiters are woodland specialists. If the bird beats a retreat into the woods instead of heading for the open, it isn't a falcon.

Where in North America Was the Bird?

If you look at the range maps in your field guide, you will discover quickly that very few bird species occur *all over* North America. Most are confined to specific regions of the continent. The borders define the species' distribution (aka range).

Distribution is one of the most obvious and determining standards in the identification matrix. Some bird species are widespread; most are more restricted and only occasionally encountered outside the boundaries of their normal range.

For example, there are four species of "golden-cheeked" warblers in North America: Townsend's, Hermit, Golden-cheeked, and Black-throated Green. All have similar traits; any might be confused with another. But Townsend's and Hermit are western species,

A bird's distribution and range can be used to help distinguish similar species. A "golden-cheeked" warbler seen in Maryland in May is most likely a Black-throated Green Warbler (top), not a Golden-cheeked Warbler (bottom), whose range is limited to Texas.

rarely seen east of the Rockies. Golden-cheeked is even more restricted in its range, breeding only on the Edwards Plateau of central Texas.

Only one of the "golden-cheeked" warblers commonly occurs in the eastern half of the continent: Black-throated Green Warbler. So if you are birding in Ohio and encounter a "golden-cheeked warbler," it would be prudent to determine first whether the field marks are consistent with Black-throated Green Warbler before considering possibilities that are far less likely.

While some birds do wander outside their normal range—particularly during migration, and more particularly in the fall, when young, inexperienced birds are migrating for the first time—birds can usually be depended on to be where they are supposed to be, when they are supposed to be there. Which brings up another important point: What you see when you go afield is not only determined by *where* you are, it is determined by *when* you go there.

When Was the Bird Seen?

When looking through your field guide, you probably noticed that the range maps are multicolored. If bird populations were static, field-guide publishers could save themselves lots of money by using just one color to show where each species is found. Unfortunately for budget-conscious publishers (but fortunately for birders,) many bird populations are not static. As already discussed, many species redistribute their entire populations over the course of a year, moving from their summer range to winter range along established migratory pathways.

For the purposes of identification, seasonal occurrence can be as useful and defining as a bird's range—a temporal line that falls between probable and improbable.

In North America, there are six "spot-breasted" thrushes: Wood, Hermit, Swainson's, Gray-cheeked, Bicknell's, and the Veery. All but Gray-cheeked occur in New York state in summer, where they are not breeders, but all may be found there during migration. (*Note:* If your field guide shows Gray-cheeked Thrush breeding in New York, it is time to replace your now-dated guide with one that recognizes the split between Bicknell's and Gray-cheeked). But in December,

American Tree Sparrow (top) and Chipping Sparrow (bottom) both have rusty caps. In summer in New England, Chipping Sparrow is a common breeder, while Tree Sparrows breed in the Arctic. In winter, it's the Tree Sparrow that's present in New England; Chipping Sparrows have flown to the South. Check your calendar as well as your field guide.

Of North America's six breeding, spot-breasted thrushes, only the hardy Hermit Thrush winters here. The others have retreated to the tropics.

any spot-breasted thrush encountered in New York (or anywhere else in North America for that matter) is almost certain to be Hermit Thrush. Why? Because among the spot-breasted thrushes only Hermit winters in North America. By December, the other five thrush species have long since migrated to the tropics, where their populations winter.

Temporal boundaries are not just barriers that hem possibility in, they are windows of opportunity, too. Knowing the migratory period for a species is not just a clue in support of an identification, it is a scheduled appointment. By knowing when to search for which species, birders can plot a strategy to intercept them.

What Is the Bird's Relative Abundance?

Some species are simply more common than others, and many that are uncommon look much like their more common kin. Probability is a very salient clue to a bird's identity, and while uncommon species (like rare coins) are avidly sought, prudence dictates that more-likely possibilities be considered and eliminated before less likely possibilities are given serious consideration.

A large red-crested woodpecker showing white flashes in the wings as it disappears through the trees might be an Ivory-billed Woodpecker, or it might be Pileated. Insofar as Pileated is common and widespread and Ivory-billed is believed to be extinct, the odds heavily favor the former.

The probability of a species' occurrence is not wholly determined by its numbers. There are other contingencies, such as weather, climate, distribution, and time of year, as well as the propensity for a species to wander. Some birds migrate great distances, some do not. Those species counted among the planet's great travelers are more likely to turn up in unlikely places than those that migrate short distances, or are basically sedentary.

The rule of thumb is simple: *If it looks like the more common of several possibilities, then it probably is.* There is a wonderful truism that applies here, none the worse for having been used before: "If you are in the prairies of North America and you hear hoofbeats, think horses, not zebras."

Having said this, probability is not determining. It is merely suggestive and supportive. Remember Bryan and the Sarus Crane. Unlikely, even improbable, is not the same as impossible.

Learning to See Critically

There is nothing fundamentally difficult about bird identification. You see a bird. Note its distinguishing characteristics. Look for its likeness in the field guide. Then cross-check your initial identification against defining particulars (like habitat and range). There is nothing fundamentally simple about this process either. Learning how to see birds critically—to note key field marks and other defining characteristics under less-than-ideal circumstances then find a bird's likeness amid ranks of images in your field guide that may in some cases differ by degrees and shades—is no easy task.

It takes discipline. It takes practice. And it takes preparation.

Many soaring hawks show blackish wing tips, but the compact shape and candle-flame wing configuration distinguish the juvenile Broad-winged Hawk.

When studying an unfamiliar bird, do not become fixated on a single obvious trait (like red on the head), assuming it alone will lead to an identification.

I can't begin to count the number of times people have asked me to help them identify a bird of prey that they saw and their first and only observation was that "it had black wing-tips." It is an apt observation, but hardly discriminating. Many soaring hawks show blackish wing-tips. What the observers failed to note, and what would have been much more useful, was the shape of the wing: Was it pointed, rounded, uniformly broad, or acutely tapered?

TALE SPOT

Learning to See: Gulls versus Terns

"I have a Laughing Gull and Forster's Tern in my scope," I announced, stepping back. "Anyone want a look?"

One member of my field-trip group beat the pack for an in-your-face study of these two classic birds of the Jersey Shore in summer. Both birds were adults in breeding (aka alternate plumage). "Tern's on the left, gull's to the right," I added, somewhat unnecessarily, I thought. But my optimism was misplaced.

"How do you tell them apart?" the viewer asked.

At first I couldn't believe she was serious. To my eyes, and to the eyes of any experienced birder, the differences between gulls and terns are manifest. "What do you mean?" I inquired.

"I mean, they both have black on the head, red bills, gray backs, and white bellies." All of these things were more or less true.

But what this new birder was overlooking were the shapes and postures of the two birds. The gull was robust, longer legged, and longer necked and so taller. The tern was slender, short legged, and no-necked and so appeared to crouch.

She had also failed to note that the bills, while both reddish, were different shapes (to be precise, the tern's bill was actually more orange than red). Gulls have thick, hook-tipped bills; terns' are thin and pointy. As for the black on the head, terns have a limited black cap. Laughing Gulls have a more extensive black hood and mask. And while the backs of both birds are indeed gray, the gull's back was charcoal gray, the tern's pale gray, almost white.

While I hope this study was helpful for my new birder, it was extremely illuminating for me. Experienced birders (even experienced birders who have been teaching new birders for decades) often fail to appreciate the perceptual gap beginning birders face: Learning to see birds critically and recognizing differences is a discipline that must be learned. But it begins by understanding that such differences exist and that they help distinguish one group of birds from the next, and one species from the next.

Finding commonality—red bill and red bill, gray back and gray back— is a mental exercise, too. But bird identification is mostly about noting differences. ■

Even birds as dissimilar as Forster's Terns (top) and Laughing Gulls (bottom) pose identification challenges for beginning birders before they learn to see critically.

Discipline—Beak to Tail

In an ideal world, a bird in the bush would be as obliging as the one in the hand. An observer bent upon identifying an unknown species would start at the bill (noting size and shape), work back to the forehead, crown, face, nape, back, wings, and tail, then return to the bill, and then study the bird's ventral side, chin, throat, belly, legs, and undertail coverts. Along the way, and in this ordered process, pertinent field marks would be noted. Also along the way, other qualifying (maybe defining) characteristics relating to behavior, vocalizations, and habitat would be noted.

Then, in real time, with the bird still in view, the field guide would be consulted, a probable identification made, and then the bird reexamined to dispel any concern and certify the initial identification.

Too often views are like this—momentary. But at least you know it's a diving bird (a duck?). And given the bold plumage pattern of adult male Bufflehead, you may already have seen enough of the bird to identify it. If not, wait. Even diving ducks must breathe.

And sometimes this is how it works in the field. More commonly, it does not. Birds in the field are rarely as disciplined as those found in museum drawers. They have free will and the ability to exploit it. The distinguishing characteristics you need to see to identify a bird are too often offered in flashes and snatches. Before everything you want to see is noted and confirmed, the bird is gone. Frustrating? Sometimes. But gratifying, too, when against tough odds you pin the name to the bird.

More and more, bird images captured by digital cameras and smartphones are augmenting and, in some cases, supplanting the identification process. Birders are shooting first and identifying later by studying the captured image, hoping it will provide sufficient information to pin the name to the bird. This may not be "field" identification, but it is bird identification.

Five Things to Bear in Mind

1. *Don't go into the field with an open mind.* Go into the field already armed with an arsenal of information you can bring to bear quickly—such as the knowledge that bill shape is useful in distinguishing terns and gulls; such as knowing that bill color is key to separating the several species of medium-sized terns; such as the discipline to note first when looking at sparrows whether they have streaked or unstreaked breasts, and for warblers, whether they have wing bars or not.

When time is short, when a glance is all you get, knowing where to focus that glance can make the difference between an identification and a missed opportunity. The way to prepare yourself is to study your field guide *before* you go into the field. Read the species descriptions. Study the plates. Know what birds you are likely to encounter and what field marks you will be called upon to note.

Studying the guide will also make it easier to reference birds quickly. When you have some skulking brown miscreant in front of you. And you want to page to the wrens. But you can't remember whether wrens come before or after swallows in the field guide.

Winter Wrens are many things—animate, vocal, fairly common, and widespread. But their virtues stop short of infinite patience.

Sooner or later, the mouselike bird is going to disappear into the tangled roots of a fallen tree (incidently, this is a useful behavioral characteristic of this mostly woodland species).

2. *Learn to look broadly before you look critically.* The identification process begins before binoculars are brought to bear. Size is something that can be measured best with the unaided eye. Family is something that is most often discernable at a glance. Ducks look like ducks, and ducks that dive beneath the surface define themselves as one of the "diving ducks." This tells you that it isn't necessary to initially consider any of the non-diving "puddle" ducks when sorting through the images in your field guide.

Nobody looks at a bird and wonders "Now which one of the 900 or so species of birds that have been recorded in North American can that be?" They look at it and wonder "What long-legged water bird is that?" or "What heron is that?" or "What swallow is that?"

Bird identification is largely a process of elimination. It starts not by noting small details but by putting each bird into a definable group—a broad-brush approach that paints birds into a corner with similar species, where they can be easily compared. The major difference between new birders and experienced birders is that experienced birders quickly place birds into broad, definable groups (then smaller and more precise groups), thus simplifying and shortening the sorting process.

3. *But learn to look critically, too.* After bringing binoculars to bear, note obvious traits first: anatomical peculiarities, color, and easily seen field marks. Some birds project very distinctive characteristics that can serve as a shortcut to an identification. Over most of North America, if you encounter an all-black bird perched atop a cattail, exposing large, red shoulder patches, you hardly need to hear its song or note the shape of its bill to identify it as a Red-winged Blackbird. But even with an identification made, you should note these characteristics anyway, because they may be very useful when you encounter this species again.

Most birds are not so obvious, however, and many look very similar to closely related kin—distinguished only by eye color, leg color, the presence or absence of a crown stripe, the shape of a bill. Approach each identification systematically, using a pattern of

Maybe ducks? No. Look at the bills—they're thin and pointed, hardly ducklike. Let's try loons, another group of water birds that swim and dive. Both birds here are in basic, or nonbreeding, plumage, but one has a diffuse neck pattern and a thick, daggerlike bill. The other has a crisply defined neck pattern and a rapier-thin, slightly upturned bill. That's all you need to distinguish Common Loon (top) from Red-throated Loon (bottom).

study that is comfortable for you. And do not become fixated on one very obvious trait, like red on the head. Many bird species (from drake Green-winged Teal to male House Finch) show touches of red on the head. Note all traits and make a systematic study of birds second nature, something you do automatically every time you see a bird. If the bird and its name do not come quickly—when the bird in the field and the ones in the book don't match—take out a notebook and describe the bird in detail, beak to tail. If you like, do a sketch. Even a poor sketch may be an asset when you later pore over the text and study various images, trying to work out the identification to your mystery bird. Me? I find sketching the bird distracting. An action that forces me to take my eyes off the bird when what I really want to do is study it. And besides, my hands are already filled with optics. The sketch I make is in my mind, thanks in no small part to the discipline instilled in me as a young birder.

4. *Use every opportunity for study.* Field guides (and apps and videos) are very useful tools. They help prepare you for field encounters with birds and later serve to organize and reinforce the information you gleaned. But if your objective is to gain identification skills, there is no substitute for studying real birds, in real time, in the real world. Whether you can identify a species or not, whether you have seen it a hundred times or more, use every opportunity to study birds in the field.

A studied intimacy with common birds will make it possible to make identifications quickly and accurately, under unfavorable conditions or great distances. It will offer a backdrop against which rare or unfamiliar species will stand out when you encounter them. It will help you identify that drab, streaky bird perched near the male Red-winged Blackbird. It's a bird that is habitually mistaken for a sparrow but is in reality a female Red-winged Blackbird. The plumage may differ, but the shape, mannerisms, and vocalization will be consistent with that species.

Becoming intimate with birds will, in short, make you a better birder. The planet's most accomplished field birders bring as much attention to bear on the birds they see all the time as they do on the ones they are seeing for the very first time. This is how they became accomplished in the first place.

Sparrow, you think? Think again. If you've invested time studying female Red-winged Blackbirds when they were in the company of their unmistakable adult male counterparts, you won't be confused now.

5. *Experience has a price; everyone antes up.* Birding is an activity that should be, above all else, fun. No person should ever go into the field worried about making a mistake or misidentifying a bird.

A bird misidentified doesn't lead to currencies collapsing or civilizations falling. Children won't starve, airline schedules won't be disrupted, the earth will continue to orbit the sun.

There isn't a birder on the planet who hasn't misidentified a bird. The main difference between a beginning birder and an experienced one is that thus far beginning birders have misidentified very few birds. Experienced birders have misidentified thousands.

Making mistakes, and learning from them, is the essence of experience. A misidentification just resets the board for your next encounter with a species. The obvious question is: "So how do I know when I've made a mistake?" For that insight, you rely on your friends—the subject of the next chapter. The text and range maps

in your field guide also help support or undermine an initial identification. As well, an identification that is particularly challenging
or frustrating should be a warning sign that you may be on the
wrong track—searching for your bird in the wrong family, struggling to jam a square peg into a round hole.

Important tip: After you encounter a new species it is very helpful
to read everything you can about it soon after. That's why you bought
all those books. Not only will this follow-up exercise support or
refute your initial identification, it will help you commit to memory
key facts about the bird now that it has become a bird you have
encountered. It's now more significant and real than all the undiffer-
entiated species you have yet to bind with the spell of their names.

Keeping Records

Most birders keep records of their encounters with birds, and all
beginning birders should. Recording the birds you find will facilitate learning through review, provide evidence that can be
reviewed later (even years later), help you see patterns of occurrence or activity, and provide a souvenir—a written snapshot of
your day afield for all time. Doing so will, in sum, track your development as a birder.

Traditionally, there are three basic formats for recording your
encounters in the field: a *checklist* (or "field card"), a *life list* (and
other composite lists), and a *journal*. Increasingly popular for this
is an online service offered by the Cornell Laboratory of Ornithology called eBird.

Checklists

The easiest and least time-consuming way to keep track of the
birds you see is to fill out a bird checklist after a day afield—an
effort that will take about five minutes on average, ten if you are
lucky. A checklist is a card that lists the birds found in a defined
area arranged in standard taxonomic (AOU) order. If your field
guide follows this order, you are already familiar with it. Widely
available (distributed free at most popular birding locations or
commercially available at nature centers and birding stores),

Filling out a checklist or field card is one of the easiest ways to keep track of the birds you find, and to help retain the memory of a day in the field.

checklists differ in terms of length, species listed, and information about each species the cards try to impart. Many are information packed, offering not just a species listing but information about a bird's abundance and seasonal occurrence as well. Not only are checklists an aid to record keeping, they provide information useful in the identification process. A checklist customized to the birds of your region is an invaluable resource.

All checklists have at least two things in common: *convenience* and *editorialized simplicity*. All the birds you might reasonably expect to see are already compiled. The birds that do not commonly occur have been omitted or are relegated to a special section on the card assigned to regionally "rare" or "accidental" species. All you have to do is put a checkmark next to the birds you find.

But you can make your sightings more meaningful by including the date, location, weather conditions, and perhaps the names of any companions. There is usually space on the checklists for "notes" or "write-in" species, too.

Some people use field cards as their sole means of record keeping, filing them as mementos of the day and a record of birds seen. Most birders take the listing reflex one step further—summarizing or synthesizing their observations on cumulative lists. Yes, there are listing software packages that can be purchased to facilitate this. They are convenient and educational, too. And don't forget eBird—Cornell's national online record-keeping service and data bank that on the one hand allows you to keep track of your personal sightings and on the other allows you to tap into the wellspring of sightings that are the sum of eBird users in your region, or anywhere in North America. (Should you be going to Arizona in August and want to know what hot Mexican hummingbirds are turning up, check out eBird Arizona.)

Another service provided by eBird is that lists are genially refereed by regional experts before being posted. Regional referees will politely question any unlikely species that you or other subscribers have reported and ask for reconfirmation—either because the bird you submitted is regionally rare or outside the dates of common occurrence. It's akin to an online mentoring service and a national species census conducted daily.

As well, some states have been franchised to maintain state-specific bird sites, which also serve as websites that often offer news of sightings and events that are of interest to birders who live in that state.

The Listing Compulsion

Part of birding's appeal is acquisition (i.e., collecting). The birds you find are yours, a token of your fortune and growing skill. Some people trust to memory, but most find greater (and more lasting) pleasure in compiling cumulative lists of the birds they see. In fact, the very act of keeping track of birds has a name. It is called "listing."

There are as many lists as there are ways to define and measure value. Some birders keep a yard list, a list limited to the birds seen in (or from) a person's yard. Some maintain state lists or county lists, lists of species recorded within these boundaries. Many birders keep a year list, a list of birds seen during the calendar year, or month lists or trip lists. Some lists are more esoteric than this.

But dear to the hearts of most birders is the life list—the cumulative list of all those species that they have encountered since the day they started birding. Some North American residents put a geographic halter on their life list—including only those species found in North America (a North American life list). Some who travel widely maintain a world list.

And while birders who do not keep lists are just as excited about seeing new birds as those who keep careful records, a simple notation in a field guide next to the picture and the name—the date and the place—not only caps the triumph but recalls it anew each time your finger falls upon that page (perhaps to make a new notation for a new life bird!).

There are any number of ways for birders to record and maintain lists, from homemade loose-leaf binders to commercially available hybrid checklist/journal/diaries that invite detailed descriptions to computer software programs and databases that not only keep track of your sightings but cross-file them any way you like.

Also, for those who are procedurally minded, there are certain standards of acceptance set forth by the American Birding Association. These guidelines, which deal with questions like the

Whiskered Tern is usually found in Europe and Asia; in North America, it's classified as a very rare vagrant. The bird shown here, an adult molting into basic plumage, was found in Cape May, New Jersey, in September 2014 and is only the third on record for the U.S.

jurisdictional legitimacy of introduced species or the accept-ability of birds heard but not seen, are not binding but are widely accepted.

Just one word of caution, for those who use a field guide as the vehicle for maintaining their life list: *Keep your record-bearing book at home, or keep updated photocopies of these pages.* Field guides, even cherished field guides, sometimes get left on lunch counters and automobile roof tops. While books are replaceable, records not indexed in memory are not.

You might also want to inscribe your name and contact infor-mation in your guide.

Journals

The most involved and, in many ways, most gratifying means of record keeping is a journal or diary that offers a detailed account of a day's birding. Information relating to weather and habitat condi-tions is essential. A detailed account of places visited and the num-bers of individuals of every species seen is important information.

Impressions and free associations are fair game in your journal. Encounters with other birders, descriptions of curious behavior (on the part of birds or birders), or aberrant plumages (again, on the part of birds or birders) is all grist for the mill. Illustrations or thumbnail sketches that highlight key points or simply enliven the pages add to a journal's significance and charm. Also, many birders post online blogs recounting their adventures afield.

There is no right way and no wrong way to keep records. There is only your way. What works and what appeals to you is all that matters.

SUMMARY

Birding can be done anywhere, but some places are more attractive to birds than others, and different species are attracted to different habitats. Bird populations shift seasonally. Regions have winter, summer, and year-round residents as well as birds that just migrate through (transient species). Bird activity is generally greatest in the early morning and late afternoon. Finding birds demands attentiveness to color, motion, and sound; seeing birds well requires patience and practice and, at times, persistence.

Bird identification is a challenge that involves sight, sound, and mind. Identifications are made by building a case for a certain species and eliminating others. Things to consider include: size, shape, plumage field marks, behavior, manner of flight, vocalizations, habitat, distribution, time of year, and relative abundance. Characteristics are best committed to paper unless you are very disciplined—that's why you carry that waterproof notepad.

Record keeping is an integral part of birding and a key learning tool. Daily lists, cumulative lists such as a birder's life list or year list, and journals are all means to this end.

I cannot emphasize enough the ease, convenience, archival significance, and tribalness of eBird—which leads us very neatly into the subject of the next chapter. ■

Resources—Dipping into the Pool of Knowledge

The Man of the Mountain

The man with the billowing white beard and flowing mane stood and extended his hand. "Floyd Wolfarth," he intoned. "Lamar Hilton," he added, inclining his head toward his seated companion, who nodded in a friendly fashion.

"Pete Dunne," I replied, deferentially, and not just because of the difference in our ages. I was twenty-four, Floyd forty years my senior. But the man standing atop this denuded outcropping of the Kittatinny Ridge in northwest New Jersey had the bearing of the mountain itself—a juxtaposition that was not far from apt. "Coon Ridge," the place of our meeting, was not merely a celebrated hawk-watching junction, a place where birders gathered each autumn to witness the river of southbound birds of prey, it was Floyd's home court. I'd learned of Coon's existence from a newly printed book about hawk watching. Floyd, I was soon to discover, was virtually synonymous with the place.

Floyd Wolfarth, retired teamster, who used to adjust his pick-up and delivery runs so he could spend his lunch hours hawk watching.

Floyd Wolfarth, who proudly allowed to having invested "five thousand hours" studying gulls in the Hackensack dumps.

Floyd Wolfarth, who was founder of the Boonton Christmas Bird Count, former Region 5 editor of "Records of New Jersey Birds," one of seventeen charter members of the August Urner Ornithological Club, and who had once birded with . . .

The Great One . . .

Roger Tory Peterson himself, with whom Floyd still "corresponded."

In short and in sum, I was speaking with one of the pillars of the birding community, someone whose knowledge of birds and birding was part of a parallel universe of information and friends that I barely knew existed.

I'd grown up in New Jersey. Learned the rudiments of birding alone. Had traveled widely in search of birds (most recently to Alaska). Studied my field guides. Worked out my share of difficult identifications and considered myself a pretty competent birder.

But I'd never considered seeking guidance or help. And I'd never dreamed that birding's true horizon lay beyond my imagination. All that was about to change.

"There's a bird, Floyd," said the seated man. "Over 'Stigs.'" Floyd raised his binoculars toward the designated landmark. I followed suit, finding the distant speck with effort (because I didn't know the geological lay of the land).

"Accipiter," said Wolfarth after momentary study, naming one of the three broad groups of hawks I knew from my book. There were buteos, the large soaring hawks; falcons, the fast, open-country pursuit artists; and accipiters, the short-winged, long-tailed hunters of woodlands.

How can he tell that's an accipiter? my experience-deprived mind demanded. The bird was just a speck turning circles in the sky, indistinguishable to my eyes from the hundreds of Broad-winged Hawks I'd been seeing all day.

It was September. Broad-winged Hawks, forest buteos, were the principle migrant, along with the occasional Sharp-shinned Hawk (a small accipiter) and American Kestrel (a tiny falcon). Broadwings had a wide white band on the tail (at least the adults did) and flew in massed flocks. Sharp-shins were small and had short, round wings. Kestrels were small and had long, pointy wings.

Most of my identifications were made at close range—as the birds made their way down the ridge and passed close enough for me to see plumage-based field marks. This guy Wolfarth had just categorized a bird that seemed beyond the limit of human conjecture, way beyond classic field-mark range.

"Watch this bird," Wolfarth commanded. "This is going to be something good," he prophesied.

The bird stopped circling, set its wings, and started gliding toward us, using the updraft off the ridge for lift. As it got closer, I began to note more characteristics—large size . . . sort of long, sort of pointed wings . . . mottled brown back . . . lots of streaks on the breast. To me it looked much like the immature Broad-winged Hawks (the ones without the white band on the tail) that I'd been seeing all day.

The bird drew abreast and circled once more to gain altitude. Then it continued down ridge—a large, brown-backed, streak-breasted bird of prey.

"Well," said Wolfarth, fixing his eyes upon me. "What did you think?"

"Broad-winged Hawk," I offered, knowing I was being tested, and falling back on probability.

"Goshawk" said Wolfarth with a disapproving look. "Unquestionable," he added to cut off debate.

Northern Goshawk, my mind repeated. A bird I'd never seen, only dreamed of someday seeing. But with this catalytic identification to guide me, all the things I had just seen but not appreciated began to fall into place.

Like the long, rudderlike tail. Like the shape—bulky but more like an accipiter than a buteo. A goshawk, I breathed. Without Floyd's help, the bird would never have been identified correctly; it would have gone down in my ledger as "unidentified" or, worse, been tabulated in with all the passing broad-wings (an opportunity lost).

Clearly this guy Wolfarth was an exceptional birder—and more. I was to discover in time that Floyd was an expert teacher, someone who excelled at passing his knowledge on to others and whose apprentices accounted for many of the best young birders in the region. (In fact, years later, Roger Tory Peterson observed to me: "Floyd Wolfarth I have always admired because he got so many young people involved in birding.")

But on this momentous day, on this spine of Kittatinny stone, I only knew that I stood in the presence of someone whose skills lay beyond my dreams, and that I'd just flunked my first exam.

As we stood, a migrant flock of chickadees swept by, moving from tree to tree, calling as they went. Among the expected chatter of Black-cappeds I picked out one call that was slurred and slower. Having just spent several weeks in Alaska, it was a call I'd grown familiar with.

"Boreal Chickadee," I announced, as the flock moved by.

"What!" said Floyd, spinning around, regarding me with an expression that suggested I'd just confessed to the murder of Jimmy Hoffa.

"Boreal Chickadee," I repeated, suddenly aware that this was New Jersey, not Alaska. And that I'd never seen a Boreal Chickadee in New Jersey—didn't even know if they occurred here.

But Floyd knew. Birder of fifty years, shareholder in the communal wisdom of the North Jersey birding community. Floyd knew well that Boreal Chickadee was a very rare winter visitor to the state and that its occurrence was linked to periodic irruptions, only five of which had occurred in the twentieth century: in 1916–17 (when Floyd was five years old, before he'd earned the Boy Scout merit badge for birding that sparked his lifetime interest), 1951–52 (the first winter of my life), 1954–55, 1959–60, and 1961–62.

The winter of 1975–76 was destined to be remembered for its impressive incursion of Boreal Chickadees too. But nobody knew this yet.

"Wa-elll," he rumbled. "Boreal Chickadee is a good bird. What made you say Boreal?"

"I heard it," I explained. "Learned the call in Alaska."

"Wa-elll, that's a good bird," he warned again. "Tough call," he added, to give me some wiggle room (in case I wanted to back down). It was clear Floyd was skeptical. Given my poor showing with the goshawk and my apparent ignorance concerning the status of Boreal Chickadee in New Jersey, his skepticism was more than justified.

The afternoon wore on. I stood my ground and listened to an outpouring of lore that flowed from Wolfarth like water from a river—names of birds I'd only dreamed of seeing, names of people and places that were part of a culture that I craved to belong, now that I knew it existed. This guy Wolfarth could be my guide if he would have me—if only I could prove I was worthy of his tutelage.

It might be that Floyd had already decided to take me under his wing. I don't know, and I never will. Floyd is gone except in spirit, except for the memories that live on in the minds of his many

It was a chance encounter with a migrating Boreal Chickadee that cemented my bond with Floyd P. Wolfarth, ushering me into the ranks of the birding community, and redeeming me for having blown the identification of my first Northern Goshawk.

apprentices. But as I've told this story before, I've always attributed our mentor-apprentice bond to what happened next, so I'll not alter the text now.

We were preparing to leave, were, in fact, leaving, when a wiry figure bounded down the trail, carrying a camera and a plastic owl decoy. His name was Fred Tilly, an avid hawk watcher and another Wolfarth protégé. He'd been photographing hawks downridge.

"Had a good bird," he said, relishing the disclosure. "About two hours ago a Boreal Chickadee went by with a flock of Black-cappeds."

Floyd looked stunned. Then he looked bemused. Then he looked at me. Tilly's credentials were known and good. Mine had just gotten better.

"That was a good call, then," said Floyd P. Wolfarth. The skepticism in his eyes was gone. I found there, instead, a new respect. And something else . . .

I'd just found my mentor.

Clubs and Chums—The Social Link

You can go birding on your own. In fact, and for reasons that will be explained, you should. But beginning birders can jump-start their entry into birding by learning from other, more experienced birders.

Experienced birders are bird identification tutors. Like Floyd Wolfarth did for me, they can take the guesswork out of identification—focusing attention quickly on key field marks, anchoring correct identifications with affirmation, correcting misidentifications before they become entrenched.

Experienced birders know how, when, and where to find birds. They can introduce you to the best local birding hot spots and tell you the best times to go there to see seasonally linked masses of birds, or birds whose appearance in your region is limited.

And experienced birders can answer the questions all beginning birders struggle with. What should I wear? What books should I buy? What publications should I subscribe to? What optics should I own? Where do I find the things and information I need, anyway?

There are, throughout the world, thousands of institutions that cater to the social and informational needs of birders. They range from international organizations to local clubs. The best way to meet other birders is through a local club or birding organization. Membership is open to all. Shared interest, not experience or skill, is the coin of the realm.

If you are a joiner, you will find that membership in a birding club will open doors you never knew were there (and that more experienced birders will be eager to hold open the doors). If you are the kind of person who prizes their privacy, you can dabble rather than immerse yourself in the birding culture—go on a few field trips, learn the location of the best local sites, and rely upon the organization's publication as your primary link to those who share your interest.

First Contact

The telephone directory has no listing for "Birding Mentors" or "Bird Clubs." But there are listings for "Bird Feeders and Houses." Under this listing, you might find a store in your area that specializes in meeting the needs of birders.

Perhaps the easiest way to locate birders in your region is to Google "bird watching" and the name of your county, state, or city. What should pop up is an array of meeting times and places, field-trip opportunities, and contact info, as well as a listing of any birding stores.

Buying Information

These stores may be independent, like the Birder's General Store on Cape Cod. They may be associated with organizations, like Los Angeles Audubon or the Cape May Bird Observatory.

They may be a franchise operating under one of several chains that cater to birders, including Wild Bird Centers and Wild Birds Unlimited.

The point is that all of these stores will be in contact with the local birding community. In some cases, they may themselves be the hub of local birding activity.

All I Know Is What I Read In . . .

Another way to get in touch with the birding community is through your local newspaper, providing it has a column that specializes in birds or nature or the outdoors. The columnist is almost certainly in contact with the local birding community—in fact, they probably post notices of meetings, field trips, courses, and events. You can glean the information you need from the column or you can contact the columnist via the paper, seeking information about birding clubs and birding opportunities in the area.

An invaluable source for birding activities in your region and across North America is the website hosted by the American Birding Association—a vocational treasure trove of information recounting summaries of "good" (rare) birds found in your region, plus contact information about North America's many bird festivals.

Your Tax Dollars at Work

Many counties and municipalities have park systems or outdoor recreation departments that offer natural history programming and have naturalists on staff. Program mainstays at all nature centers are bird-identification classes, bird walks on site, or birding field trips off site.

Community colleges and local high schools sometimes include birding or field ornithology courses in their continuing education programs. In some places, museums and zoos have a birding component, too. The people who teach these courses or lead these walks are almost certainly linked to the birding community at large. Through them, so are you.

WING BAR

Solo versus Social

Birding is an activity that can be done alone or with others. Both avenues are essential to building birding skills, and too often birders adopt one and shun the other.

Birding alone, without the guidance of more accomplished birders, prompts individuals to work out identification problems by themselves. It

You'll never find a more welcoming, genial, articulate, considerate, and avocationally focused cross section of society than North American birders. Welcome to the club!

forces an individual to look for field marks, assimilate them, and then relate what they have seen to illustrations and descriptions in field guides—which is good. These are the fundamental skills of birding.

What birding alone cannot do is impart the cumulative wisdom amassed over the course of 100 years of field birding. Unless demonstrated, it might never occur to a solo birder that high-soaring hawks can be identified by their silhouettes alone, that warblers can be distinguished by their chip notes, or that it really is possible for mere mortals to separate *Empidonax* flycatchers. Birding with other, more experienced birders gives beginners a head start and shows them where birding's skill horizon lies. It is also a good way to learn where and when to go to see birds in your region.

But there is a danger inherent in always birding with a group. By relying too often and too much on the skills of others, beginning birders sometimes grow passive. They never develop and polish their own skills, because it is always easier to rely on the superior skills of others.

The solution is a balance. Go birding with other, more experienced birders to learn the tricks of the trade. Then go birding by yourself to put these newfound tricks to the test and make them part of your personal skill set. You'll be a better birder for it. And in time, well, who knows? Maybe you'll be pushing birding's skill horizon a little farther. ▪

WING BAR

A Beginning Birder's Guide to Field-Trip and Bird-Tour Survival

It was the kind of summer dinner party tailor-made for a birder: outdoor setting, goldfinches and hummingbirds at the feeders, young Great-horned Owls calling as night fell. The raison d'etre of the gathering was a field tripper's reunion, proving that birding field trips and tours also figure among the planet's greatest social activities, bringing people with similar interests together for fun, good fellowship, and friendship.

The conversation turned, quite naturally, to birding and the highlights of trips and tours recently taken. In this spirit (and as field-trip leader) I posed the question:"What should a beginner do to get ready for a field trip?"

The response was a thought-provoking barrage of spirited "dos" and "don'ts," the list evolving as people recalled their own early days of birding and remembered recent field trips where, perhaps, a participant or two had behaved in a less-than-satisfactory manner.

Here's a list of field trip dos and don'ts straight from field-trip partici-pants (augmented by a few thoughts from the trip leader's stockpile of experience).

Dos

DO ask questions about the trip before the trip. Find out what the weather conditions will be like, how much walking is involved, how bad the "bugs" will be, whether you should bring your scope. Most organizations or tour companies will provide you with a pretrip list of what to bring and recom-mendations for how to prepare. If they don't—ask.

If you have special physical needs or limitations, DO make sure the leader knows about them before the trip. Many times such needs can be accommodated with advance notice.

DO honestly evaluate whether you are physically up to a particular trip or portion of a trip. Don't leave it to the leader to say, "I really don't think you should come on this hike—it's going to be tough." Normal birding is not particularly strenuous, and most trips and tours are suitable for anyone in good general health, but on many, if not most, there will be night ses-sions or portions with long, sometimes arduous, hikes that are optional. No one will look down on you for opting out.

DO be early, or at least on time, for the trip, or each morning of the tour. DO make sure you know how to get to the meeting place. Some leaders are ruthless when it comes to timeliness and will leave without you, but most will wait at least a little while, delaying the trip for everyone else.

DO let the leader know if there is a particular bird you would like to see. If it is a common bird but you would really like a good look at it, say so! Leaders are happiest when they make people on their trips happy. However, DON'T harp on the birds you are missing. The leader will hear you the first time.

DO feel free to ask questions about a bird—how to identify it, where it lives, what it eats. This is *your* trip, and one of the delights of birding is learning. Field-trip leaders love to have people along who are truly interested in birds and who express their interest in questions.

If someone calls out a bird and you cannot find it, DO SAY SO! Leaders and other trip participants are always glad to help you get on the bird.

If you see a bird, say a raptor, overhead, DO call out. It doesn't matter that you cannot identify it. One of the chief advantages of birding with a group is having multiple sets of eyes all looking at once.

DO learn how to give and receive directions to a bird's locations (see Directions, Please on page 261).

DO make the investment in decent binoculars. If the trip leader is calling out field marks and you can't see them, it may well be that your binoculars, not your eyes, are the problem.

DO know how to be quiet and when. Being quiet means more than not talking loudly. It means not moving unnecessarily when the group halts and planting your footsteps with quiet care when moving (stay out of crunchy leaves and gravel). Watch the leader. If he or she stops suddenly with head cocked, STOP. Undoubtedly, the leader heard a bird, maybe your next life bird.

DO stay with the leader. This is particularly true when the group is intently looking for a particular target bird or when the leader is pishing. Pishing brings birds to the pisher, and good leaders generally choose places to pish where birds are easily attracted and easily viewed.

DO wear quiet clothing in quiet colors. It can be hard to get good looks at shy birds; it becomes doubly hard with a group garbed in neon nylon.

DO be prepared for less-than-adequate bathroom facilities. This may mean long periods between bathrooms (drink less coffee), or it may mean the only bathroom will be the great outdoors (know how to handle this).

If the absence of a man-made toilet facility is a concern, ask about "pit stops" before the trip.

Don'ts

DON'T be a scope hog. Even if the leader's scope is trained on your dream lifer, step to the eyepiece, take an identifiable look, then step away to let the next person have their look. Often there will be opportunities for a more satisfying second or third look. If you've already seen the bird well with binoculars and someone in the group has not seen it at all, let that person have first crack at the scope. Here's a related DO: If the bird moves, DO try to follow it with the scope (so that the leader doesn't have to waste time finding the bird again). Here's a related DON'T. DON'T bump the scope when stepping aside for the next person.

DON'T be a complainer. If something about the trip is bothering you, carefully evaluate whether the problem is worth mentioning. If it is, discretely speak to the leader in private—to avoid possible embarrassment for you, the leader, and other participants.

DON'T monopolize the leader. A dozen or more other people may want to share in the leader's expertise, plus the leader can hardly look for birds if he or she has to spend all their time administering to you.

DON'T insist on a particular seat if traveling in a van. Offer to rotate seats with other participants (this is customary procedure on many field trips, especially when window and front seats are involved).

DON'T insist on driving your own car. If the field trip has space in the van, ride in it. If carpooling is possible, do it. The fewer vehicles involved in a birding trip, the better.

DON'T drag significant others along on a birding trip unless they are ready and willing to come and understand what is involved. Make sure they have binoculars. Disinterested people tend to drag the trip down.

—Don Freiday

In addition to being head of visitor services at Forsythe National Wildlife Refuge, Don Freiday is a consummate birder, exceptional naturalist, and popular and accomplished field-trip leader whose followers are legion. His book A Precious Place *was drawn from his regular outdoor column in the* Hunterdon (NJ) Democrat. ∎

Going Direct

There are three national organizations that cater to the information and social needs of birders: the American Birding Association, the National Audubon Society, and the Cornell Lab of Ornithology.

American Birding Association, headquartered in Delaware City, Delaware, focuses on meeting the informational needs of birders in the U.S. and Canada. Founded in 1974, ABA attracts members drawn from the most avid elements of birding. Its several publications are of excellent quality and invaluable to birders. Online: aba.org/birding.

National Audubon (700 Broadway, New York, NY 10003), founded in 1942, is a national organization whose support base and appeal is bolstered by a national system of local chapters, which hold regular meetings and orchestrate field-trip schedules. Chapters differ in terms of size, character, and orientation (some are more environmentally focused, some more bird focused). All have at least some kind of bird-watching component. Membership in the National Organization confers memberships in the local chapter. Online: audubon.org.

Not to Be Confused With . . .

State Audubon societies—in addition to National Audubon, there are a few states that have their own independent state Audubon societies.

The state societies, most of which were founded before, and are independent of, National Audubon, also differ in terms of focus and the intensity of their birding orientation. But birders living in Massachusetts, New Jersey, Rhode Island, Connecticut, and Florida might consider these institutions a primary resource and avenue to the birding community.

Cornell Lab of Ornithology orchestrates national programs involving backyard bird feeding (Project: Feeder Watch), offers a home-study ornithology course, and publishes a quarterly journal on birds and birding related topics, *Living Bird.* Online: birds.cornell.edu.

Other Organizations

In an avocation as large and diverse as birding, be assured that there are many organizations that cater to the interests of birders. Some are social in nature, allowing birders to get together to discuss matters of interest or concern. Examples include the Nuttall Club of Massachusetts, the Kansas Ornithological Society, and the Delaware Valley Ornithological Club (serving birders from Delaware, New Jersey, and Pennsylvania).

Some are informational, disseminating information to a geographically dispersed membership more than offering a structure for social interaction. Some are focused on specific interests and objectives, providing an information network for people of like mind. Examples include the Hawk Migration Association of North America, serving the interests of birders who have a particular fascination watching birds of prey at migratory concentration points, and the Purple Martin Conservation Association, committed to the protection and proliferation of this popular bird species.

State or Provincial Birding Organizations

Almost every state or province has one or more regional organizations that cater to birders. Some meet regularly, some annually or semi-annually. Some offer a regular field-trip schedule.

Most of these organizations also publish a journal or newsletter with information and host a website about bird distribution and occurrence. Often accounted among their functions are the maintenance of official state bird lists and review of bird sightings through rare-bird committees.

Another function these organizations may perform is the upkeep of bird-sighting hotlines.

State (Bird) Email Lists and Birding Hotlines

Almost every state and province has a weekly updated list of bird species tallied and news of interest to birders. State-by-state contact information is found on the ABA website. Many of these hotlines are supported by statewide organizations. Some are sponsored by clubs, Audubon chapters, and, in some cases, private individuals or stores. All are an easy link to the birding community at large and a source of information about rare-bird sightings, seasonal distributions of birds, and, frequently, programs, events, bird walks, and membership in the host organization.

Hooking into the Publication and Communication Network

There are a number of very fine publications that cater to the interests and needs of birders. Some are the communication link that binds organizations and members. Others serve only the avocational focus of subscribers.

Rather than list and describe all the journals and newsletters of state and local organizations, a simple blanket endorsement will do. Every birder should receive the publication that focuses upon the birds of their geographic region—as a resource and link to the birding community at large.

There are also several publications that cater to a national audience. All relate to birds and birders. Each differs somewhat in focus, subject, and audience.

Birding. Published six times a year and distributed to members of the American Birding Association, *Birding* is a magazine for avid birders who have a particular interest in improving their skills and whose interest in birds is continental in scope. Articles that specialize in the identification of challenging or unusual birds and or that identify new and exciting birding areas are strengths; conservation issues are a focus. New equipment and books are reviewed. Updates on bird name changes are analyzed and discussed. I will say categorically that all birders should be ABA members.

Bird Watcher's Digest. Published six times a year, this friendly, excellent magazine appeals to birders across the entire range of interest—from casual backyard birding to adventure birding—but its principal focus is the pleasure of birding. Feature articles range from the humorous and anecdotal to informative and species specific. One of the strengths of this publication is the quality of its department writers and the editorial anchoring of the publishers and staff. They are birders writing for birders, and it shows. Write

Bird Watcher's Digest, PO Box 110, Marietta, Ohio 45750. Phone 800-879-2473 or go online.

BirdWatching (formerly *Birder's World*). Published six times a year, this high-quality, highly esteemed magazine is as diversely focused as *Bird Watcher's Digest* but places greater emphasis on the nuances of birds, their behavior and biology. It is not highbrow, but it is wonderfully informative and broad in scope. Celebrated for its superior bird photography, this publication is perhaps the most visual of the birding magazines. The stable of department editors is excellent. Regular columns include "Where to Bird." Subscriptions: 800-437-5828 or go online.

Living Bird. A quarterly publication distributed to members of the Cornell Lab of Ornithology, *Living Bird* is visually arresting and written to appeal to those who want to be engaged more than diverted. It has a broad geographic focus, with particular attention paid to North, Central, and South America. Conservation and bird ecology are common themes, but birding and the needs of birders are perennial topics. Feature articles are in-depth in their approach and thoughtfully selected. As in *BirdWatching,* quality photography is a hallmark. The Cornell Lab is anchored in birding and ornithological tradition, and *Living Bird* has long served as a bridge between these parallel disciplines. Subscriptions: Cornell Lab of Ornithology, 159 Sapsucker Woods Road, Ithaca, NY 14850. Phone 607-254-BIRD or go online.

WING BAR

Birding in the Digital Age

With the advent of the internet and smartphones, there are now a multitude of websites and apps that can assist you in both bird identification and identifying locations to bird. They can also help you keep track of your sightings and tell you what birds other people in your area are seeing.

A good place for a beginner to start is the website for the Cornell Lab of Ornithology, birds.cornell.edu, which offers a wealth of information about birds. Cornell hosts eBird; it also has a bird guide online, with blogs, All About Birds, with comprehensive information on bird ID and behavior.

For beginning birders, Cornell offers a free app, Merlin Bird ID, which features the four hundred most common birds in the U.S. and Canada. The purpose of the app is to narrow down the possible birds so you do not have to look through an entire field guide. You input the date, location, colors and size of the bird, and where it was when you saw it (on a feeder, for example). Merlin then gives you a list and pictures of birds that fit your description.

There are also field guide apps available for smartphones. In addition to drawings, range maps, and text descriptions of birds, these apps include bird songs and calls. Some currently available are Sibley Guide to Birds, iBird Pro, and Audubon Birds Pro.

An app linked to eBird that allows you to easily enter your sightings on your smartphone is BirdLog, which allows you to select your location from a map, gives you a list of likely birds in the area, and, once you complete the checklist, enters the data into your eBird account. A companion app, BirdsEye, gives you a list of nearby birds reported to eBird with abundance graphs, or allows you to pick a location to see a list of birds seen there. When you search nearby birds, it also provides maps with exact dates and locations where the bird was reported. You can also access descriptions, pictures, and sounds of each bird.

Another helpful website is that of the American Birding Association, aba.org, which hosts an index of worldwide email lists for birders under the tab Birding News. People post birding-related information on the email lists, such as sightings, requests for information, and local bird club meetings.

Many other birding organizations and parks host websites and Facebook pages. These include the National Audubon Society, national wildlife refuges, local birding organizations, local Audubon societies, state and local parks, and state birding trails. An Internet search for birding in your local area will give you an idea of birding locations and resources available to you. ▨

—Janet Crawford

Janet Crawford is an associate naturalist with the Cape May Bird Observatory

Birding Tours and Workshops

Before ecotourism was a household word, birders had discovered the excitement of traveling to different areas to see new and exotic birds (and travel companies tailored to meet their interest soon discovered them). Three of the most well-established birding tour companies catering to the national and international interests of the North American birding market are Field Guides, Victor Emanuel Nature Tours (VENT), and WINGS. Many birding organizations, such as Massachusetts Audubon, have their own travel programs. There are also scores of very fine smaller or more specialty-focused birding tour companies, such as Wilderness Birding Adventures (with a focus on Alaska) and Shearwater Journeys (with a focus on ocean birds).

Most tour companies advertise in the national birding magazines and have their own websites. Tour costs can range from several hundred dollars for a long-weekend excursion to a regional hot spot to over $10,000 for a cruise to Antarctica or a three-week tour of Papua New Guinea.

Advantages

Tours offer two very compelling advantages. First, they take the effort of planning and logistics out of the hands of participants, allowing them to focus on birds and having fun. Two, they are led by experts—professional birders who are intimate with the birds of a particular region and skilled at responding to the needs of clients, whether this means helping them locate a bird, describing a bird's distinguishing field marks, or ensuring participants' safety and comfort.

Birding tour leaders are "mentors for hire," but the matter of money does not stand between them and those they take into the field. Professional bird-tour leaders lead a demanding life. Those who stay in it do so because they truly love sharing their passion and knowledge. They feed off the enthusiasm of clients. In this regard, the relationship differs little from the traditional mentor/student bond that has long been part of birding.

Planning, logistics, and coordination are handled mostly by the tour company. On-the-ground execution and meeting the needs of clients are largely the responsibilities of the tour leader.

The birding trail leads everywhere because birds are everywhere. Their interest in birds leads these birders to Trinidad, one of the stellar stops on the birding circuit.

Finding a good company and a good leader is the responsibility of the client. You can attempt this by trial and error or you can ask other more seasoned birders for their recommendations.

WING BAR

Choosing a Bird-Tour Company

A birding tour can be one of the most productive and delightful ways to enjoy the birds of an area and learn about them—if you choose the right tour. Here are some of the factors to consider when making your choice.

Leadership. This is the single most important factor. Quality leaders are essential for a successful tour. It is particularly important that the leader has extensive prior experience in the area (i.e., know the birds of that area as well as how to find them); be skilled at handling trip logistics and any surprise situations that may arise; be a good communicator, skilled teacher, and enthusiastic role model. Finally, a good leader must be a "people person" who genuinely enjoys sharing birding and natural history experiences.

Company Philosophy and Style. It is important to pick a company that has a philosophy and style of birding that most closely match your own. Important considerations include the pace of the tour and the approach to birds and nature. Some tours are very fast paced, covering lots of ground in a day and seldom spending more than two or three nights in one location. Other trips have a more relaxed pace, with longer stays at one location and time off in the early afternoon.

The philosophy of a tour influences the type of birders who attend. A tour that emphasizes getting the highest species total will be attractive to hard-core listers. A tour that emphasizes bird appreciation and study will attract birders who enjoy looking at common, widespread species as well as rare ones and who want to learn more about bird identification and the lives of birds. Some birding tours combine birding with looking at other aspects of natural history—butterflies, reptiles, amphibians, mammals, and wildflowers. Others focus exclusively on birds.

Creature Comforts. Birders vary in the level of creature comforts they desire. You should choose a bird tour that has creature comforts similar to what you want. Some birding tours stay in the least expensive places and do not include food in the cost of the tour. Other birding tours place an emphasis on quality accommodations and good food.

Reputation. You are more likely to have a good experience if you choose a tour operated by a long-established company that has a good reputation. Tours run by older established companies are likely to be of high quality. If these companies weren't doing a good job, they probably wouldn't have been in business for so many years. Such companies typically have leaders who are full-time, professional bird-tour leaders. These individuals derive all their income from leading bird tours. They are aware that repeat business is essential to their livelihood. They put the interests of clients first.

Short of signing on to a tour and seeing whether it meets your interest and needs, there are two ways of finding tour companies. The first is to send for the company's catalog listing upcoming tours. The catalog will give breadth and scope of tour options, and from articles and trip descriptions potential clients will learn much about the company and its approach. Or go online and visit the company's website.

The other way is to ask other birders. Many birders are well traveled and have used the services of more than one bird tour company. Ask for their opinions and their recommendations of companies, tours, and leaders. ■

—Victor Emanuel

Victor Emanuel is director of Victor Emanuel Nature Tours, based in Austin, Texas. Operating since 1976, VENT offers guided tours and cruises all over the planet.

Disadvantages

Tours have disadvantages, too. The first is cost. In general, measured in terms of pure cost, signing onto a bird tour is going to be more expensive than traveling to a birding destination on your own. In addition to their own expenses, clients must assume the costs of a tour company's overhead and the expense of having one or more leaders. However, if the costs are measured in terms of bird sightings per dollar spent, they go down—in fact might even mean a savings. The advantages inherent in having a well-planned tour and experienced leader will mean more birds, less frustration, and a better experience.

The other disadvantage is individual freedom. Members of a tour necessarily relinquish a measure of self-determination once they become part of a group. Individuals who are very controlling or very particular about how they believe things should (or should not) be done would do well to consider not subjecting themselves (and other tour members) to unnecessary frustration.

Consider instead an activity format that offers many of the advantages of a tour (leaders, new birds, new opportunities) with considerably more freedom.

Like attending a birding festival.

Events, Functions, Festivals

There are scores of birding festivals in North America. Sponsored by individual organizations, state and federal agencies, and chambers

Just a few of North America's 47 million bird watchers—albeit a highly skilled cross section.

of commerce, their objectives are to promote a special, local bird-related phenomenon in order to attract out-of-region birders and excite residents about a natural event that makes their region special. Festivals are an easy and productive mechanism for birders to savor the bird riches of different parts of the continent and tap into the local expertise for very little money and very little effort or planning on their part. You could spend your entire birding life simply traveling from one festival to the next, in the process savoring most of the birds of North America, and meeting most of birding's tribal leaders, too.

Some festivals have thousands of attendees; other more regional festivals enjoy relatively modest attendance. All will offer a blend of field trips, educational and information booths, indoor programs, and outdoor demonstrations, plus celebrity speakers. They often are well advertised both locally and in targeted birding publications. The American Birding Association posts notice of festivals on their website, as do several of the birding publications just discussed.

One of the great advantages of festivals is the opportunity to test and purchase optics from attending dealers.

One on One

Among all the avenues leading to the birding community there is nothing that beats teaming up with more experienced birders, one on one. Other birders are the ultimate primary resource, able to put answers to the questions that plague you. Most are very pleased to help beginners because, as you will come to learn yourself, the coin of tribute in birding's realm is not experience, and not skill, it is shared interest.

If you go to any of the prime birding locations mentioned in the next chapter you are bound to locate other birders who share your interest. You may even find a mentor.

SUMMARY

The birding community is a social and informational network that beginning birders can draw from. Points of contact include wild bird retail stores, nature centers, local bird clubs and Audubon societies, some museums and zoos, and community colleges. Activities include morning bird walks, birding courses, field trips, regular meetings, and guest speakers. Information about these activities is found in newspaper columns that feature birding/outdoor activity or via birding telephone hotlines and online.

In addition, there are national and international organizations that cater to birders as well as a vast amount of information in birding magazines and books. A number of birding tour companies, led by experts, specialize in taking customers to domestic and exotic birding hot spots. The Web is a prime link to all the social and organizational facets of birding, but the next birder you meet is a primary source of information.

Bird festivals are an excellent resource—in many ways the avocational framework that bird clubs were in the twentieth century. ■

CHAPTER 5

Expanding Horizons— Finding and Facing New Challenges

That Story about the Harrier

I was seated atop a very uncomfortable rock—the only kind there is on the North Lookout of the world-famous Hawk Mountain Sanctuary, in Pennsylvania. Before me was a vista that is emblazoned on the minds of every ardent hawk watcher on the planet . . . and two novice hawk watchers.

You could tell they were novices because of the single and not very useful pair of binoculars they were passing back and forth.

You could tell they were novices because they had an array of basic field guides spread in a semicircle around them, all turned to the pages depicting birds of prey.

You could tell they were novices because every passing Turkey Vulture became an object of scrutiny and discussion and the cause of much page flipping.

Hawk watching is challenging. Like all bird identification it relies on the use of field marks to distinguish one species from the next. But unlike most birding, identifications in the hawk-watching arena are often made at distances beyond the functional range of traditional field guides and standard field marks, such as leg color and plumage patterns.

In hawk watching, identifications are often made on the basis of overall shape (stocky versus lanky), overall color (cold brown versus warm), or the character of a bird's wing beats (quick and snappy versus sluggish and stiff). It's a subtle art, and a subjective one, too, requiring study and experience to gain a measure of competence.

For the beginner, it also requires more specialized field guides than the couple had in their array, and better optics. Lower-power binoculars in the hands of experienced hawk watchers are perfectly adequate, but beginners often need (and even experts often prefer) greater magnification to vault the distances—sometimes magnifications so great that the instruments defy hands to hold them steady.

Me? I was pretty new to hawk watching myself but clearly more experienced, better armed, and better attuned to the challenge than my neighbors. For one thing, I'd virtually memorized *Feathers in the Wind,* a book published by Hawk Mountain that focused specifically on the identification of hawks in flight. Having already discovered the need for higher magnification, I'd augmented my optical arsenal with a spotting scope mounted on a custom-made shoulder stock—a versatile combination that offered high magnification, stability, maneuverability, and portability.

I was also, I must admit, totally dedicated to the challenge at hand. Hawks had captivated me. During the autumn of 1975, I spent virtually every day hawk watching. This explains why I was seated atop Hawk Mountain under bluebird conditions—conditions that don't produce appreciable flights. It also explains why I was scanning so ardently and why, indeed and in fact, I succeeded in finding a hawk.

W a a a a y out there. A phantom form that drifted in and out of the heat waves and owed at least half its existence to the very force of my will. After several minutes of study I convinced myself that what *might* be a bird was *in reality* a bird and very probably a *hawk.* Fixing the position of the bird in my mind, reaching for my spotting scope, I managed to find the phantom in the heat and haze and concluded, happily, that I was right. The bird was eminently raptorial.

"I've got a bird," I shouted to the assembly. "Off the slope of 'One.' Half a field up. WAY out," I cautioned.

Everyone on the lookout brought binoculars to bear, including the gentleman in the birding dyad in front of me. Some folks located the bird. Most could not. You had to know where and you had to know how to look.

The guy in front of me was one of those in the majority. First he looked up . . . then he panned right . . . then left.

No joy.

He turned around, curious to see whether I was serious about there being a bird out there. Convinced by my look of concentration, he resumed his search.

The guy might not have been experienced and he might have had lousy binoculars but he was nevertheless serious about finding this hawk.

Seconds passed. The bird got closer. I began to see more and more details—suggestions that coalesced into discernible features.

For instance, the set of the wings began to appear less than horizontal; in fact, angled upward in a V. Only several raptors frequenting Hawk Mountain fly with wings in a dihedral like this. These include Turkey Vultures, Golden Eagles, Red-tailed Hawks, and Northern Harriers—slim-winged, bantam-weight predators of open spaces.

The bird I was looking at was too pale to be a vulture or an eagle (both of which appear almost black at a distance). It also seemed to have more dihedral than a Red-tailed Hawk should—particularly a Red-tailed flying in light-wind conditions. And . . . was it my imagination or did this bird rock ever-so-unsteadily in flight?

Given the gentle winds, only a bird with very light wing loading would be flying so unsteadily. A point that would eliminate the burly, even-keeled Red-tailed Hawk.

It seemed I'd narrowed the possibilities down to one. So I stuck my neck out.

"It's a Marsh Hawk," I yelled. (We called harriers Marsh Hawks back then.)

At this disclosure, the gentleman up front spun around and glowered. Turning down ridge once more, he jammed the ocular lenses of his binoculars into his eyes, fixing them once again upon the horizon.

The guy was drop-dead serious about finding this hawk.

My suspected harrier kept coming, shedding uncertainty along the way. Wings that seemed to be held in a dihedral became clearly held in a dihedral. A flight that might have been tippy was noticeably tippy. The bird's profile, such as could be seen, seemed gratifyingly long-limbed and slim.

All these traits are harrier traits.

The bird was still too far away, and the angle too acute to make out the white rump patch, the classic textbook field mark that would have certified the bird a Northern Harrier. But it wasn't necessary. By projection and deduction, via compounded hints and clues, the bird was as much a harrier at a mile out as it would be if I'd held the bird in my hand. The trick with hawk watching (as with anything else) is knowing the tricks.

Abruptly, the bird left the ridge, angling off over the valley, a classic bluebird-day maneuver. A mile off was as close as the bird was going to get. As I watched, studying the bird, trying to learn as much as I could about harrier shape, size, and manner of flight, a vagrant updraft caught it, tipping it on its side, exposing bright white underparts.

Young harriers show cinnamon underparts; adult females are tawny. But . . .

"Adult male!" I sang out. "It's an adult male Marsh Hawk!" Not so commonly seen, the bird was then, and remains today, my favorite bird of prey.

At this pronouncement, the gentleman in front of me released his binoculars, lowered his head into his hands, rocked back and forth several times, then, righting himself, leaning toward his wife, he whispered:

"I can't believe this son-of-a-bitch behind me. I can't even find this bird and he can see its genitals."

Fact: You can't see the genitals on migrating birds of prey.

Fact: If your objective is identification, and if you know the tricks, you don't have to.

And for the record, no, he didn't say *genitals*. He used another word that was a whole lot funnier.

Reaching for New Sights and Sounds

OK, you've met your basic equipment needs. You've learned the rudiments of identification—may even have gained a working familiarity with the birds that occur in your favored birding haunts. Now it's time to grow. To reach for new birds that lie beyond the scope of your present horizon.

Part of this horizon is defined by the world of sight—birds whose identity lies beyond the range of your binoculars, identification

OK, here's an adult male Northern Harrier displaying its signature white rump patch. So what if you can't see the rump patch? Welcome to birding ID's horizon.

challenges that lie beyond the scope of your present skills (and your basic field guide). Part of the horizon negotiates the world of sound—bird vocalizations that offer up a bird's identity sight unseen. Part of your expanding horizon is, in a very literal sense, geographical. The world is a big and bird-filled place. Discovery, excitement, and challenge lie in every direction.

As birders expand their horizons, they will discover a need for tools and equipment that will both facilitate their journey and open new avenues of exploration. Some of the aids are optical, some are electronic, some are informational. Most were developed by birders who pioneered the boundaries you are pushing now. All will help bring the horizon within reach.

Spotting Scopes and Tripods

Binoculars may be the primary tool of birding, but they have their limit, and sometimes this limit falls short of need. Picking up where binoculars fall short is the spotting scope.

A spotting scope is an optical tool that, via higher magnification, permits birders to study birds that lie beyond the effective range of binoculars. They are single barreled and offer a view through one eye. Fitted to a tripod or some other stabilizing platform, they allow the effective use of greater magnification, which enhances the details that can be seen at a distance.

Spotting scopes are not as quick, versatile, or portable as binoculars. They are not a substitute for inferior binoculars (birders who have inadequate binoculars and think that buying a spotting scope will make up the difference had better think again). They are also not useful for some types of birding—most woodland birding, for instance.

They are nevertheless invaluable at times—especially in situations where birds must be studied at great distances, like distant waterfowl on a lake, or when a tricky identification dictates very detailed scrutiny, like the identification challenges presented by similar small shorebird species.

Spotting scopes are also a portal to gain supernatural intimacy with birds. Some very fine instruments today can offer images of birds that are even better than those of a bird in the hand. Birding's challenges may well lie on the horizon, but discovery is often no farther than your shadow's length.

Mirror versus Prism Scopes

There are two basic types of spotting scopes: mirror (or reflecting) scopes, which use mirrors to capture and direct light, and prism (or refracting) scopes, which use prisms and lenses.

Mirror scopes are generally short, bucket shaped, and commonly have an angled or look-down eyepiece. Because of the mirrors, they are lightweight, provide good-to-excellent resolution, even at high magnification, and are exceptionally bright.

They are, unfortunately, not rugged, not waterproof, not particularly user friendly—all qualities that would render them unpopular among birders even if these types of instruments did not reverse the image (which, using mirrors, they do) or tend to burn the colors out of subjects (particularly at the center of the field).

Mirror scopes serve well for observing stars and planets, but only the highest quality (and priced) mirror scopes have ever won a place in the hearts of birders.

Prism scopes are infinitely more popular among birders because of their ruggedness, simplicity, high image quality, wide availability, and portability. Prism scopes are classically tube shaped. Many models come with a choice of an angled eyepiece (for restful long-term viewing) or a straight-through-view eyepiece (which is nominally easier to aim).

Prism scopes come in two basic size classes: those offering a smaller 60mm objective lens and those with a larger 80mm objective. The 60mm scopes are lighter and more compact; those with the larger objective offer marginally superior brightness and image quality—but much also depends upon the quality of the instrument. A superior-quality 60mm spotting scope—one that employs very high-quality glass—can outperform some lesser-quality 80mm scopes.

WING BAR

ED (HD) and APO Lenses—What It Means, What It's Worth

Lenses work because light rays bend as they pass through glass, or any other transparent material that is significantly denser than air. Unfortunately, daylight (the kind we use to see birds) is really a mix of many colors, and each color is bent at a slightly different angle when it passes through glass. If you have seen the rainbow formed by a prism you have observed this effect. Each object in the image formed by a simple glass lens is actually surrounded by a rainbow halo (reds, blues, greens, and purples) of unfocused light. Early on, lens designers discovered that if they made lenses from two pieces of glass (elements) with different densities, they could bring two colors of light (red and yellow) to the same focus. Since red and yellow account for most of the energy in daylight, in most situations you can't detect the blue, green, and purple halos that are left in the image. Most modern spotting scopes use a two-element, or achromatic, objective lens and produce an image that is clean and sharp enough to satisfy 95 percent of the time in the field. Still, that unfocused light does bleed over from one object in the image to another, muddying the colors and blurring the edges. In critical situations (at great distances, using the highest powers, or in low light), a standard achromat may show you less than you want to see of the bird.

Using something denser for one of the elements can help tighten contrast. Modern ED objectives use extra-density glass (made by adding heavy metals, or rare earths, to the glass mix). In Europe, ED glass is sometimes called high density (or HD) but it is essentially the same. Some spotting scopes use a fluorite element, made from a transparent mineral that is also denser than glass.

Scopes with ED (HD) and fluorite objectives eliminate all but a tiny bit of unfocused halos in the image. Compared to the image formed by a standard achromatic objective, the ED or fluorite image will appear sharper, brighter, snappier, and more intense. You will see the difference most in those critical situations, but the extra measure of clarity can add to your enjoyment of birds all day long. I would guess that an ED or fluorite spotting scope would show you all you want to see of the bird 99 percent of the time. You do pay a price, of course: ED and fluorite scopes can cost up to a third more than standard achromats (33 percent more money for about a 4-percent boost in image quality). Only you can figure out if that cost-benefit ratio is acceptable. [I find that most birders just suck it up and buy the best. PD]

To eliminate the last bit of unfocused light and produce absolutely the purest image, it is generally necessary to add a third element to the objective lens and use a third type of glass. Lenses that bring all the colors of daylight to the same focus are called apochromatic. They are featured only in top-end astronomical scopes and a few spotting scopes used by birders. ▨

—Steve Ingram

A resident of Kennebunk, Maine, Ingram is the former editor of Better View Desired, *a newsletter with a focus on optics and the optical needs of birders, as well as former editor of* Birding's *"Tools of the Trade" column.*

Power and Performance

Power and performance are what using a spotting scope is all about. The considerations used to measure binocular performance generally apply to spotting scopes: brightness, field of view, eye relief, depth of field . . .

But at the core of spotting scope use is power—the ability to vault distances and magnify distant objects so that tiny details can be seen. Remember, hand-shake is no longer a diminishing factor. The scope rests on a tripod, not in your hands. In an ideal, vibration-free world, image quality comes down to a simple matter of magnification and the quality of the glass.

How Much Power?

Spotting scopes offer a range of magnification most often determined by the power of the interchangeable eyepiece you buy and fit to the scope. Popular powers include 15x, 20x, 22x, 25x, 30x, 32x, 40x, and 60x. Not all manufacturers offer all these options for all instruments (and some offer even higher magnifications). In general, anything between 20x and 32x will serve for both easy

Spotting scopes range in price from several hundred to several thousand dollars. Most scopes can be fitted with an array of eyepieces offering differing magnifications; zoom eyepieces function very well and are generally preferred by veteran birders.

scanning and concerted study. Wide-angle lenses are superior for scanning. Higher-power lenses (40x and above) enhance detail at the expense of field of view.

There are also zoom spotting scopes—some with internal zoom mechanisms; most lines include a zoom lens among the array of interchangeable lens options (ranging from 15x to generally 60x). There are some zoom eyepieces on the market that offer optical performance that is every bit as good as their fixed-magnification counterparts. The field of view on some zoom eyepieces is, unfortunately, not generous, even at the lowest magnification setting. But their ability to resolve detail is often stellar. (*Note:* Reservations expressed earlier in this book about zoom binoculars do not apply to spotting scopes.)

For years, and for many reasons, the standard for spotting-scope magnification was 20x—a power that for most spotting scope makes and models provides a good, sharp, bright image that will not push the limitations of a scope past performance levels. Today, 32x is a very popular magnification.

But remember that magnification not only increases image size, it magnifies optical shortcomings. A spotting scope that offers a nice, bright image at 20x may well produce a dingy, resolution-challenged image at 40x.

What do I use? A very high-quality 80mm instrument that can take the challenge of higher magnification at no performance loss. I commonly use a 20–75x zoom eyepiece. My partiality to zooms was initiated by an experience I had looking at a severely backlit bird. Through low magnification the bird was a dark silhouette but after zooming up the magnification, thus reducing the field of view and diminishing peripheral light, I was able to note color and detail. The improved image quality wasn't related to power—it was the ability to control the amount of light surrounding the bird that gave me the improved view.

Other Considerations

Optical performance is the primary, but not necessarily the only, quality that a field-worthy spotting scope should offer. Like binoculars, there are attributes that can make a spotting scope excel, or compromise its usefulness in the field.

Depth of Field/Critical Focus

Not as critical a concern in spotting scopes as binoculars, but scopes with a shallow depth of field make studying flocks very difficult, even physically exhausting. With scopes whose image is blurred everywhere except the precise point of focus, eyes try to compensate for the instrument's shortcomings—and quickly tire. Once again, lower magnification offers greater depth of field.

Close Focus

Less a concern for scopes than binoculars. Nevertheless, there are times when a close-focusing spotting scope can be useful— for studying very subtle distinctions, such as the feather patterns that distinguish Western and Semipalmated Sandpipers or separate Cassin's and Botteri's Sparrows. The greatest advantage of close-focusing instruments, however, is the supernatural intimacy they offer viewers. While all scopes should focus down to at least 30 feet, there are some on the market that focus down to 10 feet or less!

So what? Well, imagine a cardinal or bluebird perched at 10 feet and viewed with a 32x eyepiece—it's the equivalent of looking at a living, breathing creature from a distance of less than 4 inches. Not only can you see the creature's eye, you can see your reflection in its eye. You crave intimacy? You got it. Also, wait until you try watching a honeybee gathering nectar with your close-focusing scope. It's a National Geographic special in your own backyard.

Focus Systems

Whether a ring around the barrel or, more commonly, a focus knob, the system should move smoothly and responsively. Fast focusing is not the concern with spotting scopes as it is with binoculars, since subjects are generally more sedentary. *Caution:* The focus mechanism of some spotting scopes gets stiff in cold temperatures, making it difficult to focus without moving the scope off target. If the scope you are considering seems stiff and hard to focus in the store, it will only be worse when the lubricants gel in the cold. Also, the focus systems of some instruments are very, very critical, making it difficult to attain a sharp image.

Angled Eyepiece versus Straight-Through

Whether to choose a scope whose eyepiece is angled or set parallel to look straight through the scope is a matter of preference, not optical performance. There are advantages to both systems, and these may determine which style you prefer.

Angled Eyepiece Advantages

1. Generally easier and more restful for long-term viewing because your subordinate eye is focused on the ground and your brain ignores the image it transmits.
2. The scope is set lower than your raised eyes, allowing you to scan over it (not around it) with your binoculars.
3. Two or more individuals of slightly differing heights can better share the instrument with less physical strain, acrimony, or tripod manipulation.
4. Observers can study birds high overhead without having to crouch or buy a super-extending tripod.

Angled Eyepiece Disadvantages

1. Slightly more difficult to aim and find the bird than with a straight-through eyepiece.
2. Eyepiece is more exposed to rain, mist, or snow—distorting the image in inclement weather.
3. Not serviceable on a shoulder-mount system and not as easy to use with car-window mounts.

More experienced birders tend to select the angled eyepiece design, but neither choice is wrong.

Ruggedness

Even more than binoculars, scopes must be rugged. Binoculars hit the ground by accident; spotting scopes go down routinely—victims of wind gusts, improperly tightened tripod legs, or collisions with object-challenged individuals. Scope bodies, particularly scope bodies in the larger 80mm and above class, should be housed in metal or very impact-resistant polycarb. Inexpensive plastic bodies are seductively light, but when they fall, a disturbingly high percentage break on impact. Be warned and be mindful of the limitations of a scope's warranty.

How Much $$$?

You can buy a serviceable entry-level spotting scope for around $400. You can buy a rugged and dependable spotting scope for

$650 and a really superior spotting scope for $1,200 and up. But no matter how much you spend on the scope, do not skimp on the ...

Tripod

Tripods are the literal foundation of power, the vibration-free platform that makes higher magnification possible. No matter how much over budget you go on your spotting scope purchase, do not even think of balancing things out by buying an inexpensive tripod.

Fact: You are better off buying a $400 spotting scope and putting it on a $170 tripod than you are buying a $3,500 spotting scope and putting it on a $70 dollar tripod. A light, flimsy tripod is not going to remain stable in even a modest wind, and wind-generated vibration will make a shambles of image quality.

There are high-quality, high-performance tripods made of aluminum that can be purchased for under $200. They are fairly heavy (weighing, depending upon models, between 5 and 9 pounds), but they will perform as well as light, strong graphite tripods costing over three times as much, and their weight is an asset in the wind.

Simplicity is the rule of thumb. Photographers seem to love tripods that offer multiple adjustment controls. But the ideal for birding is a spotting scope tripod that has just one lever that controls all movement of the head—panning up and down, left and right—smoothly, easily, without disconcerting skips or jumps. When you stop moving your hand, the scope stays in place.

Legs should sleeve easily and extend so that the spotting scope eyepiece will reach your eye without your having to stoop. If you travel frequently, you may want to make sure the tripod can fit in your travel bag.

There are other very useful mounts for spotting scopes: window mounts that sleeve over a half-open car window and use the car for stability and commercial shoulder stocks that optimize portability.

But a good tripod is essential, and only a few manufacturers make tripods especially designed for birding. It is not certain that your average camera store is going to carry a birder-worthy tripod—but if you do shop at one, narrow your search to tripod heads designed to pan video cameras. What you will most likely find in camera shops, however, are tripods designed for photography—ones with lots of adjustment levers and knobs.

Simplicity, stability, and *portability/weight* should define your purchase. The more you spend, the lighter the tripod will be. Graphite and basalt tripods offer stability and light weight. Tripod heads (purchased separately) that function with a single adjusting lever is what you want.

Once again, find out what other birders are using. Find out where they bought their equipment. Follow their lead.

Birding by Ear

Birds are not merely a visual presence, they are an audible presence, too, disclosing their existence, location, even their identities through sound. Many of these sounds are vocalizations that emanate from the bird's syrinx, or voice box. They include chips,

Crow, yes? But which species? The call can help you decide if it's the widespread American Crow or one of the smaller and more geographically restricted species, like Fish Crow.

grunts, wails, warbles, trills . . . and, of course, songs—one of the natural world's most celebrated offerings.

Bird sounds can also emanate from an alchemy of air and feathers (examples include the drumming of grouse and the winnowing of snipe) or from percussive manipulation (such as the hammering of woodpeckers).

The point is this: Birds make a number of sounds for a variety of reasons. Together, they form an avenue that leads to a greater awareness and understanding of birds. Separated, they are an audio fingerprint that distinguishes one species from the next. Learn which sounds are made by which birds and you've made an identification that is as accurate as any made by visual means—in many cases, even more accurate.

WING BAR

Sifting Through Sound

You pull into the parking lot at Warbler Woods and backseat Sylvia—you know, your birder friend with the perpetual smug look on her face, starts calling out birds:

"Black-and-white Warbler, Wood Thrush, Scarlet Tanager, Rose-breasted Grosbeak, Chipping Sparrow . . ." And she hasn't even gotten out of the car!

While Sylvia didn't exactly walk on water, she has performed an apparent miracle. She has identified most of the birds in the area without even raising her binoculars. Along the way her flippant audio IDs may just have discouraged every beginning birder in earshot.

To many beginners, Sylvia's auditory talents appear more like a divine gift than an acquired skill. Because most folks come to birding with little or no appreciation for birdsong, getting a handle on even the most rudimentary facts of bird vocalization may seem a daunting challenge. And anyway the name of the game is bird watching, isn't it? To be fair, the beginner already has their hands full learning the visual characteristics of birds while fine-tuning their binocular skills. Typically then, even when the birder becomes dimly aware that birdsong may be of some use in playing the birding game, he or she just lets the audio-ID challenge slide. And this is a big mistake. Let me tell you why.

Ask almost any experienced or expert birder and they will tell you that knowing birdsong is a critical component of their skill. One survey suggested that between 75 percent and 90 percent of bird identifications are based on bird vocalizations. Think of all the situations in which you are more likely to hear a bird before you see it: bitterns in a marsh, sparrows in a hedgerow, warblers in the treetops. The list goes on and on. Also, our ears are turned to 360 degrees—they constantly monitor our immediate environment; our eyes focus on only a small portion of that same area. Once you know most of the common bird songs, your ears will tell you if there is something different in the area—then you can put your eyes to work to "find" the bird. There is little debate about the usefulness of knowing birdsong—so the sooner you begin your birdsong learning the quicker you will develop into a competent birder. So, how do you get started?

I suppose most of us, largely for reasons relating to maintaining our sanity, paid little or no attention to birdsong before we become birders. Apart from the occasional crow or barnyard rooster vocalizations—bird songs are just not part of our reality. It's as though we are born with certain sensory filters, and a conscious decision is needed to remove one of those filters. As fledgling birders, however, we are soon made aware that birds are vocal critters. And herein arises the initial problem: A spring morning can offer up a bewildering symphony of bird sounds. Unfortunately for the beginner, the result is not enlightenment but sensory overload. Just as we focus on one bird at time with our binoculars, we need to retrain our hearing to focus on one bird song at a time. So a good way to get started is to learn one or two of the most common vocal birds in your area and concentrate on their songs. House Finches, Northern Mockingbirds, and American Robins are good candidates.

You also need to develop a system for representing birdsong. While the means for representing the visual characteristics of birds—size, color, plumage patterns, and so on—are familiar, methods for representing vocalization require a little practice. Two forms of representation are most helpful: description and phonetic representation.

Let's use the American Robin to exemplify both methods. The American Robin's song can be described as a lilting, up and down tune. The rhythm is singsongy. Now let's add a phonetic representation—*cheerily, cheerup, cheerily.* Try singing (or whistling) the phonetic and give it an up and down rhythm (don't worry, nobody is listening). Now we have a good representation of the American Robin's song—one that we can mentally compare to

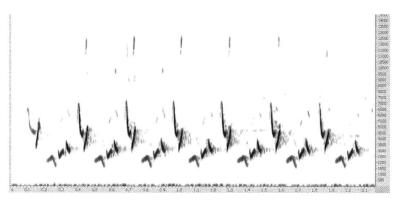

Sonograms graphically replicate a bird's song—a Carolina Wren's is shown here. Even without knowing the song, you can see that the same phrase is repeated multiple times.

the robin singing in the backyard. Just as we compare a field guide illustration to the bird in the field, we compare the birdsong representation to the song we hear. The list of descriptive words you can apply to birdsong is limited only by your imagination. Squeaky wheels, flutes, rusty hinges, whistles, ping-pong balls dropping on tables—all these are used. In my experience the more bizarre the description, the more likely you are to remember it.

Did you know that singing Bobolinks sound like R2D2 (of *Star Wars* fame) with his wires crossed? Also, if you can add emotional content to your description—for example, *the haunting song of the Veery*—this seems to reinforce the description. You will find dozens of descriptive and phonetic representations in field guides and birdsong tapes, but don't be bashful about creating your own. Many birdsong learners find that the most helpful representations are ones they have devised. Keep a notebook of birds you hear and representations of their songs. One other method for representing birdsong is to use simplified drawings. Graphical representations might include dotted lines for a trill, wavy lines for an up and down rhythm, and upward and downward pointed arrows to indicate changes in pitch.

There you have it! A crash course in birdsong learning. A few final tips: Don't try to learn too many songs at once. Start with the common birds first. And relax. This is supposed to be fun. Soon you will be suggesting to

Sylvia that she may have missed the Black-throated Green Warbler singing in the background! ■

—Dick Walton

Dick Walton is a skilled naturalist and producer of the "Birding by Ear" tapes and several natural history videos, including "Hawk Watch." Well-known on the birding (and butterfly) lecture circuit, he lives in Concord, Massachusetts.

But . . . Do Heard Birds Count?

Of course they count—whether the foundation of your concern stems from your desire to fully appreciate a bird or merely to include it on your life list. You might just as legitimately ask whether a bird that is momentarily seen and identified visually can be counted if you didn't hear it sing, or haven't yet seen it in all its various plumages.

Bird sound is not only a way to find birds; it can help you identify them, too. You often hear a woodpecker drumming before you see it.

Some species, particularly many nocturnal species, are virtual disembodied spirits anyway. They are heard, filling the night with a rich blend of sound, but rarely seen. For years I thrilled to the sound of Black Rails not far from my home without ever making an effort to see one. I didn't care to engage in any effort that might disrupt their nesting (or, for that matter, the nesting effort of other salt-marsh birds). I was content merely to listen, appreciating them for what they were, and appreciating the fact that it was my audio ability that had earned me standing. A momentary glimpse of a small black bird in a night-darkened marsh would hardly have made the encounter any more meaningful.

Awareness First

The first step in learning to identify birds by ear is simple awareness. Whether you are in the field or inside your home with windows open, train your ears to be as attentive to sound as your eyes are attentive to motion. Learn to pick up sounds that are new;

It's challenging, but if you can identify the honk of a Canada Goose, you can do all the rest—the principles are the same.

condition yourself to isolate individual songs they way you pick out individual instruments in a musical ensemble.

Nobody Starts from Scratch
Nobody who is not hearing impaired opens their ears to the world of bird sound without a clue. You probably know more than you think—can identify the raucous *caw, caw* of an American Crow or the seven-note hoot of a Great Horned Owl. Perhaps you live in the suburbs and recognize the liquid cascade of notes that is a House Wren's song or on a farm where meadowlarks sing from fence-post perches.

You have the basic foundation of an audio repertoire. All you have to do is add to it—by listening, first, to the common, everyday birds around you. The ones whose songs and sounds form the soundtrack of your world. Once you've linked the sounds to the singers—once you've reached the point that a rising and falling flow of caroled phrases automatically conjures the name *robin*, and that a rapid trill means *Chipping Sparrow*—you can move these backyard birds to the back burners of your mind and listen for new and unfamiliar sounds.

Building Your Audio Repertoire
Learning bird sounds is like anything else. The more you know, the easier it gets. The more attuned you become to the nuances of bird sounds, the easier it is to distinguish and to compare an unfamiliar vocalization to a familiar one.

Part of this heightened proficiency is linked to process. With practice you learn to hear critically, distinguishing the elements of a song—volume, pitch, frequency, cadence, phrasing—much the same way wine lovers learn to appreciate the subtle qualities of a fine Bordeaux.

Part of it is portfolio. Once you know a bird song, you can call it up from memory and use it as a comparative reference—to help distinguish and even lock away the elements of a new song. While bird songs are idiosyncratic (used for intraspecific communication), many species have vocalizations that recall or have qualities that are similar to other species.

Take, for example, Chipping Sparrow, a very common, very widespread bird whose elemental song is a rapid series of dry chip notes, all on the same pitch, all on the same frequency.

There are other birds whose song is a trill, among them Dark-eyed Junco, Swamp Sparrow, and Worm-eating Warbler. But the trill of Dark-eyed Junco is more musical than a Chipping Sparrow's; that of Swamp Sparrow is slower and more musical; that of Worm-eating Warbler is faster, dryer, more brittle with opening notes that lack volume and closing notes that lose force at the end.

Knowing the song of Chipping Sparrow offers a comparative reference. Knowing that one broad category of bird vocalizations is "trilling" helps give some structure and order to the complex world of bird sound. Now you can move on to those species whose songs are more warbled, such as Pine Warbler.

Sounds Like (Mnemonics)

Some people are audio gifted, able to hear a bird's song once and lock it into memory. Most of us are not so fortunate. We hear a song, strive to memorize it and the name of the singer, and fail to recognize it (and the singer) two minutes later.

"I've got to relearn warbler songs every spring," is such a common lament that it's a cliche among birders.

Many people find it helpful to render birdsong into rhyme—coin a phrase that recalls the pattern of a bird's song. At its most simple and accurate is the song of Prothonotary Warbler: a loud, ringing "SWEET! SWEET! SWEET! SWEET! SWEET!" Hardly more complex and no less phonetically apt is the call of Scarlet Tanager: "Chick-Burr." Or the song of White-throated Sparrow, which sings a lament to "Oh, Sweet, Canada, Canada, Canada."

Some mnemonics can be more complex and creative, including the song of Indigo Bunting: "What, what. Where, where. Here, here. See it, see it." And (perhaps my favorite) Warbling Vireo, who taunts its caterpillar prey with the boast "If-I-see-it, I-can-seize-it, and-I'll-squeeze-it, till-it-*squir-r-r-rts!*"

When You Can't Find the Words

Some bird sounds that don't lend themselves to mnemonic phrases are reminiscent of other familiar things. For example, one of the common vocalizations of the Gray Catbird is a petulant whine that sounds like a cat. The cry of Sandhill Cranes sounds like a wooden hinged gate opening. Yellow Rails make a call that sounds like two quarters being tapped together. The high, vapor-thin call of Cedar Waxwing sounds like the sigh of a screen door closing. The flight call of Swainson's Thrush might easily be confused with the call of the Spring Peeper, a small eastern frog.

But while Spring Peepers, like migrating thrushes, are nocturnal, frogs don't fly. Spring Peeper sounds emanating from the heavens over much of North America in May are much more likely to be Swainson's Thrush than frogs in flight.

It is often helpful to liken a bird call to a sound you are familiar with. To me, the rattling bugle of a Sandhill Crane sounds like a wooden gate opening.

Which Brings Up an Interesting Point

Birds vocalize all year—to communicate with other members of a flock, warn of enemies or intruders, or disclose their location. For most species, birdsong is limited first to the males of the species and then to a brief portion of the year. Most male birds are most vocal in spring and early summer, when they are establishing and defending territories and advertising for mates.

Nesting season can be very protracted in some parts of the continent, and there are some species (such as Carolina Wren) that sing all year. But over most of North America, male birds are "singing" (not "calling") from March through early July, with April through June the period when many nesting birds are in full chorus.

Off season, the audio fingerprint offered by birds might be hardly more than calls, mere fragments: single-note chips or nasal whines. Remember that, in general, only the male birds sing. So half of every songbird species' adult population doesn't advertise its presence or identity itself on the airways in song.

But for some reason, for most birds, it is the complex vocalization (i.e., birdsong) that is the easiest to recognize and remember. Learning the short utterances usually comes later for most birders and most species.

Spring and early summer are when most male birds are singing. Dawn to midmorning is prime time. One reason singing males make good subjects is because for the most part they are conspicuously perched. Prospecting birds want to be seen as well as heard.

Once your unidentified siren is located, bring your binoculars to bear. Identify the singer. Then watch and listen, fusing the image of the bird to the elements of the song in your mind.

The bond might not hold the first time, or the second, but sooner (if you are audio-attuned), or later (if you are like me) the bird and sound will be linked. You will have moved one step closer toward birding's horizon, and pushed your personal horizon just a little farther away.

No Shortage of Aids

Ornithologists and birders have tried for years to find ways of facilitating the vocalization-learning process. Descriptions and mnemonics are helpful but are not the audio equivalent of an illustration in a field guide. Bird sounds can be illustrated using sonograms, visual constructs that use lines on paper to replicate sound. They are accurate but require study and a working familiarity with birdsong to be truly useful—it's not like reading sheet music.

Next to actually watching birds vocalize, sound recordings are by far the most useful aids to gaining a tympanic toehold in the world of bird sound. There is an assortment of bird-sound recordings available online or on CDs that are unified in their high quality and divided by their focus and scope.

Some recordings, like the ensembles produced by the Peterson Field Guide Series, are offered as an accompaniment to the book. The order of bird sounds follows the order in which birds are depicted in the field guide—a utilitarian marriage that facilitates learning.

Some, like *Songs of the Warblers of North America,* produced by Donald Borror and William Gunn, have a specialized species focus. Some, like *Voices of the Peruvian Rainforest,* by Theodore Parker, or *A Bird Walk at Chan Chich,* by John Moore, have a geographic or site-specific orientation.

More useful to those who are just learning to find their way around the world of bird sound are recording packages with a species order designed to group similar-sounding birds together—to impart to listeners the sense that there is in fact an organizing structure to bird songs (those that trill, those that sound buzzy, those that use short phrases, those that repeat their notes, and so on). These facilitate comparisons of sound-alike species. The popular *Birding by Ear* and *More Birding by Ear* recordings, produced by Richard Walton and Robert Lawson and published by Houghton Mifflin, are classics.

Another new classic is a CD-ROM called *Flight Calls of Migratory Birds.* Produced by William R. Evans and Michael O'Brien, the CD successfully reproduces and graphically depicts the esoteric sounds that migrating thrushes, warblers, sparrows, and others make during their nocturnal migrations.

And don't forget birding apps that also have a sound component, as do many species accounts found online. You hear a disembodied song that reminds you of American Robin, call up robin, listen, then determine whether your vocalist is indeed a robin or something else—a species that has a robinlike song but differs somewhat (is lower pitched, perhaps, or more run-on). Time to key up orioles or tanagers.

Recordings and CDs have the advantage of being portable and easily accessible. They can be called up no matter what the season or where you are (sitting in traffic, jogging). The problem with CDs has always been that the sounds are disembodied. Without the anchoring reference of the bird making the sound, recordings commonly go in one ear and out the other without finding a home in between. DVDs or video streams that mate the sound to a visual depiction are superior educational aids.

You can also go online and Google specific species and click on their vocalizations. You want to hear what species X sounds like, you call up the section on species X and click the icon that makes it sing. The image might be stilted, or the bird depicted might be a female (not the male), but the vocalization is still backed up visually. It may even include a sonogram.

DVDs, while not interactive, have the advantage (again, so far) of being closer to life. Birds move as freely as they do in nature (since the footage was lifted from nature) and the sound that is heard most often emanates from the bird being shown. The classic, in fact the reference standard, for this method of depiction is the DVD *Watching Warblers,* produced by Michael Male and Judy Fieth. Here the intimacy is surreal—the projected situation is almost as good as being in the field.

However Nothing, Repeat, Nothing Beats REAL
The many devices that replicate bird sounds are useful and promise to get better. There are systems that use bar codes affixed to field guide illustrations that will key to and play the songs of particular birds. Newer applications allow birders to record songs in the field and have them instantly digitally translated to find a match in memory and call up an identification.

But insofar as learning to identify birds by their vocalizations is concerned, nothing is as effective as listening to real birds, in real time, in real outdoors situations. It is, after all, why you started birding in the first place.

Travel

The pioneering spirit of our ancestors endures in birding. Just as you once left your backyard in search of new birds and new discoveries, most birders are eventually inspired to take their avocation on the road, searching for birds whose "home ranges" do not overlap with theirs.

More than 900 species of birds have occurred in North America north of Mexico. In most states and provinces, fewer than half this number are accounted resident or regular transients. And while birds often turn up hundreds, even thousands, of miles outside their normal range, pursuing birds in their native environment is more productive, and arguably more satisfying, than relying upon accident and chance.

Travel . . . Where?

The flippant answer is *anywhere*—anywhere the range maps in your field guide show species that do not occur where you live and that you want to see.

As a general rule, the farther you travel from home, the more exotic the birds become. If you live on the East Coast, a trip to the West Coast will put you in touch with many new and exciting species. If you live in Alaska, you will find species that would earn the envy of every birder living in Florida. But just as Florida birders must travel to Alaska to see birds like Bristle-thighed Curlew and Yellow Wagtail, Alaskan birders must go to Florida if they hope to see White-crowned Pigeon or Limpkin.

You do not necessarily have to travel across the continent to see birds that do not occur close to home. Habitat can be as determining as distance where bird distribution is concerned. In some places, where physiographic regions are found in close proximity, a trip of 100 miles (or less) can dramatically change the birding landscape. For example, the distance between Rocky Mountain National Park and the Pawnee National Grassland of Colorado is

The famous boardwalk at Crane Creek, in Ohio's Magee Marsh, is a celebrated location for seeing migrating warblers in May.

about 100 miles. But the difference in the nesting bird life—the difference between western forest species like Hammond's Flycatcher, Western Tanager, and Lincoln's Sparrow and prairie specialties like Mountain Plover, Lark Bunting, and Chestnut-collared Longspur—is dramatic. Worlds (or at least habitats) apart, in fact.

Birds are found everywhere. If you have the time and means to travel everywhere, anytime, feel free to wander and lay claim to avian encounters that are serendipitous. Most of us don't have this latitude, however. We are limited by time and budget. We must approach birding trips with an agenda, a shopping list.

For those who must target their birding adventures, there are places and regions that have earned the title "birding hot spot." Many are places that offer easy access to large numbers of the endemic and "specialty" birds of a region. They have the advantage of being well known and documented, and are found in proximity to places that meet the needs of travelers.

Not to Be Redundant But . . . WHERE?

Many knowledgeable birders have compiled lists of the top ten or twelve birding hot spots, and while no two lists are identical, everyone will agree that the following locations offer great birding. They are distinguished by avian diversity and regional representation. Some are famous for their endemics; some host large or unusual numbers of wintering species; some are locations that attract vast numbers of migratory birds. Taken in sum, they cover most of the bird species found in North America.

NEWBURYPORT / PARKER RIVER NATIONAL WILDLIFE REFUGE / ROCKPORT, ALL IN MASSACHUSETTS

For winter specialties with an Atlantic Coast flavor. Examples: Great Cormorant, Common Eider, Barrow's Goldeneye, Harlequin Duck, Purple Sandpiper, Iceland Gull, Glaucous Gull. **Period:** Late November through February. **Contact:** Massachusetts Audubon Society. **Also recommended:** Coastal Maine / New Hampshire; Montauk Point, Long Island, New York. **Reference:** *A Birder's Guide to Eastern Massachusetts,* by Bird Observer.

CAPE MAY, NEW JERSEY

An autumn migratory concentration point famous for its songbird fallouts, hawk migration (averaging 40,000 birds of prey per year), and one-million-bird seabird migration. **Period:** August through November. **Contact:** Cape May Bird Observatory. **Also recommended:** Cape Charles, Virginia; Hawk Mountain Sanctuary, Kempton, Pennsylvania. **Reference:** *The Birds of Cape May* by David Sibley; *Birds and Birding at Cape May,* by Clay and Pat Sutton.

POINT PELEE, ONTARIO

The spring counterpart to Cape May, offering massed concentrations of spring migrants (particularly warblers) in full color and full song. **Period:** Mid-April through May. **Contact:** Point Pelee National Park. **Also highly recommended:** Crane Creek State Park, Ohio; Presque Isle State Park, Pennsylvania; Whitefish Point, Michigan.

EVERGLADES / SOUTHERN FLORIDA

A winter getaway that offers the opportunity to see many species that rarely occur outside of Florida, including Snail Kite, Short-tailed Hawk, White-crowned Pigeon, Mangrove Cuckoo, Black-whiskered Vireo. **Period:** December through February. **Contact:** Everglades National Park, also Florida Audubon Society. **Also**

recommended: Audubon Corkscrew Swamp Sanctuary, J. N. "Ding" Darling National Wildlife Refuge. **Reference:** *A Birder's Guide to Florida,* by Bill Pranty.

TEXAS COAST / HIGH ISLAND

A place with great winter diversity and celebrated for its spring songbird fallouts. Birders are courted from High Island (near Port Arthur) to South Padre Island. **Period:** December through March for wintering species; April for migrants. **Contact:** Texas Parks and Wildlife Department. **Also recommended:** Cameron Parish, Louisiana; Dauphin Island, Alabama; Dry Tortugas National Park, Florida. **Reference:** *A Birder's Guide to the Texas Coast,* by Mel Cooksey and Ron Weeks.

RIO GRANDE VALLEY, TEXAS

A verdant window into Mexico with a number of species found nowhere else in the United States, including Muscovy Duck, Hook-billed Kite, Ringed Kingfisher, Brown Jay, Tropical Parula. Key sites include Santa Ana National Wildlife Refuge and Bentsen-Rio Grande Valley State Park. **Period:** December through April. **Contact:** Santa Ana National Wildlife Refuge. **Reference:** *A Birder's Guide to the Rio Grande Valley of Texas,* by Mark Lockwood, William McKinney, James Paton, and others.

CHURCHILL / MANITOBA

Churchill offers northern and tundra species with a measure of traveler conveniences, including Willow Ptarmigan, Ross's Gull, Arctic Tern, Northern Hawk Owl, Smith's Longspur. Linked by air and rail (no highway). **Period:** June and July. **Contact:** Churchill Chamber of Commerce, Churchill, Manitoba. **Reference:** *A Birder's Guide to Churchill,* by Bonnie Chartier.

ROCKY MOUNTAIN NATIONAL PARK / PAWNEE NATIONAL GRASSLAND, BOTH IN COLORADO

A geographic package offering alpine and western forest birds (White-tailed Ptarmigan, Brown-capped Rosy Finch, Hammond's Flycatcher, Western Tanager) and prairie species (Mountain Plover,

Chestnut-collared Longspur) as well as a variety of nesting raptors. Fort Collins offers midpoint proximity to both locations (but campers will have a geographic and experiential edge). **Period:** Memorial Day through July. **Contact:** Rocky Mountain National Park and Colorado Bird Observatory. **Reference:** *A Birder's Guide to Colorado,* by Harold Holt.

SOUTHEASTERN ARIZONA
One of North America's most endemic-bird-rich regions; late summer during the monsoon season is typically the best time to view twelve hummingbird species and other species whose nesting range breaches the Mexican border at this point, including Elegant Trogon, Violet-crowned Hummingbird, Sulphur-bellied Flycatcher, Rose-throated Becard, Mexican Chickadee, Olive Warbler, Five-striped Sparrow. **Period:** May through August. **Contact:** Southeastern Arizona Bird Observatory. **Reference:** *A Birder's Guide to Southeastern Arizona,* by Richard Cachor Taylor.

SALTON SEA / SOUTHERN CALIFORNIA
A salty inland sea known for its great number of wintering waterfowl, shorebirds, and water birds as well as the periodic waif from the Sea of Cortez. Southern California is exclusive host to several species, including Yellow-footed Gull and California Gnatcatcher (coastal slopes only). **Period:** November through March. **Contact:** Los Angeles Audubon Society. **Reference:** *A Birder's Guide to Southern California,* by Brad Schram.

MONTEREY, CALIFORNIA
The deepwater currents just off Monterey support a pyramid of life whose visible tip is the millions of seabirds that gather there. Prominent among them are assorted tubenoses (albatross, shearwaters, petrels), alcids, jaegers, and assorted other coastal pelagic species. **Period:** August through September is best for shearwater species; October and November better for storm-petrels. Marine mammals are also part of the marine pyramid. While birds can be seen from shore, the best technique for intercepting great numbers and diversity is to take a day-long boat trip. **Contact:** Shearwater Journeys.

ALASKA

Hardly a hot "spot" (the boundaries encompass 586,000 square miles and span two time zones) but undeniably worth any birder's visit. The birding opportunities are varied and exhaustive. Within any birder's reach is a trip to Denali National Park and Preserve, Chugach State Park, and Homer, backed up with a coastal ferry trip to Kodiak Island and Seward for the bounty of seabirds. Birders can piggyback trips to the Pribilof Islands, Nome, or Gambell (for Asian species that overshoot). **Period:** June through August. **Contact:** Denali National Park. **Reference:** *A Birder's Guide to Alaska,* by George Weeks.

Many of these hot spots host one or more birding festivals during the year, simplifying your travel plans.

WING BAR

The Perfect Fallout

In the perfect birding world, every morning would bring a fallout. Like manna from heaven, a fallout brings songbirds (and other migrants) to earth—not just a few birds, but gobs of birds. Catching a monster fallout, whether it is in New York's Central Park, along the Texas Gulf Coast, or in a favorite birding place near your home, will be unforgettable.

Although birders are basically gamblers, betting on the possibility of a fallout day (and winning big) is not strictly a game of chance. There are several ways to ensure that you will find or be present for a fallout. Most importantly, you have to know where to look. The best places are usually the same places that are known as migrant hot spots or traps. These are also known as migrant stopover sites or places where migrant songbirds can find food or safe places to rest. They are located along coastlines of large bodies of water or in places where there are small islands of suitable habitat. For forest songbirds, these places are patches or strips of forest surrounded by unsuitable habitat, such as water, desert, farm fields, marsh, or urban development.

In cities and suburbs, fallouts occur in parks or forested patches. Some may be only a few acres in size, and sometimes smaller is better. Because habitat that is acceptable for forest birds has been eliminated in these areas, the remnant patches become the only refuges for migrants. When dawn comes, migrants look down on a sea of asphalt and concrete. The small green patches act as magnets. With hundreds or thousands of songbirds descending on a few acres of woodland or brush, the birds become relatively abundant and easy to see.

Along coastlines or rivers, the places to look are forested strips that run parallel to the shoreline. Along the Gulf of Mexico, the forests are thin strips that occupy the first sand dune. In much of the Midwest and the southwestern and western United States, the forests are thin strips along rivers and streambeds surrounded by desert or farmland. Again, these small forests act as magnets to migrants, and songbirds can pack into them in large numbers.

Trying to predict a fallout is more difficult. There are two things that you can do that will increase your odds. First, on the night before you plan to go birding, try watching the moon with your spotting scope. If it's at least one-third visible, focus your scope on it and watch. Start watching about one to three hours after the sun sets and keep watching for fifteen to twenty minutes. It won't take you long to start finding birds if there is a good migration. If you see birds moving through at a rate of one every minute or so, you have a fairly decent migration. This is a prerequisite for a fallout. The birds must be migrating.

You can also hear birds migrating overhead. Listen for the high-pitched call notes of warblers or sparrows, the burry rising or sliding yelp of thrushes, the squawk of herons. This can be a particularly productive way to test the air if, as often happens, clouds are preceding a front.

The second thing you can do to help predict a fallout is watch the television weather report or listen to the weather-band radio. Be attuned to weather that will block migration. A line of thunderstorms or rain that crosses your birding area during the night or before dawn is an obstacle to migrants. More and more birds will "pile up" at the obstacle and, in the morning, will be found in the forests below. In autumn, the rain should be located right over and to the south of you. In spring, cold fronts with accompanying showers impede migrants, as do thunderstorms. As they do when they face rain and frontal boundaries, birds that encounter adverse winds will also land.

Other conditions that create fallouts include strong winds that push birds to a coastline, such as the Atlantic Ocean. In autumn, the northwest and west winds that accompany a cold front in the eastern and southern

United States create fallouts along the coast. A bright, crisp morning a day or so after a cold front passes brings millions of birds to coastal woodlands. During the night, they are confronted by water and so fall out on the last available land. After dawn, many migrants come in off the ocean and drop into the first vegetation they encounter.

Whereas fallouts are great for birders, they are not always good for birds. The large numbers of birds you see dripping from the trees during a fallout is not normal and usually indicates that something has made them land in a particular place. In some cases, fallouts indicate a minor, or major, tragedy. For example, when thunderstorms or northerly winds ground millions of birds along the Gulf of Mexico between Florida and Texas during spring migration, there are many birds that did not make it to shore. The rain or adverse winds literally makes these birds drop into the water. Many die. Those that make it to shore land in phenomenal numbers in the narrow strip of forest that rings the gulf—the first safe landing after flying more than 600 miles without rest.

Fallouts in places like Central Park or in the ribbonlike forests along streams and rivers in the Southwest or Plains states are not as tragic. In fact, they can be good for birds, especially if the habitat provides a safe place in which to rest and eat before taking off again the next night.

Fallouts offer some of the best birding opportunities. They offer lots of birds of many different species. They usually involve migrants that are weary or energy taxed from a storm or a long night's migration. Because of this, they are usually quite easy to see and study. You won't get opportunities to see many of these species as easily as during a fallout. When you catch one, don't squander the opportunity. Use every moment. Finding the right place and being there at the right time is critical for success. Knowing the conditions that make for a fallout can maximize your chances of catching a perfect one. Remember, however, that no matter how much you plan for and learn about the conditions that precipitate fallouts, you will also need some luck. ■

—Paul Kerlinger

Paul Kerlinger, former director of the Cape May Bird Observatory, is a writer/consultant living in New York City whose specialties include birding economics, bird migration, and fly fishing. He is author of How Birds Migrate *and* Flight Strategies of Migrating Hawks.

The Weather Channel's Doppler radar can also be used to detect large bird movements and migratory fallouts. If the radar in the hours leading up to dawn shows patchy green along coastlines and there isn't a cloud in the sky, it is likely that what the radar is picking up is the "bounce" from massed concentrations of birds. In some places, flocks of migrating hawks and birds entering and leaving winter roosts also appear on weather radar.

Other Notable Birding Sites and Spectacles

While the dozen hot spots discussed offer great birding and, taken in sum, the chance to see most of the bird species that regularly occur in North America, there are many other locations that provide great birding, and some that offer up spectacles that are unrivaled. These great bird spectacles might involve one or a handful of species and may occur for only a few short days or weeks. Nevertheless, for those interested in birds, they are worth seeing.

COPPER RIVER DELTA, CORDOVA, ALASKA, FOR SHOREBIRDS

In early May, approximately six million migrating shorebirds (principally Western Sandpiper) gather on the mudflats outside Cordova, drawn to a surfeit of tiny mollusks. An annual festival celebrates the spectacle. Contact: Cordova Chamber of Commerce.

CORPUS CHRISTI, TEXAS, FOR HAWKS

From mid-September through October, hundreds of thousands of birds of prey migrate past Corpus Christi and the hawk-watch located at Hazel Bazemore Park. Ninety percent of this flight passes between September 25 and October 4. Twenty-two species of raptor can be seen. Contact: Corpus Christi Convention and Visitors Bureau.

DELAWARE BAY, NEW JERSEY, FOR SHOREBIRDS

From May 10 through June 5, more than half a million Red Knots, Ruddy Turnstones, Sanderlings, and Semipalmated Sandpipers gather on the shores of the Delaware Bay to feast on a bounty of horseshoe-crab eggs. Contact: Cape May Bird Observatory.

This hardly looks like a birding hot spot, but winter gull watching at Niagara Falls is a hallowed tradition and productive way to study this challenging bird group.

NIAGARA FALLS, NEW YORK, FOR GULLS

When winter closes over the north, the open waters below the falls attract thousands of gulls of many species and in a range of age classes and plumages.

PLATTE RIVER, NEBRASKA, FOR CRANES

In March, the Platte River is a major staging area for hundreds of thousands of migrating Sandhill Cranes. Contact: Hall County Visitor's Bureau.

WING BAR

Little-Known North American Birding Hot Spots

Birders are creatures of habit. When going on birding trips out of town we tend to go to the same places that most other birders have visited. That makes sense much of the time: Most of these places do indeed provide some of the best birding experiences possible. We also visit these places time and time again because many of them are written up in the popular bird-finding guides, valuable books that tell you exactly how many miles to go down a certain road to see certain species. But too many birders rely too heavily on these books. It is also important to be able to recognize habitats, microhabitats, habitat limits and outposts, and what makes a good migrant and vagrant trap. Armed with such knowledge birders can discover other extremely worthwhile destinations. There are many excellent birding areas that remain unappreciated and which observers have largely ignored.

The following are my top choices for the best "little-known" birding sites and regions in North America.

Atlantic Provinces of Canada

OK, OK, I know this is hardly a single birding location. But what I want to emphasize is the incredible potential and track record that various islands and peninsulas in Newfoundland, New Brunswick, and Nova Scotia have in spring and especially fall for turning out good numbers of migrants and oddball vagrants from the West and South and even Europe. Places like St. John's and the Avalon Peninsula; Miscou and Grand Manan Islands; and Brier, Cape Sable, and Seal Islands and the Halifax/Dartmouth area. In addition, beautiful Prince Edward Island just gets no respect. (Also, add Monhegan Island, to the south, in Maine, to this list).

Bluff Point, Connecticut; Cape Charles, Virginia; the Outer Banks, North Carolina

The Cape May area richly deserves its well-known reputation as an autumn migratory hotspot. Other, lesser-known sites along the East Coast include Bluff Point and Cape Charles, where one can witness a similar sort of early-morning rush of hundreds or perhaps thousands of land-bird migrants (mostly warblers) as that seen in Cape May. The Outer Banks are fairly well known for water birds and offshore pelagics, but the migrant passerine potential there in fall has never been fully tapped.

Great Lakes Peninsulas

As a spring migration hot spot for migrant land birds, Point Pelee, Ontario, is well known . . . perhaps too well known, as crowding in May has become a problem there for many birders. But what is not well known is that Pelee is also very good for fall migrants in late August and early September. Elsewhere around the Great Lakes there are several excellent spring or fall migrant traps. Whitefish Point on Michigan's Upper Peninsula is well known, as is Minnesota's Duluth area. But Crane Creek State Park in Ohio was, for many years, a sleeping giant (during the past few years, however, it too has become fairly crowded during peak periods in May). Tawas Point State Park, along Michigan's Saginaw Bay, Lake Huron, is a rising star.

The Gulf Coast East of Texas

Most everyone has heard about the splendid migrant trap at High Island, which in April may be inundated with trans-Gulf migrants, and birders. Dauphin Island is also well-known. But equally good as these areas are the Cameron Parish area of southwestern Louisiana (Holleyman-Sheely Migratory Bird Sanctuary is a convenient public-access destination to visit) and Fort Morgan, in Alabama, just to the east of Dauphin. And how many folks actually give High Island a visit later in the spring—in May—or during the fall?

New Mexico

Yes, yes, just like my Canadian Maritime choice, this one is a bit broad. But New Mexico is clearly one of the best, most underbirded states in the Union. The southwest corner (near Silver City) supports many, but not all, of the same Mexican specialties found in adjacent southeastern Arizona. The water-birding at places such as the Bosque del Apache and Bitter Lake National Wildlife Refuges is excellent; Rattlesnake Springs Preserve, near Carlsbad Carverns National Park, is a great migrant oasis; and there are water- and land-bird traps scattered throughout the state's arid west and eastern plains. The northern mountains are pretty good, too.

White Mountains, Arizona

Only a few hours' drive north of the fabled canyons of southeastern Arizona lie the higher, moister, conifer-covered White Mountains. This beautiful region supports a number of breeding resident species with affinities closer to those of the Rocky Mountains, including Three-toed Woodpecker, Gray Jay, American Dipper, and Pine Grosbeak. Next time you visit the Sky Islands southeast of Tucson in summer, give the Whites a try as well.

Great Basin Oases

Far from almost any major population center, this is an area rich in water- and land-bird migrants and out-of-range vagrants. It's an arid region pock-marked with isolated stands of deciduous trees, such as willows, poplars, and cottonwoods, that are found in small towns, along streams, and at ranch yards. Isolated lakes and reservoirs beckon over-flying water birds. These oases draw in large numbers of migrant flycatchers, thrushes, vireos, warblers, tanagers, grosbeaks, buntings, and sparrows, and some interest-ing breeding species.

Some of the best sites are in Nevada (Corn Creek "Oasis" at the Desert National Wildlife Refuge headquarters, north of Las Vegas; a roadside rest-stop just west of Tonopah; and Stillwater National Wildlife Refuge and the Carson Lake Wetlands, east of Reno), northern Arizona (Pipe Spring National Monument, Page, and Ganado), western Utah (Beaver Dam Wash and Fish Springs National Wildife Refuge), and southeastern Oregon (the Malheur National Wildlife Refuge headquarters). ■

—Paul Lehman

Paul Lehman is a tour leader for WINGS, consultant, former editor of Birding *magazine, and a student of North American bird distribution and identification. He divides his time between San Diego California; Gambell, Alaska; and the rest of North America.*

No Shortage of Places, No Shortage of Guides

These locations represent just the tip of the iceberg. Virtually every state and province has a surfeit of well-known and not-so-well-known birding spots. More importantly, most states and provinces have one or more printed bird-finding guides to help you find these locations.

Most guides are independently written and published, although a number are part of the very excellent Birdfinding Guide series published by the American Birding Association. Allowing for artistic license, all guides offer (at least) directions, maps, descriptions, and tips for selected birding sites. Many bird-finding guides provide information relating to the geology and human history of the target area as well as information about other aspects of natural history.

Guides tailored to your region may often be found in general bookstores as well as nature and visitor center shops. Travelers targeting a birding destination who want to plot their trip around information in a guide can order books online.

The World at Your Fingertips

Being fortunate to live in a bird-rich continent, North American birders can easily overlook (for a time) the fact that while there are about 800 species of birds that regularly occur in North America, there are about 10,000 species found on Earth. With the exception of the South Pole, there are few locations on the planet were birds do not regularly occur. There are many countries, particularly those near the diversity-rich equatorial region, that host more than twice the number of bird species found in North America.

Unfortunately, not all these bird-rich areas are field-guide rich. In fact, some countries celebrated for their bird diversity are still without a basic field guide.

Nevertheless, many field guides and even bird-finding guides do exist for such celebrated locations as Kenya, Costa Rica, Peru, Africa, Australia, Papua New Guinea . . . and new guides that will fill key geographic gaps are in the works.

Those interested in visiting countries in Northern Europe (which have a long birding tradition) will find many excellent field guides and no shortage of exceptional birders.

But No Matter Where You Go . . .

There you are, engaged by birds that beg to be savored. Travel is a means to greater discovery, greater skills, and greater awareness. But never forget that challenge and discovery lie no farther than your own yard. Birds whose plumage makes them look one way at one time of year can look like an entirely different species after a molt from alternate to basic plumage (American Goldfinch, for example) or from juvenile to adult plumage.

Some birds, such as gulls, go through three or four different plumages on their way to full adulthood plumage, and many species viewed during the process of molting can look like nothing you will find in a basic field guide.

Which explains why there are very focused guides that specialize on species groups. And why birders can spend their entire lives perfecting their field identification skills and never stray far from home.

If you aren't careful, the birding trail might lead you to the very ends of the earth. Bylot Island, in Arctic Canada, is not quite the end, but you can see it from there without a spotting scope. LINDA DUNNE

That scope will be useful in spotting an Ivory Gull, a rare Arctic specialty.

Mastering Difficult Identifications

If bird identification were easy, we could master the challenge in short order—and then go on and try to find something else to engage our minds and our lives. Relax. Bird identification is not so simple. No matter how adept you become, there will always be identification challenges that test the limits of your abilities, or a tantalizing possibility that flies just beyond the reach of your present skills.

The very finest field birders on the planet encounter birds that defy identification, and these are the ones they love most . . . because these are the encounters from which they stand to gain the most insight.

No Shortcuts

The only way to become a better birder is to go birding with the objective of discovering new things and improving your present skills. It takes time. It takes study. It takes focus. It takes a lifetime. Enjoy it!

When you see a bird you cannot identify, *study it.* Apply the basic skills of birding. Earn the privilege of its name.

When you see a bird that you can identify, *study it even more closely.* The best way to recognize an uncommon species is to become intimate with the ones you see all the time.

Whenever the opportunity for study presents itself—a seasonal gathering of shorebirds, two very similar waterfowl species wintering together (Greater and Lesser Scaup, for example)—don't hurry off. Use the time for study. Note the differences that distinguish species while they are manifest and bank them for that more challenging encounter that is bound to occur sometime in the future.

TALE SPOT

Shorebird Summer

In 1977 I was a good hawk watcher and a fair birder but a failure when it came to identifying shorebirds. Oh, I had a handle on most of the species in the medium-sized category. Pear-shaped, long-billed, and feeding like a sewing machine: Dowitcher (not so plump and not so long-billed but longer-legged). Yellowlegs (Greater or Lesser). But that was about the extent of my knowledge.

All those peeps—the small sandpipers. All those different plumages. All those molting birds. It was a veritable avian chimera! But it was also July, prime time for southbound shorebirds in New Jersey, and I'd made up my mind to learn 'em or die—which might have been the end of this story had it not been a dry summer, and had Bunker Pond in Cape May Point State Park not been reduced to mudflats and shallows: perfect habitat for shorebirds. Visitor traffic was constant, another plus. The birds had become habituated to people, allowing long-term viewing at very close range.

So every lunch hour for several weeks I staked myself out at the edge of the pond—butt plastered to the sand, eye fused to the eyepiece of my spotting scope—studying the feeding masses. At first it was all I could do to distinguish those elemental field marks that are the foundation of field guide ID.

Little with yellow legs—Least Sandpiper. Little with black legs—Semipalmated Sandpiper. But in time I began to note more subtle distinctions. Like how Least Sandpipers were overall browner and liked to keep their feet on the mud, even on dry land. Like how Semipalmateds were grayer backed and generally stayed in the water, or at least the wetter mud. Like how dowitchers probed but yellowlegs stabbed. Like how . . .

"This sandpiper has a bill that's drooped like a Least, but the legs are black like a Semipalmated. In fact, it looks like a Semi except for the long, drooping bill—like Western Sandpiper is supposed to have. But if it's Western then shouldn't it have red feathers on its shoulder?"

And it did! Just one or two that hadn't molted out yet. I would have missed them before, and never seen them at all without a spotting scope.

After a while I got to the point where I could accept the normal range of variation between birds of a species. I even reached a point where I could recognize individual birds in a flock.

So when my life Stilt Sandpiper arrived—a very worn adult that showed only a trace of barring on the underparts—I realized, quickly, that it was too lean to be a dowitcher, not lanky enough to be a Lesser Yellowlegs, and that it had to be . . .

"So what are you seeing?" a voice inquired. The voice belonged to one of Cape May's very experienced birders, a man whose skills I admired. I'd been so intent on my study I hadn't realized he'd joined me.

"Stilt Sandpiper," I said proudly.

"I didn't see any Stilt Sandpiper out there," he said flatly. "Where?"

"In with that group of dowitchers," I said, more pleased with one-upping one of the elders than anxious about my identification—although anxiety would have been justified.

"That's not a Stilt," he said. "That's Lesser Yellowlegs."

Stunned, I studied the bird again. Tried to superimpose the image of a yellowlegs over what I was seeing—but the name and the shape wouldn't match.

"But look at the curve on the bill," I insisted, pointing out the single mark that most easily distinguishes Stilts from Lesser Yellowlegs. Look at that barring." The bird was up to its belly in water. The legs, which would have been greenish, not yellow, could not be seen.

"No, that's a yellowlegs," he repeated, firmly. And then another birder showed up, who, after study and a short debate, sided with the more experienced birder.

I still believed I was right. A couple of days earlier, I might have been confused, might have second-guessed my identification—but not now. In the past couple weeks, I'd gained more than just a solid grounding in shorebird identification, I'd gained a measure of confidence, too.

No, I wasn't confused. But I was a disappointed that I'd managed to find a "good" bird all by myself and couldn't share the excitement.

There wasn't any reason to make an issue of our differing opinions. Besides, lunch hour was up. I said my good-byes, wishing both birders good luck, and left the veteran to his study. The man was a careful observer, which is why his skills and reputation were so good.

The next day, I returned to the pond for another lesson in shorebird ID and was surprised (no, let's be honest, dismayed) to find the elder birder there ahead of me. Mumbling a greeting, I plopped down and buried myself in the task at hand.

"Your Stilt Sandpiper is still here," he said with an offhandedness that could not mask the significance of this admission.

Birds often don't play fair. This adult Stilt Sandpiper transitioning into basic plumage might be mistaken for a yellowlegs because its legs are not visible. Or maybe it's a dowitcher . . . except the bill seems a bit too short. And do I see traces of fine barring on the sides?

"That's good," I said reflexively (and not inaccurately). "Where?" I invited, letting him guide me to the bird.

Twenty-one years later, I don't mind saying that whenever I think back to that moment it still feels good. Not because I was right. And certainly not because he was wrong. But because an identification problem tough enough to stump an elder had come my way, and I had mastered it.

So, in time, will you. ■

Specialty Books for Specialty Birding

There are scores of specialized field guides, books that offer the best information available relating to the identification of different bird groups. So narrow a focus allows an attention to detail that would be impossible to house in a general field guide. Some of these guides describe plumages, in age classes and between closely allied species, right down to individual feathers.

But for some species, that is the level where the line gets drawn between species—and between a correct identification and a wrong one.

Very few birders become as intimate with these guides as they might with their basic field guide, but they are invaluable resources and reference tools. Something to turn to when a tricky identification hangs in the balance. Something to study to brush up on key marks before going into the field.

While there is no upper limit to the number of specialty guides that a birder needs, for those who take birding seriously, there is a lower one. Here is a list of specialty guides that over most of North America are most useful and most frequently used, and most definitely deserve a place in your birding library.

Kaufman Field Guide to Advanced Birding, by Kenn Kaufman. An exceptional utilitarian and easy-to-read guide that groups similar species and explains how to distinguish one from the next.

Ducks, Geese, and Swans of North America, by Guy Baldassarre. The newly updated revision of the classic work written by Francis Kortright, later revised by Frank Belrose.

Hawks of North America, by William Clark and Brian Wheeler. Part of the Peterson Field Guides series, this book covers North American Birds of Prey with an emphasis upon plumage. Also recommended by these authors: *A Photographic Guide to North American Raptors.*

Hawks in Flight, Second Edition, by Pete Dunne, David Sibley, and Clay Sutton. Differs from *Hawks of North America* by placing emphasis upon North America's migratory birds of prey and identifications based on shape and manner of flight.

Hawks from Every Angle, by Jerry Liguori. Represents the masterwork of North America's premier hawk watcher and a boon to all incipient hawk watchers. Also by this author (or in conjunction with): *Hawks at a Distance* and *The Crossley ID Guide: Raptors* (with Richard Crossley).

Petrels, Albatrosses, and Storm-Petrels of North America, by Steve Howell. Written by the noted authority on the identification of oceanic birds. Accurate and dependable in its depictions and descriptions. A benchmark book, as is, by the same author, *Molt in North American Birds,* a Peterson Reference Guide.

The Shorebird Guide, by Michael O'Brien, Richard Crossley, and Kevin Karlson. A simple, thorough, user-friendly treatment of a notoriously challenging, popular, and widespread bird group.

The Warbler Guide, by Tom Stephenson and Scott Whittle.

Waterfowl, by Steven Madge and Hilary Burn. Covering a group of birds notorious for extralimital excursions, the book is thorough in its treatment.

Other Resources Birders Cannot Live Without

Birds are more than an identification challenge. They are animate creatures. Knowing more about them makes them more real and more alive. There are many books that delve into the natural history of birds, some extensively. Here is a basic sampling of books that will broaden your awareness and pleasure.

The Birdwatcher's Companion, by Christopher Leahy. Subtitled "An Encyclopedic Handbook of North American Birdlife," the book is a handy reference for terms and topics that map the world of birds and birding.

Birds of North America. Initially a printed biological treatment covering all of North America's breeding birds. Now available online. Don't second-guess this: You need access to *BNA.* Order it now.

The Birder's Handbook, by Paul R. Ehrlich, David Dobkin, and Darryl Wheye. A species-by-species natural history synopsis of North American birds interspersed with sidebar insights that focus upon the biology and behavior of birds.

Lives of North American Birds, by Kenn Kaufman. A companion reader to both the Peterson Guide and the Kaufman Guide, and every other general field guide.

Ornithology, by Frank B. Gill. Birding is not so removed from the parent ornithology that birders can avoid a fundamental understanding of birds, what they do and why. This text, written by an eminent ornithologist (and birder), is lucid and thorough.

And in the self-serving category: I am pleased to direct your attention to *Pete Dunne's Essential Field Guide Companion,* a supplemental field guide whose focus is the behavioral hints and clues that basic field guides don't have room for.

SUMMARY

Once birders have mastered the basics they can expand their horizons—reaching for birds that are more challenging to identify, farther away, or not even visible at all— distinguishable by vocalizations alone. Spotting scopes, specialized field guides, and birdsong recordings are tools that facilitate the learning process.

Horizons are geographical, too. Distant locations offer new and unfamiliar species. There are dozens of celebrated birding hot spots in North America, and many more throughout the world. Most North American locations are described in bird-finding guides that offer detailed instructions for birding key areas. Most of the popular birding locations on the planet have at least one field guide that is specific to that country or region and its birds. ■

Tips to Better Birding

At Birding's Horizon Line (Standing with Will)

We were standing, silent as pillars carved from shadow. We being me and my World Series of Birding teammates—Pete Bacinski, Don Freiday, and Will Russell, director of WINGS, one of North America's finest bird-tour companies.

Around us was the midnight-darkened Vernon wetlands. Before us, 24 hours of limit-pushing birding. Above us, a sky filled with stars, clouds . . . and the nocturnal flight calls of migrating birds.

"Lincoln's Sparrow," said the shadow who was Will, putting a name to a single-note utterance whose source was somewhere overhead.

"If you say so," I said (but only in my mind). All of us had heard the sound. Only Will was skilled enough to identify it.

"Black-billed Cuckoo," he said a moment later.

"Got it," the three of us chanted—the nocturnal flight call of Black-billed Cuckoo has a quality that is reminiscent of the bird's more commonly heard daytime vocalization (a sound all of us were familiar with).

But in the next minute Will's audio identification skills out-stripped our abilities again.

"Ovenbird," he said to the stars, pinning a name to a disembod-ied call note.

Will Russell is on everyone's short list for finest field birder in North America, and among a handful who are pushing the limits of birding's horizons by exploring the frontiers of sound. When asked about his birding skills, he answers, simply, "I work at it."

At one time, the audio-frontier line was drawn by birds singing rings around their territories. Birders struggled to decipher the myriad sounds, but in time, ears and minds learned to distinguish this species from that.

Then the frontier moved on to single-note utterances (because most birds don't sing most of the year, and every new generation needs new challenges). Limit-pushing birders listened to chips and call notes that left the beaks of birds and lodged them in their minds.

Now the frontier has moved again, beyond the safety net of sight to the nocturnal flight calls of migrating birds. Today's pio-neers spend hours listening to and recording the flood of sounds, and then more hours in sound laboratories decoding the disem-bodied noises, linking them by deduction and compounded skill to the birds that made them.

Will stands among them—at birding's high-water mark. But it's a big beachhead. And not all of it has been mapped, or even explored.

Birding is a lifelong adventure, and one of its components involves the sharpening of skills—as a means to finding more birds, as an objective that continually challenges us. There are no shortcuts to proficiency, just as there is no danger of mastering all there is to learn about birds and birding.

The horizon is not fixed. It moves all the time. This is not to say there are not techniques widely used by birders that will speed less-experienced birders down the road to greater proficiency (and maybe help avoid some bumps along the way).

The balance of this chapter will expound upon some of these tricks. To save you frustration, to increase the pleasure of birding . . . To help you find more birds and get to birding's frontier faster. Your talents are needed there.

Tips for Equipment

Protecting Binoculars When It's Wet

Inclement weather doesn't send birds indoors—and if you are prepared, it won't send you there either. Some of the best birding occurs in rainy conditions (for reasons that will be explained later in this chapter) but some of the toughest birding, too.

Optical performance in particular is quickly compromised by rain—another way of saying that when your binoculars get wet, all you'll see is a blur. One of the easiest ways to keep rain off the ocular lens is by attaching a commercial rain guard—a loose-fitting cap made of plastic or hard rubber that attaches to the binocular strap and can be seated over the ocular lenses as needed.

Note: Some rain guards supplied by binocular manufacturers are too tight to slip on and off easily, some so poorly designed that they will not fit over the lenses when the eyecups are rolled down. Rain guards aren't like car parts. They aren't necessarily specific to one binocular. Sometimes guards made by other companies for other instruments will serve you better.

Or you can make your own: Take a piece of chamois cloth (approximately 5 by 5 inches, or large enough to drape over the ocular lenses). Make two slits spaced to fit the two ends of your binocular strap. Sleeve the straps through the slits.

If you don't have a rain guard—or don't care to be bothered with one—you can help keep water droplets off lenses by wearing binoculars bandolier fashion, beneath an arm, where they will be better protected from the elements. Or you can hold your hand over the eyecups to shield them from rain.

Do not press your hands over the eyecups, sealing them, however. In cold weather the moisture from your hand will condense on the outside of the lenses, fogging them. Leave a gap for ventilation and your lens shouldn't fog.

Slipping binoculars inside a loose-fitting rain jacket (Napoleon Bonaparte fashion) is also common practice.

Once raised to the eyes, objective lenses are also vulnerable to rain. The best defense is to buy binoculars with objective lenses that are slightly recessed so that rain falling sideways won't hit the glass.

Objective lens rain guards can also be made of 3- or 4-inch PVC pipe with a diameter just wide enough to sleeve over the barrel. When dry, the tubes encircle the barrels; when it rains, the tubes can be drawn out, telescope fashion, offering objective lenses 2 to 4 inches of shielded protection.

Shifting your grip forward, grasping the binoculars so that hands shield the objective lens, will give you short-lived protection—perhaps enough to get a glimpse of a fast-receding bird whose suspected identification is good enough to prompt you to withdraw your optics from the protective confines of your jacket.

One last thought: If your ocular lenses have water droplets on them, you can still see your target—it will just be pocked by dark dots. A quick swipe with a cleaning cloth will probably only smear the lens, making it impossible to see anything. When wiping the rain drops off your lens make sure you have time and a dry enough cloth to do a thorough job—otherwise just tolerate the raindrops; peer through them.

What to Do When It's Cold

Winter temperatures are tough on optics, and this means frustration for birders. And temperatures don't even have to fall below freezing before problems occur.

One of the most common problems is fogging of the external lenses of binoculars. This situation sometimes occurs when non-eyeglass-wearing birders bring cold optics up to their eyes for a prolonged scan. In cold temperatures, moisture transpires from the eyes and condenses on the lens.

To prevent this hold your eyecups slightly away from your eye sockets, perhaps resting just the top of the eyecups on your eyebrows, leaving the remainder of the eyecup rim open and ventilated. Keep this technique in mind if you're considering buying binoculars that have flared eyecups designed to block peripheral light. They do block the light—but they block ventilation, too. Another way ocular lenses become fogged is when you breathe on them. There are two ways to prevent this. First, use your rain guard. A second option is to lengthen your binocular strap—the more distance between your exhaled breath and the lens, the less fogging you will encounter.

The fogging that is the hardest to combat occurs when binoculars are carried from the cold into a warm car. For immediate relief, try carrying a chamois cloth or clean cotton handkerchief, something to wipe the lenses. Or try placing the binoculars on the dashboard, over the defroster, and turning the heater and air-conditioner on simultaneously. Not only will you get moisture-dissipating heat, you will get dry heat.

This technique can also be used to temporarily "cook" moisture out of rain-soaked binoculars if the fogging is internal.

The most drastic, and most effective, way of keeping your binoculars from fogging when you get into a warm car is don't. (i.e., don't warm the car). Keep your heat off and the windows open. You might not be comfortable, but at least your lenses won't fog.

What to Do When the Bird's Too Close

There may be nothing more frustrating than having a bird so near at hand that you cannot adjust your focus close enough to see it clearly. Under normal circumstances, at distances under 20 feet, familiar or distinctly marked birds can be identified without binoculars.

But what about in rainy conditions? Or twilight conditions? Or in deep woodlands that cast a shadow over detail? What about birds that are partially obscured by leaves and grass—showing you only a wing, a cheek, or part of a breast? If only you could get your binoculars to focus 2 or 3 feet closer, you could see these disjunct parts and piece an identification together.

Well, sometimes you *can* cut 2 or 3 feet off the minimum focus of your instrument. How? By using the individual eyepiece

adjustment and turning your binocular into a temporary super-close-focusing monocular.
Step 1: Focus as close as possible using the center focus wheel.
Step 2: Close one eye and peer through the barrel controlled by the individual eyepiece adjustment ring or wheel. *Step 3:* Turn the ring to focus down on the bird. Depending on make or model you can usually gain 2 or 3 feet of focus distance—and sometimes this is close enough to see the detail you need. Just don't forget to return the diopter to its proper setting.

Binoculars in the Hands Merit a Bird in the Bush

Less experienced birders in the company of very accomplished birders are often astonished at the rapidity with which experienced hands bring their binoculars to bear.

Yes, it's a practiced reflex. Yes, it may be linked to youthful reflexes and eyes unhindered by age. But often the reactive time gap between newer and more experienced birders is a matter of anticipation and preparedness. What experienced birders know that beginners often don't is *where* and *when* a bird is likely to appear—insight that allows preparation for a split-second reaction.

The ability to read a habitat is something that birders gain with experience. Sorry, no shortcuts here. But beginners can do two things to help cut down their reaction times. Both relate to how binoculars are handled.

First, when approaching an area that looks promising—the edge of a marsh where shorebirds teem, or a surefire woodland pocket that always holds a migrating warbler or two—hold your binoculars with one or both hands wrapped around the barrels, ready to bring lenses to your eyes the instant you see movement. By eliminating the need to reach for your binoculars and then bring them to bear, you can cut your reaction time in half.

Here's another trick: When approaching your chosen vantage point (some point short of flush distance) prefocus your binoculars to fall within the anticipated range. You don't need to bring them to your eyes to do this. Just move the wheel all the way to the closest focus setting and then focus back to a distance that approximates the anticipated range.

Your estimated point of focus need not be perfect. You may have to make minor adjustments once your binoculars are brought to bear. But prefocusing sure beats having to go through the entire range of a binocular's focus in order to get a clear image (with some binocular models this is a matter of making multiple revolutions of a focus wheel). When split seconds count, time spent spinning your wheel is time you can't afford.

Meet Them at the Landing Zone

Getting binocular views of flushed birds in flight is an art, one that requires practice and binoculars with field of view and depth of field suited to the task. These attributes do not define many instruments (including, maybe particularly, many fine 10x instruments).

Rather than pushing your (or your binoculars') limits, here's another way to catch sight of a bird you've flushed. Try guessing where the bird is going to land and be prepared to bring your binoculars to bear on this point when it does.

This is not as improbable as it sounds. You see the bird so you know where it's heading. You can fairly guess that if the bird is aiming for a prominent bush or stalk or wire or sign in an open landscape, that is where it's planning to land.

Even if the bird is heading for a wall of trees or a hedgerow, anticipate that the bird is going to take some prominent perch in the open. If the bird disappears into the foliage, you lose. But if the bird momentarily lands in the open to see who the intruder is and you aren't prepared, you really lose.

Vibration Kills

Wind is the mortal enemy of all spotting scope users. It makes tripods vibrate, scopes dance, and image quality go all to hell. Heavy tripods are better at bucking the wind than light tripods, but no portable tripod is vibration free.

There are a few things that scope users can do to reduce wind-induced vibration, however. Placing a hand (or a couple of fingers) on the scope and pressing down will marginally and temporarily improve image quality.

Retracting the tripod legs (the mechanical equivalent of trimming sail) will also help. The shortened scope can be placed on the hood of a car (which will add elevation, and at 2,000 pounds, is more stable than a 5-pound tripod). Or in very windy conditions, the scope can be set close to the ground and used from a sitting position. If a car is handy, use it as a windbreak.

Tips to Better Technique

Working the Crowd

Birds, as you already know, or will soon discover, are not always perched where they can be seen. Beginning birders confronted by some skulking songbird have two choices. *One:* Approach for a better vantage (and risk flushing the bird). *Two:* Wait and hope the bird will eventually show.

But there is a third alternative that can often be used to good effect. It involves mimicking the alarm or scolding calls of birds in an effort to draw them closer, or into the open. This response is called mobbing. The technique, "pishing."

Pishing isn't foolproof, and it is not universally applicable (many European birds, for example, respond not at all). But over much of North America, done properly, pishing will give birders an attractive advantage. Sometimes the results can be spectacular. Birds from over a hundred yards may be drawn in, sometimes to within arm's reach.

First, realize that pishing (by which I mean all manners of onomatopoeic squeaks, squeals, *shhhh*es, and stuttering slur*sss*) doesn't have to whip all birds within earshot into a mobbing frenzy. All pishing needs do is incite one or two easily piqued species (chickadees, titmice, and nuthatches in particular are notoriously pish prone). It is their excitement and scolding vocalizations that draw a crowd of more reticent species. (I actually have a whole book in print dedicated to this useful but arcane art, complete with a tutorial CD: *The Art of Pishing,* published by Stackpole Books.)

Different birders have different pishing techniques. My own standard repertoire is a three-part ensemble composed of (1) a

Chickadees are most notoriously prone to respond to pishing.

standard "pish" sequence, (2) a predator imitation, and (3) a squeal call.

The basic pish sequence sounds like a cross between the *psh, psh, psh* Aunt Mable uses to call her cat and the scolding utterances of an apoplectic titmouse. Phonetically rendered, it's *PursssEEE, PursssEEE, PursssEEE; PursssEEE, PursssEEE, PursssEEE,* and it's usually given in a series of three. The best way to get a sense of what you are trying to sound like is to pay attention to the scold call of a titmouse, then mimic it.

The pish sequence (continued for 20 seconds or so) puts birds on notice that there is something rotten in bird-dom—an intruder, maybe a predator. To reinforce this idea, follow the pish sequence with a predator imitation (Eastern Screech-Owl, Barred Owl, Northern Pygmy-Owl, Northern Saw-whet—whatever species is common to the area).

Then I play my trump card. I cut loose with a long, plaintive squeal call, the sort of sound a starling might make to protest the inopportune embrace of a Cooper's Hawk.

The squeal call is produced by placing the middle and index finger to your lips and producing a loud, prolonged (held for one to three seconds), high-pitched kissing sound. The noise is made by drawing air through tightly compressed lips. The fingers create a resonating chamber.

Done properly, the squeal call will almost pull the fillings out of your teeth—and attract birds the way accident scenes attract onlookers. Once you have incited a mobbing action, you can keep excitement levels high by repeating the sequence, or mix up the order to suit.

I have, over the course of many years, used this sequence (or elements of it) to draw all manner of birds into the open, including such notoriously reticent species as Sedge Wren, LeConte's Sparrow, and Connecticut Warbler.

I have also lured a dozen foxes, three weasels, two mink, two bobcats, one skunk, innumerable horses, cows, pigs, one duck hunter, and one very perplexed bunch of British birders on the Isles of Scilly.

Pishing is not by any means guaranteed to draw birds to your side. In fact, there are times when a bout of spirited pishing will have the opposite effect—as the late Dr. Harold Axtell once observed, "Pishing will do one of three things: It will attract birds, scare them away, or do nothing." There are things you can do to increase your chances of success. If you are trying to lure woodland species, it is better to step beneath the canopy than try to lure birds into an open field. Birds might be gullible, but they are also bound to habitat.

It also pays to be persistent. Once you incite a mob, give it five minutes to draw the attention of less pish-prone species.

Finally, with regards to pishing, several cautionary notes. First, pishing is intrusive. Don't overdo it, and consider not doing it at all in very heavily birded areas. Pishing not only intrudes upon the lives of birds, it intrudes upon the aesthetic threshold of fellow birders.

Second, there are times when pishing should be avoided altogether—such as during nesting season, at dawn, and on cold winter mornings. The energy reserves of birds may be sorely depleted after a cold night. Offer half-hardy species a chance to feed before tweaking them. If you draw energy-depleted birds into the open, you may be pushing them past their limits, and you are most certainly inviting their demise at the talons of some bird-eating hawk (which, incidentally, also responds to pishing). *Be responsible.* When birds begin to lose interest, or when you've gotten the look you need, stop.

Final warning: Do not under any circumstances pish in places where visibility is poor and large predators such as Grizzly Bears are found. Be warned, and be mindful.

Sometimes Just a Little Chip Will Do

Pishing is not universally effective. Many birds will sooner freeze or flee than approach, including many sparrow species. For sparrows and other pish-proof species, try imitating a "chip" note—a single, sharp, call note that can bring even the most reticent sparrows to attention.

To produce this sound, press the middle and pointer fingers to your lips and give them a short, sweet, loud, high-pitched kiss. As with the squeal, the fingers serve as a resonating chamber. Done properly, the chip should sound like a stone skipped on ice.

Timing and position are key. Best results are had by walking up to a sparrow-ish looking spot (best identified when a group of feeding birds abruptly flushes into the brush). Stop where you are. Wait 30 seconds or so for the birds to calm down. Then bring your fingers to your lips and *chip.*

One chip is usually all it takes to get skulking sparrows to pop for perches—the vantage they need to see what the problem is. Periodic irregular chips may keep birds in view for a short time (but sparrows have very short attention spans).

The chip note, done in sequence at one-second intervals, will also draw warblers into view. It also seems very effective at rebooting a mobbing action after birds lose interest in pishing.

But once again, don't overdo it. Remember that birds have their own lives to live. You are just an observer.

Knockdown Pish

How many times have you seen a small passerine zip by, just overhead, flying too fast to bring binoculars to bear? Haven't you wished there were some way to get it to land on a handy perch, where you'd have a fighting chance?

Well, there is. You can often get passing birds to land by making an alarm call: a single, emphatic *PSEWSH* (a truncated pish) or a two-note *PSEW-PSEW*. This is bird Esperanto for "look out!" Rather than be the only obvious target in an open sky, flying birds will often take evasive action, dropping like a sinker to get out of harm's way. Sometimes after an evasive dive the bird continues on its way. But often they take an open perch to investigate.

If the bird continues on, you are no worse off. If it falls for your trick and perches, so much the better.

Talking Owl

Despite a range limited to the eastern half of North America, the Eastern Screech-owl, with its distinctive whinny call, seems to pique birds all over North America. You can imitate this call all by itself, or as part of a pishing sequence, to incite a mobbing reaction—so long as (A) you can whistle and (B) you are not dissuaded by what you are about to read.

Screech-owls have two classic vocalizations: a tremolo, the characteristic communication call; and a descending whinny, a defensive territorial call. To make either call, first listen to a recording of a screech-owl. Know what you are trying to imitate before you attempt it.

Next, work up a gob of saliva (the more viscous the better). Locate it on the middle/back of your tongue. Tilt your head back slightly. Elevate your tongue toward the roof of your mouth. Whistle. The force of the whistle passing over and through the saliva sets up a mini-wave action that breaks up the whistle, causing it to warble. Yes, the description is disgusting, but that's how you do it. The tremolo is simply a matter of keeping the whistle's pitch low and even. The whinny requires changing the whistle's pitch.

If creating a passable screech-owl call is beyond you, you can try substituting the call of a saw-whet owl (in the East) or Northern Pygmy-Owl (in the West). Both are short, regular, whistled toots. Saw-whets use single notes; pygmy-owls often double them.

The Power of Pause

More than to sound, more than to color, birds react to motion. Under many circumstances, a cautious or stationary observer is more likely to see birds and get better looks than a carelessly mobile one.

People who maintain window feeders know this to be true. Sit quietly and birds ignore your presence. Rise to leave or make a sudden motion, and birds flee. The difference between feeding stations and field situations is that birders rarely see the birds that flush as they advance. The reaction time of birds is so much faster than our own that all birders see is an empty trail where seconds earlier there were birds.

If mobile is your nature, try pausing for a minute (or two or three) whenever you turn a corner. Give flushed birds a chance to return to normal behavior patterns.

Better yet: Pinpoint locations that habitually hold birds—sunny woodland edges on cool mornings, bottlenecks or junctions between adjacent woodlots, water sources on hot afternoons, brushy borders that always hold sparrows. Walk quietly to that spot. Make yourself comfortable. Watch the show.

Bring a blanket, a chair, a folding stool. Bring lunch and a beverage. Not only will birds quickly acclimate to your presence, their subtle movements will not be masked by your own. It is far easier to detect movement in vegetation when your own activity isn't obscuring it.

If you use the power of pause, you'll increase the number of birds you see in the field. (Only the doctor who prescribed more exercise might gainsay this technique.)

Directions, Please

Often more difficult than finding birds is pointing them out to other birders. "It's right there" doesn't offer much guidance, and all too often the accuracy of this assertion only becomes apparent after the bird flies.

If the bird is stationary, find some orienting feature in close proximity to your target: a bunch of leaves that are darker than the rest, a patch of flowers, a boulder if the bird is on the ground. Tell your fellow birders how far above, below, left, or right the bird lies from the orienting mark. At close range, estimate the distance in standard linear feet.

If the bird is far away and standard units of measure (feet or yards or meters) become conjectural, estimate the bird's distance from an orienting point in "fields of view"—the view offered through your binoculars. A bird sitting on a hillside might be "half a field left of the red barn." A bird flying overhead might be "two fields above the horizon."

Don't forget to say which direction the bird is flying, either "left" or "right." (For some reason birders seem unnecessarily and redundantly compelled to express direction by saying that a bird is moving "left to right" or "right to left." If a bird is flying left, it stands to reason that it's coming from someplace to the right. Right?)

Objects on the horizon can also be used to orient hopeful observers to birds closer at hand. "The bird is going to be in line with that ship . . . *now*" is an often-heard phrase at a seabird watch or on a pelagic birding trip. In the absence of ships or navigational markers, pelagic birders often use the hands of a dial clock to direct fellow birders. Using the bow (front) of the ship for 12 o'clock, a bird slightly right of the bow might be at 1 o'clock. A bird directly astern lies at 6 o'clock.

Birds flying high overhead present their own peculiar problems of orientation. Clouds are a hawk watcher's best friend. They offer not only a silhouetting backdrop but a reference point, too.

Hawks: Putting Yourself in Fortune's Path

Identifying hawks in flight is a tricky pursuit—and it is only the second half of a challenging two-step process. Before distant birds of prey can be identified, they must be found!

The first step is placing yourself in opportunity's way. During migration, birds of prey move on a broad front, but their movements are directed and their numbers concentrated by what are called "leading lines." These include mountain ridges, like the one straddled by Hawk Mountain, where birds of prey are drawn to energy-conserving updrafts. They also include shorelines, which are the causal agent behind the concentrations seen over such famous locations as Duluth and Cape May. All birds of prey use thermals—rising columns of warm air—to gain easy lift. Oceans and large lakes represent thermal-poor habitats, so many birds of prey avoid them, electing instead to follow the contours of the coast.

Weather conditions also affect hawk movement and the numbers of birds that might be seen at a certain place. In the spring (as early as February in some locations), birds of prey pulse north in waves, pushed by warm, southerly breezes. If these broad-front movements intercept an approaching cold front, the wall of stormy weather moving ahead of the front concentrates migrants along its edge. Hawks will run up along the edge of the squall line the same way they skirt the edge of an ocean or lake.

In the fall (beginning as early as late July in some places), cold fronts trigger the migratory urge, propelling hawks (and other migrants) south. For some thermal-dependent species such as Broad-winged Hawk these cold fronts not only drive birds south, they carry them. Northwest winds associated with the passage of a front sweep migrating birds with them in the same way that a person swimming across a river is propelled downstream. This is another reason why coastlines act as migration corridors. Birds are ferried to the coast like flotsam in a flood, and they pile up, sometimes in vast numbers.

Finding Hawks

At most hawk-watching locations, migrating hawks fly predictable routes that are affected daily by geography, wind, weather, time of day, and (of course) season. Once you've located one bird and plotted the pattern of its movement, chances are more will follow.

Scanning with binoculars is the important first step. A good technique is to pan the horizon in the general direction from which you anticipate hawks will approach. The full scan should be around 120 to 160 degrees. Now raise your binoculars a full binocular field above the horizon and backtrack, covering the sky above the initial sweep, then repeat the process one more time. Three sweeps is generally enough to map the sky—unless your binoculars have a critically small field of view (in which case you should buy new binoculars).

From midmorning to midafternoon, particularly on days marked by excellent soaring conditions, hawks fly higher at many locations, and the effectiveness of scanning the horizon diminishes. When birds are high, try scanning directly overhead with binoculars and the unaided eye. Not only are approaching birds closest at this point but the angle of view offers a full ventral profile (more surface area), making the birds easier to see.

Blue skies (disparagingly called "broad-winged blue" by some hawk watchers) swallow up birds of prey. With little contrast and little to focus on, eyes peering into the blue prefocus to a point less than 50 feet out. High-flying birds are easily overlooked. If there are clouds (or even jet contrails), scan these. Your eyes will have something to focus on, and hawk silhouettes stand out against a white backdrop. Cumulus clouds offer a special advantage. They are the visual tips of the rising columns of warm air hawks ride aloft. So not only do cumulus clouds show off hawks to best effect, they attract them!

Some birds of prey are easier to see than others. Large, dark birds (vultures and eagles) and birds with contrasting plumage (Osprey) stand out. Pale or pastel-plumaged birds (adult Cooper's Hawks) melt into the sky. Since birds of a feather do tend to migrate together you can use obvious birds to disclose the presence of less contrasting ones. If you find a distant, high-soaring vulture, watch it. You may be surprised to see other birds materialize around it (now that your eyes have been calibrated for the proper distance and are fused to the right section of sky).

If the eye-catching raptor you've latched onto is in a glide, a good trick is to direct your binoculars along the bird's flight path to pick up any birds moving ahead of the first. Then backtrack, pick up the bellwether bird, and scan along the bird's wake. There may be birds coming up behind as well.

Reaping the Bounty:
Being Where the Birds Are

In the breeding season, woodland songbirds are fairly evenly distributed throughout appropriate habitat, their apportionment and location dictated by the territorial prerogative. An attentive birder should be able to find nesting species at fairly regular intervals just by strolling along and listening.

But in spring and fall, when birds migrate, and in winter, when many species stop defending territories, woodland birds may be very irregularly distributed. There will be long stretches with nothing, then suddenly . . . WHAM! You are into birds. Woodland birding in fall and winter, therefore, is often a matter of finding and working multispecies flocks.

In migration, search for nomadic bands of warblers and vireos moving through the canopy in search of insect prey. Brightly plumaged species like American Redstart or hyperactive birds like Golden-crowned Kinglet will draw your eye and tip you off to the presence of a mixed flock. Be alert, too, for the subdued chatter of a flock: the call notes of warblers, the monotonous rantings of nuthatches, the ethereal incantations of Golden-crowned Kinglets.

In winter, mixed flocks of hardy and half-hardy species move like a hungry cloud through the woods. Their presence is usually heralded by the telltale notes of chickadees and titmice, but be alert for braying jays or a nuthatch whose calling is pointed and incessant. It may indicate the presence of a roosting predator and an ad hoc flock-to-be (as a mobbing action evolves).

There is, of course, rhyme and reason to the distribution and movement of birds. Birders can increase their chances of running into flocks by using their heads as well as their feet. On cool mornings, seek out woodland edges that are exposed to the sun. Insect (and bird) activity will be greatest here. In winter, birds like warmth, too. A thicket with a southern exposure that is protected from the wind is nearly perfect. Add a trickle of open water and it is ideal.

Feast or Famine

The distribution of birds across the planet is not evenly apportioned. As birders know, sometimes you can travel great distances and not encounter anything that rates a raised binocular.

But the flip side of paucity is bounty. Sometimes birders encounter great (even great, great) concentrations of birds. These don't happen by accident. Be assured that if large numbers of birds are all sitting or flying in one place at one time there is cause. Being savvy to these catalytic causes will help you cash in on some great birding experiences.

At the heart of many, perhaps most, bird concentrations is food. Whenever nature rings the dinner bell, birds stand first in line.

Sometimes these banquets are predictable, and annual, such as the great concentration of horseshoe crabs and shorebirds on the beaches of Delaware Bay every May. The crabs emerge to deposit their eggs on the beaches—and one million energy-taxed migrating shorebirds gather to feast.

Sometimes the banquets are impromptu, prompted by conditions. A coastal storm, one large enough to stir the bottom and deposit large numbers of mollusks onto beaches, is certain to draw a host of hungry gulls in a day or two. A reservoir drawn down by summer drought is a magnet for southbound shorebirds, who will short-stop their migration to forage along the muddy banks.

Birds move as their needs and conditions dictate. When conditions change—when all the food is consumed—birds move on. If an opportune condition exists one year (a raptor-encouraging high rodent population that attracts large numbers of wintering hawks and owls) and fails to materialize the next (the rodent population crashes) hawks, and you, need to go someplace else. No food, no concentration.

But when you do find a concentration of birds, play it for all it's worth. A condition that attracts birds will attract more birds, day by day, and the chances of finding species that are new and uncommon to the region are heightened.

When the condition changes, and the birds move on, take the hint. Time to move along yourself—and look for another auspicious opportunity.

Many birders seek out great migratory spectacles such as the half million northbound shorebirds found along the Delaware Bay in May (top), or the hundreds of thousands of Sandhill Cranes that flock to the banks of Nebraska's Platte River in March (bottom). LINDA DUNNE

Playing the Conditions

Many birders schedule their activities according to the calendar: hawk watching in October, search for owls in December, scan for rare gulls in January, look for early migrants in April. And this is good. It keeps birding diverse. It keeps birding fun. It plays the temporal card to a birder's best advantage, maximizing success.

But while a familiarity with the natural calendar is important, playing the conditions is paramount to making the most productive use of your time afield. Often it is meteorological conditions not the calendar that determine where a birder should spend the day.

Say it's November and blowing a northwest gale. You'd planned to search your local patch for lingering southbound passerines or irruptive northern species, but wind and woodland birding is an unproductive combination. Give up? No—change plans. Head for the leeside of a lake or reservoir, where water birds will be seeking shelter from the wind. If rain preceded the front it might well have knocked late-migrating water birds (loons, grebes, scoters) out of the sky and onto inland lakes.

Or consider going to a hawk-watch site. The peak of the migration may be over, but over much of North America, birds of prey continue to migrate (or at least relocate) through December (even into January). A day on "the ridge" or "the coast" or "the point" may garner treasured looks at eagles, cold-weather buteos, or . . . who knows? Maybe that rare Arctic falcon you've been looking for all your life.

Or say it's February. You'd planned on heading for the local winter-gull hot spot, but the winds are southerly and unseasonably warm. Maybe you should head for a migrant trap instead and search for unreasonably early migrants that have been stimulated by the warm weather to push the calendar by migrating early. Late winter warm fronts vault seasons, ferrying waves of early migrants (crows and raptors) and birds whose early appearance is totally at odds with the calendar. The gulls will still be there tomorrow. But a Purple Martin or Common Nighthawk in February is a red-letter entry in any birder's ledger.

Working Flocks—Finding the Odd Bird Out

Some birds stand alone. Happily, many do not, and the flocking tendency of birds can be used to your advantage. Rare and uncommon species are often found among more common ones, offering direct comparison.

The first thing to do when coming upon a flock of gulls (or shorebirds, or waterfowl, or blackbirds . . .) is to identify the familiar birds that constitute the bulk of the flock. This will give you a standard to compare any individuals that do not conform to this baseline uniformity. For instance, a bird that stands slightly taller or is noticeably stockier or whose color differs by a shade. These differences don't require concerted study. They are the things that naturally draw your eye. So relax. Let your eye be drawn. The study comes later.

Even beginning birders can see manifest differences—a snowy-colored second-winter Glaucous Gull standing among an

Looks like a lot of Bonaparte's Gulls—must be food around somewhere. What a great opportunity to scan for a Little or Black-headed Gull, two European species that sometimes mix with the North American Bonaparte's.

assortment of mocha-colored first-winter Herring Gulls, or an adult Lesser Black-backed Gull amid the considerably larger and darker-backed adult Great Black-backed Gulls.

The odd bird out may also betray itself by being slightly off to one side, slightly away from the body of the flock, or maybe the birds in the flock avoid the outsider, causing a slight gap in the ranks.

But sifting out birds that differ only slightly from the balance of the flock—finding, for instance, the slightly larger Black-headed Gull or the more petite Little Gull hidden among a resting flock of Bonaparte's Gulls—requires more than a glance. It requires that a birder be aware of possibility, must know that these two uncommon species may sometimes be found among flocks of Bonaparte's Gulls, and search accordingly.

It's anyone's guess how many rare birds have been passed over because an observer didn't think to look. For that matter, it's anybody's guess how many extralimital vagrants you are destined to find because now you do.

TALE SPOT

Missing the Crane for the Gulls

My friend and fellow hawk watcher Clay Sutton was approaching. Suddenly he stopped and started scanning through a flock of gulls about 70 yards away. Not being much of a "gull man" I'd all but ignored the assemblage. Clay, however, likes gulls almost as much as he likes hawks. "So how long has that been here?" he asked offhandedly.

"How long has what been here?" I asked uneasily.

"That," he said, pointing toward the gulls but at the single Sandhill Crane standing in their midst.

"I don't know," I admitted. Intent as I was on migrating hawks, I'd never so much as glassed the gulls, thus overlooking an unusual bird for Cape May.

While anyone can pick a crane out of a flock of gulls, you still have to try. My failing was gross inattention. ■

Want Birds? Just Add Water

All living things need water, and birds are no exception. They use it to drink, bathe, cool off, and some rely upon aquatic habitats to provide prey. For birders, finding birds is often a simple matter of finding open water.

This is particularly true in desert climates wherever a parched landscape gives way to a lush oasis. The number and diversity of resident species increases along watercourse edges. Migrating birds, searching for habitat that meets their needs, home in on these green retreats—and they are not terribly particular about the water's source.

Well-watered desert golf courses and sprinkler-maintained highway rest areas are magnets for migrating birds. Some of the finest birding on the planet can be had along the edges of sewage facilities serving desert communities.

In the prairie plains of the American West, where desiccating winds and the summer sun take the song right out of the mouths of grassland birds, one of the best ways to find endemic species is to stake out a livestock water trough or tank in the late afternoon. When the worst of the day's heat is done, sparrows, longspurs, and other grassland specialties gather to drink. A quiet and strategically placed observer can get wonderful views.

Winter, Too

Water is important to birds in winter, too. In fact, in areas gripped by winter's cold, birds concentrate wherever open water may be found.

Sometimes when temperatures plunge below freezing, open water survives in pockets on inland lakes and in swift-flowing rivers and streams. Ducks, grebes, loons, and other water-dependent birds, frozen out of one area, seek out and crowd into those open places that remain. Often, open pockets are kept ice-free by the action of the birds themselves. A community lake or golf course pond populated by geese or swans (the icebreakers of the Anatidae) may draw unusual species after the freeze.

Even water in lesser amounts can be highly attractive to winter birds. Hardy birds like sparrows, finches, and juncos, and even half-hardy species like robins and towhees, concentrate in the habitat bordering tiny springs and trickle-sized streams. A seep or irrigation ditch in a snow-covered field may harbor snipe or Killdeer (I once found a woodcock foraging on the bare earth beneath a dripping outside faucet; everything else was snow covered).

Of course the ultimate open-water mechanism is the waterfall—whether the man-made kind associated with hydroelectric dams or the natural kind, like Niagara Falls. In northern areas, the combination of open water and winter-killed fish that characterizes the base of hydroelectric dams can give rise to the birding highlight of the year. Hundreds, even thousands, of gulls gather at such opportune locations. Birders scan through the flocks, searching for unusual species. It's cold birding, but the possibility of finding something truly rare—a Slaty-backed Gull or a Ross's Gull—warms the heart.

Watching Birds Watching Birds

You might own the best optics on the market. You might have 30 years of experience, be able to pick Thayer's Gull out of a flock half a mile away, know the flight call of every eastern warbler. But next to the detection skills of the creatures you seek, you are strictly junior varsity.

Don't envy them. Use them. Train yourself to be attentive to the behavior patterns of birds and let their bird-finding skills lead you to some great encounters.

One of the most obvious and productive examples of birds finding birds is the penchant woodland birds have for mobbing roosting owls. Chickadees, titmice, and jays are the habitual indicator species of these antagonistic interactions. Any scolding harangue is worth investigating and may lead to an in-your-face encounter with a . . . Northern Pygmy-Owl . . . Northern Saw-whet Owl . . . Long-eared Owl . . . whatever your luck (and their antipredator instincts) bring.

Yes, in warm weather, their angst could be focused on a rat snake, but you're going to tell me that the possibility of a pygmy-owl isn't worth a sleuth?

Mobbing is something birds do in flight, too. Icterids and starlings will "ball up" over a soaring raptor. The tight-packed, wheeling

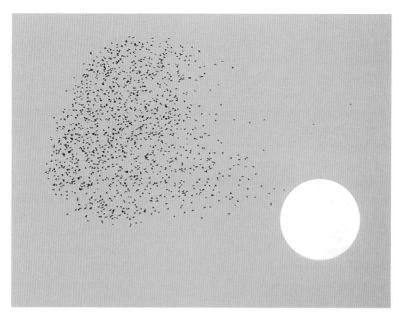

In migration, some species fly in tightly packed flocks; others are not so massed. Shown here are migrating Red-winged Blackbirds over Cape May.

flock appears and disappears like a puff of smoke on the horizon but the signal it sends is clear: "Psssst, look here for a bird of prey too distant to be picked up by casual scanning alone. Hey, Mr. or Ms. Birder, it's below us."

In coastal areas, where vast numbers of Tree Swallows are common in the fall, kestrels signal their approach by drawing an angry entourage—the thickened clot of birds in the otherwise uniform distribution shows where the kestrel is. A raspy snarl from a swallow or martin says the same thing.

Approaching Merlins announce their arrival (and their identity) by boring little bird-free holes through the flock. Swallows treat Merlins differently than they treat the lighter, smaller, less dangerous kestrel.

If you are watching a flock of shorebirds and they crouch and freeze, look up. There's a raptor up there somewhere. Count on it. If the frenetic activity around your bird feeder suddenly stops, or if your usually busy trays are quiet on a cold morning, start scanning the trees. You've got another hungry bird coming to your feeders, one that doesn't eat seed.

And if you do find that perched raptor and it cocks its head and looks up, do likewise. In days of yore, falconers intent on capturing passage birds relied on tethered shrikes to give advance warning of approaching hawks. The detection technique is even called "shriking," and it is possible that the very name is traceable to the vocalizations emitted by a raptor-piqued shrike.

Not all bird-seeking-bird interactions are antagonistic. Soaring birds will seek out, and lead attuned observers to, other thermal-dependent birds. By focusing on large soaring birds (pelicans, storks, vultures) observers often discover smaller, less obvious birds soaring with them (Anhingas or small soaring raptors).

The opposite is also true: Sometimes smaller soaring birds will alert you to the presence of a larger species. Scanning the bottom of a cloud one spring day I became aware that a line of "ants" was streaming in from below and then spreading out across the cloud face (translation: high-flying, migrating Broad-winged Hawks homing in on a thermal). An individual bird would have been invisible but the massed flock was enough to draw my eye.

As I watched, a long plank slipped through the mass of ants. No head, no tail—just a thin, dark plank (translation: adult Bald Eagle flying so high the white head and tail were invisible). I never would have seen the plank had I not been focused on the ants.

It might just be me. There might not be any cause-and-effect relationship. But it seems that once I find one woodland bird I find more. Certainly everyone is familiar with the concept of feeding flocks, assemblages of several species that forage through brush and woodlands. But even birds I do not think of as flocking birds seem to like company.

If, for example, I find a wintering catbird—suddenly I note a Hermit Thrush not far away. It seems to work for water birds, too. If I see a Pied-billed Grebe after navigating a bird-free stretch of marsh, why is this the place that I'll also find a gallinule, Least Bittern, maybe a rail? Is it just that now I'm focused? Or is it that birds derive security from having other birds around? Yes, it could be just a nice cozy place, but I think there is more to it than that.

Or look at it this way—why is it that in a near-empty train station a commuter elects to sit in close proximity to another patron instead of seeking out the most distant bench?

For my part, for safety or shared advantage, or for whatever reason, I believe that birds of different species prefer to be near each other (and that attentive observers will find more birds by being attentive to this).

There is a flip side to this tendency. A delicious trick that can be used to great effect when searching for Snowy Owls. These northern wanderers are habitually found on beaches, and beaches, at most access points, run two ways. Choosing the wrong direction can add hours to a search for a reported Snowy Owl (a bird that is almost certain to make the local birding hotline or web page).

My technique, founded upon the bird-finding skills of other birds, is this: Scan the beach for gulls, which tend to distribute themselves fairly evenly along a shoreline. But what I'm looking for is not a concentration of gulls, and not even a nominal allotment of gulls. What I seek is a stretch of beach distinguished by the *absence* of gulls. That will be the stretch of beach distinguished by the presence of a large white owl—and no gull wants to share it.

SUMMARY

There are no shortcuts to becoming a better birder. There are, however, tricks that experienced birders use that make it easier to find, see, and identify birds. Some relate to getting the most out of equipment. These include keeping lenses unfogged in wet or cold weather, keeping spotting scopes steady in wind, using the individual eyepiece adjustment knob to cut the minimum focus distance, and cutting reaction time by keeping optics in hand or anticipating where a bird will land. Other tips relate to techniques such as pishing to attract birds, pausing as a means of locating birds, offering bird-locating directions to other birders, finding hawks, using the vocalizations of resident birds to find migrant flocks, using weather conditions to predict where concentrations of birds will occur, using the magnetic quality of water to lead you to birds in summer and winter, learning the value of probability as an aid to identification, and using the bird-finding skills of birds to lead you to other birds. ■

Ethics and Responsibilities

Looking for Baird's Sparrow (Walking on Eggshells)

We were 20 abreast and 3 deep, part of the ABA convention in Minot, North Dakota, and moving through knee-high, bird-rich prairie grasslands. From lions stalking gazelle to Broad-winged Hawks searching for thermals, fanning out in an interception line is a time-tested technique used by hunting animals—acting in concert to find whatever it is they seek.

What we were seeking was Baird's Sparrow, a handsome prairie species distinguished by an array of streaks on the back, a beaded necklace on the breast, chestnut-touched scapulars, and a rich buff about the head and nape.

The bird was also distinguished by its very restricted range— limited, in the breeding season, to the northern prairie states and southern portions of the prairie provinces of Canada. This bird was a target species, one of the reasons more than 500 ABA members had converged on Minot. This is why we moved so eagerly and with such focused intent.

We were in pursuit of a bird that had been heard but not seen. All eyes were focused well ahead, trusting that the grasslands were free of ankle-twisting obstacles, or that the tall prairie grass would buffer any fall. Suddenly, I felt a bump . . . maybe a tug beneath my left foot. Looking down, I found a female Sharp-tailed Grouse flailing on the ground, the tips of three outer flight feathers of one wing pinned beneath my boot. Horrified, I lifted my foot, releasing the bird, which tried to fly but could not. The wing was injured, possibly the result of my incaution, or possibly the injury was caused by one of those walking ahead. Not that it mattered. When you hunt as a tribe, you share the fortune of the tribe—good and bad. The bird was injured. We were responsible.

To make matters worse, in the spot where the grouse had been, a ground nest containing nearly a dozen eggs was exposed. Several of the eggs were broken.

Concealment and sitting tight is part of the nest-defense strategy of many open-country birds. The grasslands of North America are a treasure trove of birds, all of them the successors to a long line of survivors. Clearly a strategy of stationary concealment does work—but not all the time, and not this time. The commotion had drawn the eyes of the group. Only those closest had any sense of what had happened. I offered an explanation. Assumed responsibility. Urged caution.

"OK," one of the leaders intoned. "Let's keep going, but let's be careful. There are lots of nesting birds out here."

And we were more careful, as careful as people walking through tall grass filled with cryptically colored birds can be. We saw the sparrow, well and without further incident. At least, that's what we think and hope.

Keeping Birding Safe for Birds

Harming birds is the very antithesis of what motivates birders. Yet birds are sometimes injured, and their lives are sometimes disrupted, by the efforts of those eager to appreciate them. Not unduly, not indefensibly, not terminally—but disrupted nevertheless. Shorebirds feeding to fuel their long flight to the arctic are forced to relocate when approached too closely, a waste of time and energy. Birds responding to pishing can be blindsided by hunting hawks.

And while many more ground-nesting birds have been injured by grazing buffalo and harvest combines than will ever be discomfited by birders, that doesn't mean that birders should not make every effort to minimize their impact on the creatures that are the object of their attention.

Common Sense

Most of the effort involved in not causing harm to birds involves no effort at all. As already discussed, if your proximity to a bird seems to be causing stress, *back off.* The bird is telling you that you have stepped over a line responsible birders don't cross.

If you are pursuing a bird whose identify puzzles you, once you've gotten the look you need, stop.

If you are adept at pishing, don't overdo it. And don't do it at all in very cold temperatures, in places where large numbers of bird-eating hawks are concentrated, or during the breeding season, when birds are otherwise occupied.

It is, of course, unusual for a bird to be stressed by a birder's attention. Birds vote with their wings. In most cases, when pressed too hard, birds simply leave.

Recorded Playbacks

Birds on territory will respond both positively and negatively to recordings of their songs. Positively, because they will boldly approach what they assume to be a rival in their territory. Negatively, because while defending their territory birds become highly agitated. And while trying to confront a phantom rival, they are not able to apply their energy more productively—by attracting a mate, foraging, or being vigilant for real threats. Repeated use of playbacks by multiple individuals targeting individual birds compounds these deleterious effects.

Abuses notwithstanding, there are times when playback recordings are less intrusive and less disruptive than other means birders might employ to gain a glimpse of a bird. In particular, in the hands of a skilled tour leader whose objective is to offer groups of birders a look at shy forest species, judiciously employed playbacks are less intrusive than pishing (which is not species specific) or marching a group through a sensitive natural (perhaps chigger-infested) area.

The ethics of using recorded playbacks is, and will continue to be, a growing concern as more and more people go afield with apps that include vocalizations. Until more is known about recorded playbacks and their effects, and until guidelines are established, the prudent action for individual birders to take is no action. Leave the gadgetry at home and enjoy birds on *their* terms. Watching birds was never meant to be like finding your favorite TV show with a remote. The gratification inherent in spotting and identifying birds is directly proportional to the challenge met and mastered.

My recommendation: Don't use recordings to attract birds. There are few species and occasions where patience and diligence will not gain the satisfying look you need without resorting to gadgetry.

The Etiquette of Birding

Birders are a society, and in any society, there are standards of behavior and etiquette that apply. If you want to benefit from the wisdom of the tribe, it is important not to alienate the tribe or its leaders.

Courtesy

One of birding's most fundamental ethics is the ethic of sharing. The classic greeting between birders of long acquaintance, or strangers meeting in some birdy place, is "What are you seeing?" or "Have you seen anything (good)?"

If you find a bird that excites you, chances are it will excite others, too. It is incumbent upon you to let others know—whether that someone is met on a trail or seen in the parking lot later, or who may be visiting tomorrow.

Finding a "good" bird doesn't necessarily obligate you to stand at the gate and offer an accounting to every newcomer (unless you have discovered a North American first, your identity is known, and you want to preserve your good standing within the birding community). But in many popular birding locations bird sighting ledgers are maintained. In them, birders record the date, location, and particulars relating to noteworthy birds—both to document occurrences and share their good fortune with others. And don't forget eBird.

Documenting Rarities: Courtesy's Next Level
Birds that are very unusual or desirable should be reported to local birding leaders. Birds that have been designated review list species by a state or region's Rare Bird or Bird Records Committee invite a detailed description, a "species write-up," so that a record of the sighting might be held on file. A documenting photo is always welcome, and in the case of first state records is sometimes mandatory.

But How Do I Know If a Bird Is Rare? How Do I Report It?
Most birding locations and states have checklists that include all the birds likely to be found in an area as well as a determination of the bird's abundance, calibrated by season. While there is no universal designation system or code, in most cases birds are designated as Abundant, Common, Uncommon, Scarce, or Rare on a checklist for a specific area. Those designated Rare rate disclosure. Any bird not found on the checklist (or possibly included in an appendix and listed as Accidental or Hypothetical) also rates disclosure and invites documentation submitted to the proper records committee. These committees are sometimes independent groups drawn from among a state's most experienced birders, or the committee might be associated with a statewide organization. Contact information is commonly printed on the checklist.

Do I *Have* to Report Rare Birds?
No, you don't have to. Birders are a community, a tribe, not a totalitarian state. But rare birds are, by definition, rare. For the sake of

those who share your interest, and as a way of offering compensation for knowledge that you have drawn from the birding community at large, reporting rare birds is just something all birders should do as a matter of courtesy.

You say you haven't tapped the resources of the birding community? Think again—do you think the elements of this book were spun from air?

Courtesy to Nonbirders

If you were to search the world over, you would be hard pressed to find a community of people more genial and considerate and less troublesome than birders. Ironically, it is the very benign nature of birders and their activity that sometimes causes birders to inconvenience nonbirders.

Since they harbor no thoughts of troubling anyone with their activity, they are frequently oblivious when they do.

The American Birding Association has established a Code of Ethics (See page 299) that establishes standards all birders should strive to emulate. These standards apply to birds, the environment, and the broad rights of others.

In addition, and as someone whose birding is conducted in a place where the lives of thousands of birders and nonbirders overlap, I recommend and emphasize the following:

1. Private property means just that. Benign intent is not a passport to trespass.
2. Being quiet is simple courtesy. In residential areas, before 10 A.M., keep voices low and vehicle noises to a minimum.
3. Never, never, never stop your vehicle in a traffic lane to view birds—*not even for a moment.* Always pull completely onto the shoulder to conduct your study. No shoulder? Drive on.
4. Be careful to not point optics toward people or houses. It is rude. It is discourteous. It is intrusive. It is likely to be misunderstood.
5. Be courteous and deferential to people engaged in other wildlife-related pursuits. They are allies, not rivals (yes, I am speaking specifically of hunters).

6. Express gratitude to individuals, institutions, and businesses that go out of their way to accommodate your interest or needs.

7. Share your excitement with nonbirders. Let them know how important open space and the natural environment are to you and to wildlife.

WING BAR

The Honored Badge of our Order

Bird watching and bird conservation are irrevocably bound. One of bird conservation's most effective tools is economic persuasion. Birders spend hundreds of millions of dollars every year in pursuit of birds, much of it on travel-related expenses.

Communities that enjoy proximity to birding areas reap the economic benefits of visiting birders. The beneficiaries range from restaurant and motel owners and gas station attendants to muffler shop managers, drug-store proprietors, and counter clerks who dish out ice cream on hot days.

These people are also the ones who affect regional land use decisions via the voting box and by word of mouth. When they recognize the percentage of their trade that comes from birders, they quite naturally become sympathetic toward maintaining natural areas. The problem is that when birders remove their binoculars, they look pretty much like everyone else. Their interest in a region's natural attractions goes unnoticed.

The solution is simple: *Wherever you go, wear your binoculars.* Bring them into the restaurant. Sling them under an arm when you saunter into the convenience store. Birding and binoculars are synonymous. And never miss an opportunity to tell the person serving you what you are doing in their area and why.

Some birders have even gone to the trouble of printing up "business" cards. Left on lunch-countertops or in hotel rooms they spell out our interest and intent. While wording varies the message is the same: "Hi. I'm a birder attracted to your area because of its natural resources. Protect your open space, and the birds who live there, and I'll be back." ▪

Conservation

You cannot be interested in birds and not concern yourself with their protection or welfare. Similarly, you cannot be concerned about birds and not be protective of the environment that sustains them.

Whatever your political leanings, however much your opinions are molded by other salient social, philosophical, and economic concerns, one thing is certain. The environment is not just one more interest competing among many.

The environment is the playing field on which all other interests compete. Rule number 1: protect the playing field.

Over much of the planet, even in our own backyards, many bird species are playing a losing game. For them to have a viable place in this world of our making, it is incumbent upon birders to take their side of the field and support efforts that will ensure their survival.

There are many organizations that have a conservation mission and a primary interest in birds who are actively courting your membership. They differ in terms of geographic scope, species orientation, and approach to meeting the needs of birds (research, habitat protection, legislative action, environmental education).

All were spawned by some manifest need that defined their original goals and objectives. Some have roots that go back over a century or more—tapping the wellspring of concern and need that was the foundation of the conservation movement (and modern birding itself).

As explained in the first chapter, birders are hybrids, the product of a marriage between ornithologists and nature lovers (aka conservationists). While much has changed in the hundred years since this union was formed, one thing has not: the need to protect birds and their habitat. We are the fortunate beneficiaries of a hundred years of conservation-mindedness and lucky to live in this age of great bird diversity. But unless this conservation-mindedness continues, all the gains of the past will become Pyrrhic.

WING BAR

Choosing Your Allies

While many organizations have my sympathy, only a few enjoy my support. My resources are limited, and I find that I must be selective, pick and choose favorites—organizations that share my specific interests and whose effectiveness assures me that my support will be used to best effect.

You are an intelligent person. You can fairly assess merit and your interests. But as someone who has worked within the bird conservation community for more than 30 years, I have determined some specific qualities I look for when deciding which organizations to support.

"Environment" is a broad term, used in promotional literature to cover everything from air quality to habitat protection to lawn care. The first thing I suggest doing when looking through an organization's promotional literature is to determine what its mission is and whether it is in accord with yours.

Personally, I prefer organizations that dedicate funds and effort toward natural habitat procurement and legislative action.

I also like organizations that have a global awareness but a defining focus—on a specific group of birds or critical habitat. Some organizations with a global perspective have internal bureaucracies to match. When perspective expands, interests and issues do too, often at the expense of mission.

More issues mean more internal competition for time, talent, and resources. More competition means more friction and more time needed to bring resources to bear when issues arise.

It means, in short, that unless a large conservation organization is very focused and very specific about its mission (and some are), a lot of environmentally dedicated funds are going to get eaten up internally.

This is also why I commonly favor small- to medium-sized organizations, and relatively young organizations—those whose original focus has not been diluted, those that already have operational infrastructure in place but still have fire in their bellies.

Older, established organizations go through cycles. When they have an inspired director, a committed and engaged membership, or a galvanizing cause, they can be a potent environmental force. But in between those times large groups have a tendency to go into dormancy; their mission becomes perpetuation. Those periods of dormancy may last decades. People support them on the basis of past accomplishments, not current performance—which is fine, provided you aren't concerned about getting as much environmental bang for your buck as possible.

How do you tell if an organization is in output mode or hibernation? Read the letter of invitation or, if you are already a member, scan the communications. If the focus is on what has been accomplished in the past or the material is big on "threats" but weak on specific actions being taken to address those threats, be cautious. If the focus is on what actions the group is engaged in now, and if this action is in fundamental accord with your environmental interests, give them your support.

I do not like scare tactics. I do not like letters that tell me that *X* amount of habitat is being lost every minute or that unless I act right now the "blank, blank" is doomed.

Nor do I favor organizations whose operational focus is primarily confrontation. Every conservation action goes through five stages: (1) determination of a problem, (2) study and fact finding, (3) confrontation, (4) resolution, (5) redress. Confrontation gets headlines, thus it gets support, but it doesn't get results all by itself. I prefer to support organizations that work toward solutions and don't engage in theatrics.

Something that will lose my support very quickly is the abuse of the "appeal." Organizations that send me lots of urgent letters asking for money tell me that either they don't know how to manage money or are wasting too much on the dollar trying to raise the next dollar. I want to be a partner, not just a pocket.

My rule of thumb when it comes to management and budget is simple: The more money used for mission, the better. Which brings up another point. I want the organizations I support to be responsive to me. I don't want a phone tree that cuts me off if I don't know the right extension. What I want with my call is to reach a person with whom I can communicate and discuss my concerns.

I also want to hear about the organization I support. If the only time I learn about an organization's "good work" is through the organization's literature, I'm not impressed. If I see its name in print—in newspapers and magazines—offering testimony at a hearing or organizing an event that fosters environmental awareness, it tells me I've picked a winner.

There is one more quality I look for. That thing is attitude. I want the conservation organizations I support to be positive about the future and believe that their efforts will make a difference, will make a better world for all the planet's denizens. An organization that is all doom and gloom is already admitting defeat. That is not how I regard the future, or the future of birds, birding, or this environmentally diverse planet. Defeatism is not an attitude I care to foster or support. ■

Home Free

Yet and still, and as said earlier in these pages, if your primary—even sole—interest in birds is to enjoy the birds of your own back-yard, that is a marvelous, life-enriching ambition.

But what was just said about supporting bird conservation still stands. The birds of your yard do not understand property lines,

Worth its weight in calamine lotion. A Prothonotary Warbler is one of the golden rewards of a lifetime spent birding. As this southern species might characterize your encounter: *sweet, sweet, sweet, sweet, sweet, sweet, sweet, sweet.*

and many of "your birds" are only yours for part of the year. They are elements in a time-share agreement with people preserving habitat somewhere else on this bird-rich planet.

One Final "But"

But if you do join the many millions of birders who have taken the birding trail in search of feathered treasure (both gold and ivory), it may lead ultimately to an encounter with something as stunning as a Prothonotary Warbler (aka Golden Swamp Warbler). Or it will take you very literally to the ends of the earth—maybe to Baffin Island, edge of the Arctic ice cap, and home to the Ivory Gull. Having read this book, you now have the skills to tell which is which.

SUMMARY

Birders should always make the welfare of birds their first concern. Common sense and a sensitivity to the stress levels of birds is usually all that is required. Using recorded calls to attract birds may be effective but is not encouraged. Offering detailed descriptions of rare birds is standard practice. Birders should maintain high ethical standards and not use their avocation as an excuse to infringe upon the rights of others. Conservation of birds and their habitat is every birder's concern; supporting organizations that work toward these ends is in every birder's interest. ■

Glossary of Terms

Accidental. A bird not native to a region and, as a result, seen and recorded at intervals spanning several years or more.

Accipiter. One of a group of mostly forest-dwelling hawks that specifically target birds as prey.

Alignment, of Binoculars. The relative focus points of each of a pair of binoculars' barrels. Binoculars that are in proper alignment have barrels calibrated to fall on the same point; binoculars that are out of alignment have barrels that fall on different points, creating a blurred, distorted, or double image.

Alternate Plumage (or Breeding Plumage). The usually more colorful plumage some species sport during the breeding season.

Anatidae. Family of birds that includes ducks, geese, and swans.

BAK-4. Barium crown; the superior of the two grades of glass most commonly used in midpriced optics; BAK-4 glass has a higher density and less distortion as light passes through it.

Ball Up. An expression used by hawk watchers to describe the tightly packed flocking behavior of birds (most notably starlings and blackbirds) as they harass a bird of prey.

Basic Plumage (or Winter Plumage). The typical plumage of adult birds outside the breeding season (when, in some birds, it is replaced by a brightly colored one).

Bill-Sweeping. A technique used by many feeder birds in which less desirable seed is moved aside by the bill in order to reach more favored seed types.

Bird of the Year. A bird born in the current calendar year; also called a hatching-year bird.

Bird Sighting Sheet (or Ledger). A sheet displayed at popular birding areas used by birders to report unusual or significant sightings.

Bird Watcher. Any person who enjoys watching birds.

Birder. Any person who actively seeks out birds for pleasure and challenge.

Black-Oil Sunflower Seed. The small black sunflower seed favored by a diverse number of bird species.

BK-7. Boro-silicate; glass that's not as dense as BAK-4 glass and is therefore less expensive and inferior in quality.

Breeding Plumage. *See* Alternate Plumage.

Breeding Species. *See* Summer Resident.

Broad-Front Movement. A migration pattern in which birds are dispersed across a wide geographic area.

Buteo. The group of medium- to large-sized soaring hawks; buteos are mostly open-country birds, and most species in this genus are not bird-eating specialists.

Call (or Call Note). Typically a single-note vocalization, which can be used to identify a bird; not to be confused with a bird's song.

Canary Seed. A small, pale seed used as filler in less expensive seed mixes and not especially favored by seed-eating birds.

Cavity Nester. Any one of a number of birds that raise their young in the protective confines of a tree cavity. These include woodpeckers, nuthatches, and chickadees, as well as some flycatchers, swallows, wrens, waterfowl, falcons, and owls.

Center Focus. The focus mechanism of binoculars—most often controlled by a wheel—that simultaneously adjusts the images seen in both barrels.

Checklist. A list of the bird species found in a defined geographic area. Checklists can be as large as the ABA Checklist (which includes birds of the United States and Canada) or as specific as one tailored to the birds found in a local refuge or park. Checklists typically follow the taxonomic order sequence established by the AOU.

Class. The large biological grouping that includes all living things that have in common a fundamental, unifying, and distinguishing characteristic. In the case of birds, whose class is Aves, that characteristic is the presence of feathers.

Close Focus. The near limit at which binoculars or a spotting scope can offer a sharp image.

Clutch. The eggs laid by a bird in a single nesting effort.

Cold Front. The leading edge of a colder air mass, commonly associated with an approaching high-pressure weather system and often featuring squall lines or storms. Cold fronts concentrate migrating birds ahead of an area of bad weather; in fall, they often spur birds to migrate after their passage.

Common Name. The English name applied to a bird species that is widely accepted by birders.

Cracked Corn. One of the generally less desirable filler items often found in less expensive seed mixes; grackles and blackbird species are nevertheless partial.

Degrees of Arc. Units of measure that describes the linear value of binoculars' field of view.

Depth of Field. The distance, measured near to far, in which objects seen through binoculars are in focus. A generous depth of field facilitates finding birds in woodlands; a shallow depth of field makes it more difficult.

Dihedral. The uplifted, or V-shaped, wing configuration characteristic of some soaring birds.

Distribution, Normal. *See* Normal Range.

Double Clutch (also Triple Clutch). A reproductive strategy in which birds will lay two (or more) sets of eggs during a breeding season as a way of increasing nesting success.

Dripper. Any elevated container that releases water in droplets for the purpose of attracting birds.

Drumming. A sound resulting from the rapidly beating wings of a male Ruffed Grouse, made to attract a mate. The sound is reminiscent of a rubber ball bouncing to a stop.

ED Glass. Extra dense; this glass is even heavier and denser than BAK-4 glass, resulting in superior light transmission. ED glass is synonymous with premium optics. Also known as HD (high definition) glass.

Elements. Any of the optical components (lenses and prisms) housed in a pair of binoculars or a spotting scope.

Empidonax **Flycatchers.** A genus of small, active, and very similar-looking flycatchers. It is notoriously difficult to identify the members of this group in the field.

Endemic Species. A species confined to a specific geographic region. Example: Island Scrub-Jay, closely related to Western Scrub-Jay, is found only on Santa Cruz Island, California.

Epaulet. A shoulder adornment, most often referring to the red shoulder patches of Red-winged and Tricolored Blackbirds.

Ergonomic. Thoughtfully designed to comfortably fit a user's hands.

Eye Point. The actual point at which the image projected through binoculars is focused. Binoculars with a high eye point are required for eyeglass wearers, whose eyes are necessarily set back a bit from the surface of the ocular lenses.

Eye Relief. The distance, measured in millimeters, between the ocular lens and the top of the eyecup.

Eyecups. The short, rubber (sometimes plastic) tubes on binoculars that surround the ocular lenses and generally touch the viewer's face when the instrument is used.

Eyepiece. The lens used to peer through when fitted to a spotting scope. Usually interchangeable, eyepieces have varying degrees of power for different magnification needs.

Exclusionary Feeder. A feeder designed to prevent unwanted birds (or other animals) from reaching food items.

Exit Pupil. The diameter of the shaft of light passing through one of a binocular's barrels, measured in millimeters. Exit pupil can be calculated by dividing the diameter of the objective lens by the power of the instrument.

Falcon. One of a group of fast, open-country birds of prey that specialize in capturing prey in flight.

Fallout, Migratory. A phenomenon, usually meteorologically linked and coastal in nature, in which large numbers of migrating birds are forced to land in restricted confines. Fallouts last only a day or two but may involve millions of birds deposited in areas as small as an offshore island or as large as a coastline.

Family. The taxonomic group between Order and Genus that incorporates birds of similar traits.

Feeder. Any manufactured or modified device used to dispense seed or other food items to birds.

Field Card. *See* Checklist.

Field Guide. A light, portable book that uses pictures and descriptive text to help birders identify birds in the field.

Field Mark. Any characteristic relating to plumage, shape, or anatomy that can be noted in the field and used to distinguish one species from another.

Field of View. That section of the world that can be seen through binoculars or a spotting scope.

Field Quality. The resolution and consistency of a binocular image as seen across the entire field of view.

Filler Seed. Any of the less expensive or less desirable seed types sometimes included in mixed birdseed to reduce cost.

Flax (or Flaxseed). A filler seed used in inexpensive seed mixes and largely ignored by birds.

Flight Feathers. Those feathers associated with the wing and tail that facilitate a bird's flight. These include primaries, secondaries, tertials, and rectices (or tail feathers).

Flush Distance. The point at which a bird will no longer tolerate a birder's approach and so flies away.

Focus System. The mechanism that controls how optical instruments move the point of focus to maintain a sharp image.

Focus Wheel. The preferred mechanism for adjusting binoculars' point of focus.

Genus. The taxonomic grouping between Family and Species that groups birds with very similar characteristics.

Good Bird. Colloquial term for a very unusual or sought-after species.

Hotline (or Sighting Sheet or Email List). A regularly updated message service that summarizes sightings of rare and sought-after birds in a state or region. Directions are usually offered and status updates made if warranted.

Hot Spot. Any location that enjoys widespread acclaim as a place to see rare, unusual, or particularly large numbers of birds. Hot spots can be local or international.

Hypothetical Sighting (or Hypothetical Record). An encounter with a bird that for one or more reasons is only conditionally accepted by reviewers.

Image Quality. The standard of what a viewer actually sees when looking through an instrument; image quality is the product of optics and the stability of the image.

Icterid. A member of the Icterid family, also known as the blackbirds, including grackles, orioles, meadowlarks, blackbirds, cowbirds, and others.

Individual Eyepiece Adjustment. The mechanism for changing the focus of just one barrel of binoculars (usually a wheel or knob), making it possible to customize an instrument to account for the small differences between a user's eyes.

Insectivorous. A bird that eats insects exclusively, or nearly so.

Interpupillary Distance. The distance between the ocular lenses of binoculars. For the instrument to offer a single, strain-free image, the interpupillary distance must match the distance between the eyes of the user.

Irruptive Species. A bird whose migrations or redistributions are infrequent and unpredictable.

Half-Hardy Species. A bird that remains in the colder regions of North America during the winter months but whose ability to withstand cold is frequently pushed to, and sometimes beyond, its tolerance.

HD Glass. *See* ED Glass.

Hopper Feeder. A platform feeder with an attached food reservoir.

Hummingbird Feeder. A specialty feeder that dispenses sugar-water solution to attract hummingbirds.

Leading Lines. Geographic features that hawks and other migrating birds orient along. Examples include coastlines and mountain ridges.

Leaf Bathing. The avian equivalent of sponge bathing; birds will use dew or water droplets on leaves as they would standing water.

Lens. An elliptically shaped pieces of glass that magnifies images.

Lens Coating. Thin layers of magnesium fluoride or other chemicals baked onto the surface of lenses and prisms to prevent light from being reflected when it strikes glass.

Lumping. A taxonomic reinterpretation in which two bird species formerly thought to be separate, distinct species are reclassified as a single species. For birders, lumping represent a loss of one bird on the life list.

Life Bird (or Lifer). A species encountered by a birder for the first time and added to a life list.

Life List. The cumulative list of all species identified by a birder since the day they started birding.

Local Patch. The place, usually close to home, that you frequently bird and whose nuances you are familiar with.

Magnification. The degree to which an object is enlarged when seen through binoculars or spotting scope. The amount of magnification is measured in "powers of magnification."

Marine Binoculars. Binoculars to be used on board a ship and so must be able to withstand frequent dousing with salt water and occasional drops onto the deck. Usually heavy, marine binoculars are not recommended for birding.

Migration. A twice-yearly redistribution across the surface of the planet practiced by many bird species.

Migrant Trap. Any geographic area that attracts or concentrates migrating birds due to its environment, setting, and location. Examples: a peninsula or a wooded park in an urban setting.

Millet. The seed from proso millet grass; favored by birds, particularly sparrows and doves, in both its white and red varieties.

Milo. The seed from sorghum; appeals mainly to doves and some sparrows.

Mini-Binoculars. Small, lightweight instruments popular among backpackers but mostly unsuitable for birding.

Mister. Any water-dispensing device that sprays a fine mist; misters are particularly attractive to birds when set up in places where water can collect on leaves.

Mixed Birdseed. A seed mixture that combines a variety of seed types in an effort to appeal to a wide variety of birds. Mixed seed ranges widely in quality and appeal, depending on its ingredients.

Mixed Flock. Any flock that contains more than one species. Usually refers to a wintering or foraging migrant flock that includes year-round residents.

Mealworm. The larval form of the Yellow Mealworm Beetle; mealworms are particularly attractive to non-seed-eating birds such as bluebirds and wrens.

Mnemonic. Words that mimic or resemble the song or call of a species. Example: "Teakettle, teakettle, teakettle" (one of the common songs of Carolina Wren).

Mobbing. A defensive reaction in which birds of one or more species gather to drive away a predator (either real or presumed).

Nest Box. A man-made structure built to replicate a natural tree cavity and sized to meet the requirements of a particular cavity-nesting species.

Nocturnal Flight Call. A vocalization that nocturnal migrants emit during flight, and also, infrequently, during daylight hours.

Nocturnal Migrant. Any one of a number of bird species that migrate primarily or exclusively during the hours of darkness.

Normal Range. The geographic space that encompasses all of a species' breeding and/or wintering range. Also known as Distribution Range.

Objective Lens. The binocular or spotting scope lens closest to the object being viewed.

Ocular Lens. The binocular or spotting scope lens closest to the user.

Order. The taxonomic grouping between Class and Family that incorporates birds that share fundamentally similar traits. Example: Passerines, the "perching" birds, include many different bird families, including flycatchers, larks, swallows . . . and warblers, tanagers, sparrows.

Ornithology. A branch of biological science specializing in the study of birds.

Passerines. The Order of birds that includes all "perching" birds; more than half the bird species found on earth belong to this Order.

Passage Bird. A bird engaged in its first migration.

Peanut Feeder. A specialty feeder designed to dispense peanuts or peanut parts.

Peanut Kernel. The shelled peanut, whole or halved; this "seed" type is very popular with Blue Jays and titmice.

Peep. A nickname for any small sandpiper species.

Pelagic Bird. Any of a diverse group of birds (including shearwaters, petrels, and albatrosses) that spend most of their lives at sea.

Permanent Resident. Bird species that are nonmigratory and remain in one area or habitat type all year. Many permanent residents are often common feeder birds, and some form the base of wintering or foraging flocks.

Phase Coating (or Phase Corrective Coating). A chemical coating applied to the elements of roof prism binoculars in order to correct the light-wave shift inherent in the roof prism design.

Physiographic Region. A geographic area distinguished by a common geographic character (example: coastal plain).

Pishing. An onomatopoeic term used to describe the scolding calls used by many bird species engaged in a mobbing action.

Platform Feeder. The simplest of bird-feeding structures, platform feeders are flat, open surfaces that hold food items.

Power. *See* Magnification.

Porro Prism. The "classic" wide-bodied binocular design.

Prism. One of the glass components in binoculars and most spotting scopes; its function is to redirect the shaft of light as it moves through the instrument.

Range of Focus. The number of revolutions required for a binoculars' focus wheel to move the point of focus from close as possible to infinity. For birding binoculars, the ideal range is about one full turn.

Range. *See* Normal Range.

Range Map. Graphic depictions that show the summer, winter, and migratory distribution of a bird species.

Rapeseed. One of the filler seed types.

Raptor. A bird of prey, including include hawks (diurnal, or daytime, raptors) and owls (nocturnal, or nighttime, raptors).

Rare Bird Committee (or Bird Records Committee). A panel, usually associated with a state or provincial organization, that reviews documentation relating to the sighting of rare and uncommon birds and administers the state or province's species list.

Rarity. Any bird not commonly found in a specific area.

Reflecting Scope. A spotting scope that uses mirrors to gather light; reflecting scopes are popular among astronomers but less so among birders.

Refracting Scope. A spotting scope that uses prisms and lenses. Slimmer and generally more rugged than a reflecting scope, refractors are the preferred scope among birders.

Relative Abundance. A comparative value that measures the prevalence of one species against another, usually as a means of establishing the probability of a bird's occurrence.

Relative Brightness. A measure of an instrument's brightness determined by squaring the diameter of the exit pupil.

Relative Light Efficiency. A measure of instrument brightness that attempts to give numeric weight to coated lenses by taking relative brightness and adding 50 percent of this value.

Resolution, Binocular. The capacity of an instrument to discern detail.

Review List Species. Any species that a records committee has determined to be rare enough to warrant documentation and committee review.

Roof Prism. The slim, very popular type of binocular known for its ergonomic design and ruggedness.

Scanning. A method of search in which binoculars are panned across a lake, horizon, or sky.

Scientific Name. The Latin (sometimes Greek) binomial unique to every species. Example: *Turdus migratorius* (American Robin). Since common names are not universally accepted and are therefore open to confusion, a bird's scientific name is the preferred reference among ornithologists.

Seasonal Occurrence. A measure of a species' abundance or occurrence as it relates to a particular season.

Shorebird. One of a group of mostly migratory species that includes sandpipers and plovers but not herons, gulls, and terns.

Shotgun Ornithology. A branch of bird study that relies on collecting bird specimens as a means of gaining intimacy and insight.

Shriking. An archaic term for one bird's warning of another bird's approach. Tethered shrikes were once used by falconers to alert them of a hawk's approach.

Soft Part. Curiously, the term used for a bird's bill, feet, or legs.

Song (or Birdsong). A simple or complex but often lengthy bird vocalization that usually includes multiple notes and is uttered mostly by males during breeding season.

Sonogram. A graphic depiction of a bird's song that replicates the pattern sounds and pauses with lines.

Species, Bird. The most basic of taxonomic groupings; at this level of differentiation, a bird is genetically distinct from all other birds except one of its own species.

Splitting. A taxonomic reinterpretation in which two forms of a species originally thought to be genetically similar are, after more consideration, determined to represent two separate species.

Spotting Scope. A single-barrel optical aid whose advantage is higher magnification and whose primary function is the study of very distant birds or the detailed study of birds that are very difficult to separate from similar species.

State Bird List (or Provincial Bird List). Cumulative list of species found in a particular state or province.

Subspecies. A taxonomic level below the species level that serves to recognize regional or genetic variation within a species. Example: Hermit Thrush, *Catharus guttatus*—the subspecies common to the East is *Catharus guttatus faxoni;* the larger, grayer, paler *C. g. auduboni* is found throughout most of the mountain West (another distinct subspecies, *C. guttatus guttatis,* is darker, breeds in Alaska, and usually winters in California).

Suet. The fat that surrounds beef kidney; energy rich, this food is popular among woodpeckers, chickadees, and other species.

Summer Resident. A species that is native to an area in summer; usually synonymous with Breeding Species.

Sunflower Seed. A very popular seed type favored by the majority of seed-eating birds (of the two types, black-oil sunflower seed is usually preferred by more species over striped sunflower seed).

Syrinx. The avian "voice box."

Tail Wagging. A behavioral characteristic in which a bird pumps its tail up and down.

Taxonomy. The science of grouping and ordering living things.

Taxonomic Order. The arrangement of birds according to their physical traits, beginning with the species assessed to be most primitive and concluding with those assessed to be most evolutionarily advanced.

Telescope. See Spotting Scope.

Territory. The geographic area that a bird claims and will defend.

Thermal. Rising column of air caused by uneven heating of the earth's surface; thermals are sought by soaring birds, who will ride the columns aloft, gaining height with little energy expense.

Thistle Feeder. A specialty feeder (actually a modified tube feeder) that effectively dispenses the tiny thistle seed.

Trip List. List of species recorded during a day afield.

Tube Feeder. A cylindrical feeder that dispenses seed from ports that open on the sides.

Twilight Factor. Another measure of binocular brightness, this one giving weight to higher magnification; to calculate, multiply power by the diameter of the objective lens, then determine the square root of this number.

Understory. The vegetative layer lying between the canopy and the forest floor. Many of the plants in this zone offer food and cover to birds.

Vagrancy, Vagrant. The penchant that birds have for wandering great distances from their normal ranges.

Vignetting. The distracting black flashes binocular users see most often when the interpupillary distance or eyecups are not properly adjusted.

Water Birds. Broadly speaking, any bird species usually associated with ponds, estuaries, or marshes and that actually stands or swims in water.

Warm Front. The leading edge of a warm air system moving into a region; warm fronts promote movements of spring migrants, called "waves."

Whisper Song. A subdued or truncated rendition of the song a bird uses on territory. Whisper songs are sometimes uttered during migration and in winter.

Window Kill. The death of a bird after striking glass; a deplorable number of birds are killed every year this way.

Wing Flicking. A behavioral trait common to some species (most notably some flycatchers and kinglets) where the wings are opened, or "flicked," rapidly, and almost imperceptibly, then returned to a folded position.

Winnowing. A sound made by snipe during their courtship.

Winter Resident. A bird that is common to an area in winter.

Yard List. The cumulative list of all bird species identified in (or from) a yard (birds flying over a yard count too!).

Year List. The cumulative list of all bird species encountered during one calendar year.

Zoom Binoculars/Scope. An instrument whose magnification can be increased or decreased. In binoculars, this feature compromises performance (and is generally regarded as the sign of an inferior product), but in high-quality spotting scopes, a zoom eyepiece is optically precise and in some situations (e.g., when birds are severely backlit) very useful.

ABA Code of Ethics

American Birding Association Principles of Birding Ethics

1. **Promote the welfare of birds and their environment.**

1(a). Support the protection of important bird habitat.

1(b). To avoid stressing birds or exposing them to danger, exercise restraint and caution during observation, photography, sound recording, or filming.

Limit the use of recordings and other methods of attracting birds, and never use such methods in heavily birded areas or for attracting any species that is Threatened, Endangered, or of Special Concern, or is rare in your local area.

Keep well back from nests and nesting colonies, roosts, display areas, and important feeding sites. In such sensitive areas, if there is a need for extended observation, photography, filming, or recording, try to use a blind or hide, and take advantage of natural cover.

Use artificial light sparingly for filming or photography, especially for close-ups.

1(c). Before advertising the presence of a rare bird, evaluate the potential for disturbance to the bird, its surroundings, and other people in the area, and proceed only if access can be controlled, disturbance can be minimized, and permission has been obtained from private landowners. The sites of rare nesting birds should be divulged only to the proper conservation authorities.

1(d). Stay on roads, trails, and paths where they exist; otherwise keep habitat disturbance to a minimum.

2. **Respect the law and the rights of others.**

   2(a). Do not enter private property without the owner's explicit permission.

   2(b). Follow all laws, rules, and regulations governing use of roads and public areas, both at home and abroad.

   2(c). Practice common courtesy in contacts with other people. Your exemplary behavior will generate goodwill with birders and nonbirders alike.

3. **Ensure that feeders, nest structures, and other artificial bird environments are safe.**

   3(a). Keep dispensers, water, and food clean and free of decay or disease. It is important to feed birds continually during harsh weather.

   3(b). Maintain and clean nest structures regularly.

   3(c). If you are attracting birds to an area, ensure the birds are not exposed to predation from cats or other domestic animals, or dangers posed by artificial hazards.

4. **Group birding, whether organized or impromptu, requires special care.**

   Each individual in the group, in addition to the obligations spelled out in Items #1 and #2, has responsibilities as a Group Member.

   4(a). Respect the interests, rights, and skills of fellow birders, as well as those of people participating in other legitimate outdoor activities. Freely share your knowledge and experience, except where code 1(c) applies. Be especially helpful to beginning birders.

   4(b). If you witness unethical birding behavior, assess the situation and intervene if you think it prudent. When interceding, inform the person(s) of the inappropriate action and attempt, within reason, to have it stopped. If the behavior continues, document it and notify appropriate individuals or organizations.

Group Leader Responsibilities [amateur and professional trips and tours]

4(c). Be an exemplary ethical role model for the group. Teach through word and example.

4(d). Keep groups to a size that limits impact on the environment and does not interfere with others using the same area.

4(e). Ensure everyone in the group knows and practices this code.

4(f). Learn and inform the group of any special circumstances applicable to the areas being visited (e.g., no sound devices allowed).

4(g). Acknowledge that professional tour companies bear a special responsibility to place the welfare of birds and the benefits of public knowledge ahead of the company's commercial interests. Ideally, leaders should keep track of tour sightings, document unusual occurrences, and submit records to appropriate organizations.

Please follow this code. Distribute it and teach it to others.

Additional copies of the Code of Birding Ethics can be obtained from ABA. The ABA Code of Ethics may be reprinted, reproduced, and distributed without restriction. Please acknowledge the role of ABA in developing and promoting this code.

Bibliography

American Ornithologists' Union Checklist of North American Birds. 7th ed. Lawrence, Kans.: Allen Press, 1998.

"Bird Observer." *A Birder's Guide to Eastern Massachusetts.* Colorado Springs, CO: American Birding Association, 1994.

Buff, Sheila. *Birding for Beginners.* New York: Lyons & Burford, 1993.

———. *The Birder's Sourcebook.* New York: Lyons & Burford, 1994.

Bull, John, and John Farrand. *The Audubon Society Field Guide to North American Birds, Eastern Region.* New York: Chanticleer Press, 1977.

Chapman, Frank M. *Birds of Eastern North America.* New York: D. Appleton, 1895.

Chartier, Bonnie. *A Birder's Guide to Churchill.* 3rd ed. Colorado Springs, CO: American Birding Association, 1994.

Choate, Ernest A. *The Dictionary of American Bird Names.* rev. ed. Boston: Harvard Common Press, 1985.

Clark, William S., and Brian K. Wheeler. *Hawks of North America.* Boston: Houghton Mifflin, 1987.

Coe, James. *Eastern Birds.* New York: Golden Press, 1994.

Connor, Jack. *The Complete Birder.* Boston: Houghton Mifflin, 1988.

Cronin, Edward W. *Getting Started in Bird Watching.* Boston: Houghton Mifflin, 1986.

Dunne, Pete, David Sibley, and Clay Sutton. *Hawks in Flight.* 2nd ed. Boston: Houghton Mifflin Harcourt, 2012.

———. *Optics for Birding.* Cranston, R.I.: Swarovski Optik, 1992.

Ehrlich, Paul R., David S. Dobkin, and Darryl Wheye. *The Birder's Handbook.* New York: Simon & Schuster, 1988.

Farrand, John, Jr. *How to Identify Birds.* New York: McGraw-Hill, 1988.

Forshaw, Joseph, Steve Howell, Terence Lindsey, and Rich Stallcup. *Birding.* Time-Life Books, 1994.

Gill, Frank B. *Ornithology.* 2nd ed. New York: W. H. Freeman, 1995.

Grant, P. J. *Gulls—A Guide to Identification.* 2nd ed. San Diego, CA: Academic Press, 1997.

Griggs, Jack. *All the Birds of North America.* New York: HarperCollins, 1997.

Hale, Alan R. *How to Choose Binoculars.* Redondo Beach, CA: C & A Publishing, 1991.

Harrison, Peter. *Seabirds—An Identification Guide.* 2nd ed. Boston: Houghton Mifflin, 1985.

Hayman, Peter, John Marchant, and Tony Prater. *Shorebirds—An Identification Guide.* Boston: Houghton Mifflin, 1986.

Holt, Harold R. *A Birder's Guide to Colorado.* 4th ed. Colorado Springs, CO: American Birding Association, 1997.

———. *A Birder's Guide to Southern California.* Colorado Springs, CO: American Birding Association, 1990.

———. *A Birder's Guide to the Texas Coast.* Colorado Springs, CO: American Birding Association, 1993.

Kaufman, Kenn. *Advanced Birding.* Boston: Houghton Mifflin, 1990.

———. *Lives of North American Birds.* Boston: Houghton Mifflin, 1996.

Kerlinger, Paul. *How Birds Migrate.* Mechanicsburg, PA: Stackpole Books, 1995.

Leahy, Christopher. *The Birdwatcher's Companion.* New York: Gramercy Books, 1982.

Lethaby, Nick. *A Bird Finding Guide to Alaska.* Publisher uncited. 1994.

Peterson, Roger T. *A Field Guide to the Birds.* Boston: Houghton Mifflin, 1934.

———. *Eastern Birds.* 4th ed. Boston: Houghton Mifflin, 1980.

———. *Western Birds.* 3rd ed. Boston: Houghton Mifflin, 1990.

Pranty, Bill. *A Birder's Guide to Florida.* 4th ed. Colorado Springs, CO: American Birding Association, 1996.

Reed, Chester A. *Guide to the Land Birds East of the Rockies.* New York: Doubleday, Page, 1909.

Reed, Chester A., Harry F. Harvey, and R. I. Brasher. *Western Bird Guide.* New York: Doubleday, Page, 1913.

Robbins, Chandler S., Bertel Bruun, and Herbert S. Zim. *Birds of North America.* New York: Golden Press, 1966.

Scott, Shirley L., Ed. *Field Guide to the Birds of North America.* Washington, DC: National Geographic Society, 1983

Sibley, David. *The Birds of Cape May.* 2nd ed. Cape May, NJ: Cape May Bird Observatory, 1997.

Stokes, Donald and Lillian Stokes. *The Complete Birdhouse Book.* Boston: Little, Brown, 1990.

———. *Field Guide to Birds, Eastern and Western Regions.* 2 vol. Boston: Little, Brown, 1996.

Taylor, Richard Cachor. *A Birder's Guide to Southeastern Arizona.* 4th ed. Colorado Springs, CO: American Birding Association, 1995.

Thompson, Bill, III. *Bird Watching for Dummies.* Forster City, CA: IDG Books Worldwide, 1997.

Udvardy, Miklos D. F. *The Audubon Society Field Guide to North American Birds, Western Region.* New York: Chanticleer Press, 1977.

Wetmore, Alexander. *Song and Garden Birds of North America.* Washington, DC: National Geographic Society, 1964.

———. *Water, Prey, and Game Birds of North America.* Washington, DC: National Geographic Society, 1964.

Zim, Herbert S. *Birds.* New York: Simon & Schuster, 1949.

Index

Page numbers in italics indicate photographs, illustrations, and charts.